Quebec City

Second Edition

Stéphane Guimont-Marceau
François Rémillard

Travel better, enjoy more

ULYSSES

Travel Guides

Offices

CANADA: Ulysses Travel Guides, 4176 St. Denis Street, Montréal, Québec, H2W 2M5, ☎(514) 843-9447 or 1-877-542-7247, ≈(514) 843-9448, info@ulysses.ca, www.ulyssesguides.com

U.S.A.: Ulysses Travel Guides, 305 Madison Avenue, Suite 1166, New York, NY 10165, ☎1-877-542-7247, info@ulysses.ca, www.ulyssesguides.com

EUROPE: Les Guides de Voyage Ulysse SARL, 127 rue Amelot, 75011 Paris, France, ☎01 43 38 89 50, ≈01 43 38 89 52, voyage@ulysse.ca, www.ulyssesguides.com

Distributors

U.S.A.: BHB Distribution (a division of Weatherhill), 41 Monroe Turnpike, Trumbull, CT 06611, ☎1-800-437-7840 or (203) 459-5090, Fax: 1-800-557-5601 or (203) 459-5095

CANADA: Ulysses Travel Guides, 4176 St. Denis Street, Montréal, Québec, H2W 2M5, ☎(514) 843-9882, ext.2232, 800-748-9171, Fax: 514-843-9448, info@ulysses.ca, www.ulyssesguides.com

GREAT BRITAIN AND IRELAND: World Leisure Marketing, Unit 11, Newmarket Court, Newmarket Drive, Derby DE24 8NW, ☎1 332 57 37 37, Fax: 1 332 57 33 99, office@wlmsales.co.uk

SCANDINAVIA: Scanvik, Esplanaden 8B, 1263 Copenhagen K, DK, ☎(45) 33.12.77.66, Fax: (45) 33.91.28.82

SWITZERLAND: OLF, P.O. Box 1061, CH-1701 Fribourg, ☎(026) 467.51.11, Fax: (026) 467.54.66

OTHER COUNTRIES: Ulysses Travel Guides, 4176 St. Denis Street, Montréal, Québec, H2W 2M5, ☎(514) 843-9882, ext.2232, ☎800-748-9171, Fax: 514-843-9448, info@ulysses.ca, www.ulyssesguides.com

Canadian Cataloguing-in-Publication Data (see p 4).

© June 2002, Ulysses Travel Guides.
All rights reserved. Printed in Canada
ISBN 2-89464-514-7

"Dans la ville où je suis né,
le passé porte le présent
comme un enfant sur les épaules..."

*"In the town where I was born,
the past carries the present
like a child on it shoulders..."*

Robert Lepage
Le Confessionnal

Research and Writing	**Cartographers**	**Photography**
Stéphane G.	André Duchesne	*First Page*
Marceau	Yanik Landreville	Superstock
François Rémillard	Patrick Thivierge	*Inside Pages*
		Y. Tessier/
Publisher	**Artistic Director**	Reflexion
André Duchesne	Patrick Farei (Atoll)	P. Quittemelle/
		Megapress
Copy Editing	**Illustrations**	S. Schanz/
Eileen Connolly	Myriam Gagné	Megapress
Jacqueline Grekin	Lorette Pierson	T. Philiptchenko/
		Megapress
Translation	**Layout Assistant**	R. Edgar/
Janet Logan	Isabelle Lalonde	Megapress
Cindy Garayt		Louise Leblanc/
		Commission de la
		capitale nationale
		Perry Mastrovito/
		Reflexion

Ulysses Travel Guides acknowledges the financial support of the Government of Canada through the Book Publishing Industry Development Program (BPIDP) for our publishing activities. We would also like to thank the government of Québec for its SODEC income tax program for book publication.

Canadian Cataloguing-in-Publication Data

Main entry under title:

    Québec City
    2nd ed.
    (Ulysses Travel Guide)
    Translation of: Ville de Québec.
    Includes index.

    ISBN 2-89464-514-7

    1. Québec (Quebec) - Guidebooks. I. Series.

FC2946.18.R4513 2002   917.14'471044 C2002-940778-8
F1054.5.Q3R4513 2002

Write to Us

The information contained in this guide was correct at press time. However, mistakes can slip in, omissions are always possible, places can disappear, etc. The authors and publisher hereby disclaim any liability for loss or damage resulting from omissions or errors.

We value your comments, corrections and suggestions, as they allow us to keep each guide up to date. The best contributions will be rewarded with a free book from Ulysses Travel Guides. All you have to do is write us at the following address and indicate which title you would be interested in receiving (see the list at the end of the guide).

Ulysses Travel Guides

4176 St. Denis Street
Montréal, Québec
Canada H2W 2M5

305 Madison Avenue
Suite 1166, New York
NY 10165

www.ulyssesguides.com
E-mail: text@ulysses.ca

Table of Contents

List of Maps

Map Symbols

✈	Airport	Ⓗ	Hospital
✪	Capital	🄯	Tourist information (seasonal service)
	Funicular	❷	Tourist information (permanent service)
	Train station		Car ferry
	Bus station		

Symbols

≡	Air conditioning
bkfst incl.	Breakfast included
⇌	Fax number
ℨ	Fireplace
⊖	Fitness centre
½ b	Half board (lodging + 2 meals)
K	Kitchenette
pb	Private bathroom
≈	Pool
ℜ	Restaurant
ℝ	Refrigerator
△	Sauna
sb	Shared bathroom
✿	Spa
☎	Telephone number
⚹	Wheelchair access
⊛	Whirlpool
🚢	Ulysses's favourite

Attraction Classification

★	Interesting
★★	Worth a visit
★★★	Not to be missed

Hotel Classification

$	$100 or less
$$	$100 to $150
$$$	$150 to $200
$$$$	$200 or more

Unless otherwise indicated, the prices in the guide are
for one standard room, double occupancy in high season.

Restaurant Classification

$	$10 or less
$$	$10 to $20
$$$	$20 to $30
$$$$	$30 or more

The prices in the guide are for a meal for one
person, not including drinks and tip.

All prices in this guide are in Canadian dollars.

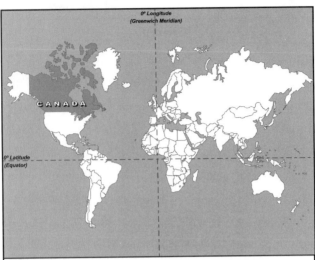

🌐 *Where is Québec City?*

QUÉBEC
Capital: Québec City
Population: 7,500,000 inhab.
Area: 1,550,000km²
Currency: Canadian dollar

QUÉBEC CITY
Population: 505,000 inhab.
Area: 552km²

Travel better, enjoy more
ULYSSES
Travel Guides

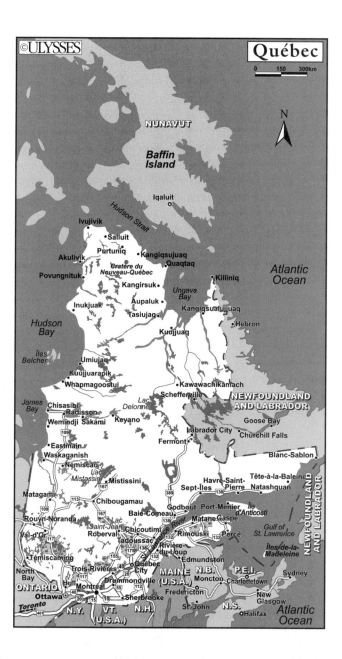

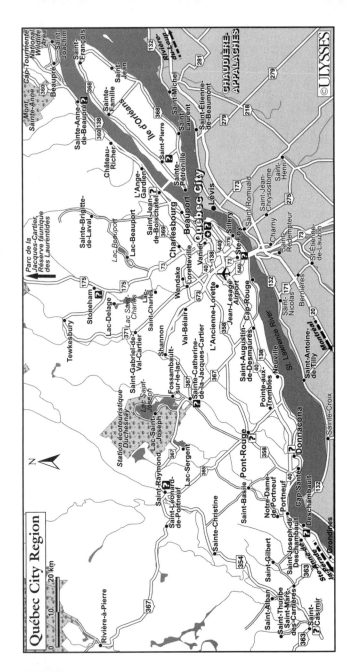

Québec City Region

© ULYSSES

Portrait

Québec City is an exceptional town. Not only is it rich in history and architecture, it is also set amidst a magnificent natural landscape.

Compared to other cities in the world, Québec City is not old; however, it is one of the oldest cities in North America and the oldest in Canada. The Haute-Ville (upper town) sits on a promontory, Cap Diamant, which is more than 98m high and juts out over the St. Lawrence River. Jacques Cartier called this rocky outcrop "Cap aux Diamants," believing he had discovered diamonds here. But he quickly learned that these precious stones were only common iron pyrites. Nevertheless, Cap Diamant became the future site of Québec City when Champlain established a fur trading post and fortified buildings, creating the settlement known as "Abitation."

This site played a strategic role in New France's defence system. Here the river is only 1km wide, and it is this narrowing of the St. Lawrence that gave Québec City its name "Kebec," an Algonquin word meaning "place where the river narrows." Perched on top of Cap Diamant and the site of major fortifications from very early on, the city is now dubbed the "Gibraltar of North America."

This fortification did not succeed, however, in driving back the English troops, who finally captured the city during the Battle of the Plains of Abraham. Yet, the French colony managed to retain its cultural identity after the Conquest. Well protected inside its walls, Québec City's heart continued to beat, making it the centre French Canadian culture in North America.

In 1985, in order to preserve and promote Québec City and its cultural treasures, Unesco declared the city's historic area – the only walled city in North America, – the first World Heritage Site in North America.

This "Vieille Capitale," often simply called "Québec" by the Québécois, is the soul of French speaking America. Thousands of tourists visit it every year and marvel at the city's many charms, its European atmosphere and its inhabitants' *joie de vivre* and hospitality. The architecture and narrow cobblestone streets give the city its character. A romantic place that always fascinates, Québec City has been a source of inspiration to artists for more than three centuries. It is a delight to both the eye and the soul. This little gem is one of those irresistible cities, and whether you visit in the summer, winter, spring or autumn, you cannot help but succumb to its charm.

History

The First Europeans

The first Europeans to reach the coast of North America were the Vikings who explored the region in the 10th century. They were followed by whalers and fishers in search of cod.

However, beginning in 1534, Jacques Cartier made three journeys that marked a turning point in this segment of North American history and were the first official contacts between

France and the New World. Cartier's mission for the king of France, François I, was to discover a passage to the East and find the gold and other riches that France so badly needed at the time. After Cartier's failure to fulfill his mission, France abandoned these new lands, considering them unimportant.

A few centuries later, the considerable profit to be made in the fur trade rekindled French interest in New France. In 1608, Samuel de Champlain chose the site where Québec City is now located to set up the first permanent trading post. Champlain was surprised not to find the Aboriginal people that Cartier had described following his journeys. During this time, the sedentary Iroquois, who farmed and hunted, had moved south and were replaced by the nomadic Algonquins who lived by hunting and gathering. The Algonquins became France's main allies. Unlike the Iroquois, they did not have a very strong sense of

JACQUES CARTIER
1534

ownership and did not resist when the French settled in their territory. The Algonquins agreed to take part in the fur trade with the French.

To understand Québec City's place in history is to appreciate all the advantages of its location. From atop of Cap Diamant, the city occupies a strategic location overlooking the only waterway leading to the North American interior. When Samuel de Champlain established the first permanent outpost to trade furs and built a fort around the few existing buildings here, it was primarily because of Cap Diamant's strategic advantages. Here, the river narrows considerably and it is easy to stop passing ships. Champlain had a wooden fortress built here, which he called "Abitation." It enclosed the trading post and the homes of various fur traders.

During that first harsh winter in Québec, 20 of the 28 men posted there died of scurvy or malnutrition before ships carrying fresh supplies arrived in the spring of 1609. When Samuel de Champlain died on Christmas Day, 1635, there were about 300 pioneers living in New France.

Between 1627 and 1663, the Compagnies des Cents Associés held a monopoly on the fur trade and ensured the slow growth of the colony. Meanwhile, French religious orders became more and more interested in New France. The Récollets arrived first, in 1615; they were replaced by the Jesuits, who began arriving in 1632.

The 17th Century

Despite the presence of significant tributaries nearby—water being the only efficient means of transport and communication at this time—Québec City was never able to profit as much from the fur trade as Montréal or Trois-Rivières. Throughout the 17th century, merchants, farmers and craftspeople came to settle in Québec City and its surrounding region. The city's economy diversified, partly because of its port (which became one of the busiest in the world), its shipbuilding yard and its lumber, which was exported mainly to France. The fur trade, however, remained the leading area of economic activity up until the beginning of the 19th century.

During the 17th century, Québec City became one of the most important centres of commerce in the New World. It was the apex of the economic triangle formed by Acadia, New France and Louisiana and would become the seat of French power in America. Also, since religious institutions and political powers looked for protection inside the walls of the Haute-Ville, Québec City quickly became the political, administrative and military centre of New France.

Many colonists settled in the town. The Basse-Ville (lower town) developed rapidly, expanding to the point where it was necessary to fill in parts of the St. Lawrence River to gain more land. At this time, the risk of fire was great because of the proximity of the buildings and the use of wood as the main construction material. In August 1682, flames devastated Québec's Basse-Ville, and the city was later rebuilt according to new standards requiring stone instead of wood for building construction. Unfortunately, a number of inhabitants did not have the money to abide by these new requirements and were forced to build outside the city walls, creating the first suburbs. Most of the stone houses in Vieux-Québec today date from this period.

The French-British Rivalry

The economic and strategic importance of Québec City made it a choice target very early on and the capital of New France had to defend itself against a covetous England. These conflicts between France and England had repercussions in the North American colony. Declarations of war and peace treaties were, in fact, the result of European politics and did not correspond to the preoccupations of the colony. Consequently, the citadel fell in 1629 when it was attacked by British forces led by the Kirke brothers, but it was quickly returned to France in 1632.

During the 18th century, the French-English rivalry increased as their colonies developed. The ever increasing pressure of British forces in New France finally resulted in the infamous Battle of the Plains of Abraham, part of the Seven Years' War. Arriving near Québec City in July 1759, General Wolfe's troops captured the town on September 13 of the same year, before reinforcements could arrive from France. During the night, the English climbed Cap Diamant to the west of the fortified walls and in the morning, to the great surprise of the French, they were on the Plains of Abraham. The battle began and ended a short time later with the defeat of the Marquis de Montcalm's troops at the hands of General Wolfe; neither general survived.

The British Regime

The Treaty of Paris, signed February 10, 1763, sealed the French defeat by officially giving New France to the British, marking the end of the French colony in Canada. Under the British Regime, Québec City was transformed. For French Canadians, the Conquest meant that they were now under British rule and ties between the colony and France were cut off, leaving Québec an orphan. Significant changes occured as the English took the situation in hand and replaced the francophones in political and administrative positions. Many of New France's well-to-do inhabitants decided to return to France at the suggestion of the British government. However, most of the inhabitants and small merchants could not afford the journey and had no other choice but to remain in the British colony. The summit of Cap Diamant was also where the English set up their government, which now

A Brief Summary of Québec's History

More than 12,000 years ago: Nomads from Northern Asia cross the Bering Strait and gradually populate the Americas. With the melting of the glaciers, some of them settle on the peninsula now known as Québec: these are the ancestors of the Aboriginal nations of Québec.

1534: Jacques Cartier, a navigator from Saint-Malo in Brittany, France, makes the first of three explorations of the Gulf St. Lawrence and the St. Lawrence River. These were the first official French contacts with this territory.

1608: Samuel de Champlain and his men found Québec City, marking the beginning of a permanent French presence in North America.

1663: New France officially becomes a French province. Colonization continues.

1759: Québec City falls to British forces. Four years later, the king of France officially relinquishes all of New France, which now has a population of about 60,000 colonists of French origin.

1837-1838: The British army suppresses the Patriotes rebellion.

1840: Following the Durham Report, the Union Act seeks to create an English majority and eventually assimilate French Canadians.

1867: This year marks the birth of Canadian Confederation. Four provinces, including Québec, sign the agreement. Six others eventually follow suit.

1914-1918: Canada participates in World War I. Anglophones and francophones disagree about the level of participation of the country. Canada comes out of the conflict very divided.

1929-1939: The economic crash hits Québec hard. In 1933, unemployment reaches 27%.

1939-1945: Canada participates in World War II. Once again, anglophones and francophones are divided on the issue of conscription.

1944-1959: Premier Maurice Duplessis leads Québec with a strong hand. This period is known as the *"grande noirceur,"* or "great darkness."

1960: The Liberal Party is elected, marking the beginning of the *Révolution Tranquille*, or Quiet Revolution.

October 1970: A small terrorist group, the Front de Libération du Québec (FLQ), kidnaps a British diplomat and a Québec cabinet minister, igniting a serious political crisis.

November 1976: The Parti Québécois, a party favouring independence for Québec, wins the provincial election.

May 1980: A majority of the Québec population votes against holding negotiations aimed at Québec independence.

1982: The Canadian Constitution is repatriated without Québec's consent.

June 1990: The failure of the Meech Lake Accord on the Canadian Constitution is poorly accepted in Québec. Following this, opinion polls show that a majority of Quebecers are in favour of Québec sovereignty.

October 22, 1992: The federal government and the provinces organize a referendum on new constitutional offers. Considered unacceptable, these are rejected by a majority of Quebecers and Canadians.

October 30, 1995: The Parti Québécois government holds a referendum on the sovereignty of Québec: 49.4% of Quebecers vote "yes" to a sovereignty project and 50.6% vote "no."

had the task of managing a considerable portion of North America.

Like the rest of the colony, Québec City was able to resist British assimilation thanks to the Catholic Church and very limited anglophone immigration until the arrival of the Empire Loyalists from the United States. Sheltered behind its walls, Québec City remained almost completely francophone for a long time.

However, the situation changed rapidly when the American War of Independence came to an end and the Empire Loyalists, faithful to the British Crown, left the United States to settle on British soil. Many of these new arrivals chose Québec City and Montréal, radically changing the look of the capital, which then saw its anglophone population grow considerably.

In addition to this emigration of Empire Loyalists, many immigrants arrived from the British Isles to settle in Québec City and work in factories or as stevedores in the port. Among them were a significant number of Irish immigrants who had an important common trait with the local population: the Catholic religion. Anglophones represented approximately 40% of the population in the Québec City region, which at that time was seeing significant economic growth. This great anglophone immigration, however, was offset by a large influx of francophones from rural Québec.

The 19th Century

The beginning of the 19th century was marked by a period of prosperity, primarily as a result of Napoleon's maritime embargo against England, which then suffered from a great lack of raw materials. This demand made Québec City an important trade link between the colony, the West Indies and England. Québec City's port, with its various shipyards set up by the French Regime, continued to develop until the invention of iron hulls and the digging of the channel in the St. Lawrence, enabling heavy-tonnage ships to reach Montréal, thus eliminating any advantages for Québec City. From then on, Québec City's importance began to decline in favour of Montréal, which had an excellent railway system that further helped establish it as the centre of industrial and economic power in Québec and Canada.

The 20th Century

Although Québec City lost its economic importance at the beginning of the 20th century and was now limited to light industry such as footwear, among others, it continued to play a significant role in politics and administration as the capital of the province of Québec.

This state of affairs continued until the Révolution Tranquille (Quiet Revolution) in the 1960s. This "revolution" in Québec marked the end of a long period spent under the yoke of religion and tradition, and set the province astir. Morals and institutions were modernized; political habits changed. The province of Québec saw the size of its government increase remarkably and Québec City, at the centre of this wave of change, was transformed as well.

At the same time, the nationalist movement made its appearance in Québec as the province's francophones expressed their desire to end the anglophone minority's control over the development of Québec society. During this period, Québec City's anglophone population began to decline, making up only 1 or 2% of the region's total population.

The reduction of the State and the decentralization of power in favour of Montréal and the regions affected employment stability in the area. Although unemployment in Québec City is fairly low, the city now relies mostly on its great industrial and technological potential. In fact, Québec City has a market of more than 500,000 consumers. Tourism is also an important source of revenue with various tourist attractions such as Vieux-Québec, Mont-Sainte-Anne and Montmorency Falls. But one of the most promising areas of economic development remains the advanced technology sector that includes biotechnology, computers, optics and telecommunications.

Portrait

Politics

Political life in Québec City is deeply marked, monopolized even, by the duality between two levels of government: the federal government and the provincial government. To gain a better understanding of the political situation in Québec, one must first comprehend its historical context. Québec City is the cradle of French culture in North America. The Canadian Confederation, created in 1867, had important consequences for all franco-

The Summit of the Americas

From April 20 to April 22, 2001, Québec City was under siege. The reason: the third Summit of the Americas, which brought together 34 of the continent's 35 heads of state (Cuba was not invited). The main topic was the creation of an immense free-trade area that would include the 800-million residents of the Americas, from Ellesmere Island to Tierra del Fuego. But the FTAA (Free Trade Area of the Americas) faces a great deal of opposition. Many researchers, intellectuals, militants and others believe that this agreement would cause tremendous losses for the people. The summit thus mobilized groups protesting against the talks that were held behind closed doors, excluding the very populations most affected by these discussions. To consolidate these "closed doors" and make sure all participants remained safe, a wall (named "the wall of shame" by locals) was built around the large security perimeter, in the heart of Vieux-Québec. This 3m-high, 4km-long fence somehow managed to keep the protesters at bay. In addition, the significant police force that had been deployed for the event drowned the city in a cloud of tear gas not once, but several times. Along with these feverish protests, a long, peaceful march attracted several thousand people.

Parallel to the Summit of the Americas, which was only for heads of state, was the second Peoples' Summit of the Americas, organized by the Hemispheric Social Alliance. This summit gathered over 2,000 participants from NGOs, unions and social organizations from all over the Americas who came to reiterate their opposition to the FTAA and try to find alternative solutions.

The protests slightly shook up the summit, resulting in the ratification of a democracy clause. Its significance is rather limited, however, since the word "democracy" was not officially defined. Furthermore, the negotiations go on and certain members—the U.S. being at the top of the list—wish to adopt the FTAA in 2005. But if these leaders truly believed in democracy, wouldn't they hold referendums asking the people to approve the FTAA?

phones in Québec. One of the most significant was the minority position in which it placed the French Canadian population, whose culture differs from the anglophone majority in Canada. The government set up in 1867 was a copy of the British model, giving legislative power to a Parliament elected by universal vote. The new constitution introduced a two-tiered regime composed of the federal government and the provincial government. In Québec City the parliament is called the National Assembly while in Ottawa this role belongs to the House of Commons. As a result of this new division of power, the minority position of francophones in Canada was confirmed. In Québec, however, their authority increased thanks to the creation of a provincial state, which would manage the major areas francophones have always tried to preserve, such as education, culture and French civil law.

Québec has always been in favour of provincial autonomy as opposed to a centralized federal government. From the first years of the Constitution, politicians like Honoré Mercier pushed for more autonomy for the provinces. Among other things, he claimed that only in Québec were the rights of French Canadians efficiently respected. However, when he became premier, he praised the French Catholic character of Québec without questioning federalism. From then on, the influence of Québec's political leaders and the ethnic and linguistic tensions between francophones and anglophones gave Québec an increasingly active role in the struggle for provincial autonomy.

In the last 40 years, the relationship between the federal government and the province has taken a different turn. In fact federal-provincial exchanges have been intense and rather tumultuous since the Quiet Revolution. The 1960s even saw the creation of an extremist group, the Front de Libération du Québec (FLQ), that demanded Québec independence. The group's political activities resulted in the 1970 October Crisis, during which Québec was subjected to the War Measures Act and the Canadian army was brought in.

The various Québec governments that have since followed have all been considered protagonists for a distinct language and culture and have all claimed a special status as well as increased power for Québec. The Québec government believes it understands the needs of the Québécois population better than the federal government and demands the right to greater autonomy, power and resources.

The event that would radically change the political scene was the election of the Parti Québécois in 1976. This party succeeded very quickly in uniting the sovereigntists forces, particularly because of the personality and charisma of its founder, René Lévesque. This political party, whose *raison d'être* was Québec sovereignty, proposed the 1980 referendum on the question of statehood and asked the Québec people for permission to negotiate sovereignty-association with the rest of Canada. The Québécois voted 60% against sovereignty-association. The same party, with Jacques Parizeau as leader, would again ask Québécois to express their opinion on the same question on October 31, 1995. This time the results were much closer – 50.6% of the population voted against the Québec government's independence project while 49.4% declared they were in favour. In the eyes of many, the issue was once again postponed but it remains present today in most political speeches.

The attitude of Québec's political leaders regarding relations between the state and the economy changed radically when Jean Lesage's Liberal Party came to power in the 1960s. This redefinition of the state's role in the economy disrupted the social, political and economic life of the province, particularly in Québec City. The number of employees in the public administration sector grew from 15,000 to 45,000 between the 1960s and the 1980s. This new direction, mapped out by the Quiet Revolution, was generally maintained throughout the 1960s, 1970s and even the 1980s. Québec's political leaders were inspired by their liberal European counterparts, supporting the Keynesian principles of a welfare state, making it a major participant in the economy and a partner in private enterprise. The presence of a large public administration provides the Vieille Capitale region and its inhabitants with steady, well-paid jobs.

The government's new economic role increased the presence and importance of francophones within the Québec economy. This phenomenon was due particularly to growth in the public and semi-public sectors and the state's contribution to the private sector. The rise of francophones was felt in all sectors of the economy but mostly in the areas of finance and public administration. However, this kind of state intervention on the part of Québec City or Ottawa has its drawbacks. Since the beginning of the 1980s, the Canadian and Québec governments, increasingly restricted by tight budgetary constraints,

have found it more and more difficult to apply their interventionist politics and have incurred high budget deficits each year.

To fix this situation, radical, difficult decisions had to be made. To reduce the deficit, powers were decentralized and the cost of the public service was reduced by eliminating jobs and raises. This created a problem since the Québec City region's economy is strongly oriented towards the service sector. However, these cuts were eventually compensated for by growth in other sectors, showing that the dynamism and ingenuity of the region allow it to quickly and successfully adjust to an unfavourable situation.

The current mayor of Québec City, Jean-Paul L'Allier, was re-elected for the fourth time in the fall of 2001. The premier of the province of Québec is Bernard Landry, the head of the Parti Québécois, while Liberal party chief Jean Chrétien leads the federal government.

Economy

The historic and romantic aspects of Québec City are so often emphasized that it is easy to forget that this city is the province's second

Portrait

most important economic centre. Situated on the banks of the St. Lawrence River, Québec City has more than 500,000 inhabitants. Its economy is strongly oriented towards the service industries and public administration, which employ about 85% of the population. A significant increase in employment has also taken place in areas such as tourism, finance and business, at the expense of manufacturing.

The colossus that the Québec public administration represented was a result of the Quiet Revolution. Supporters of the principles of a welfare state wanted to make the Québec State a major player in the economy and a partner in private enterprise. Subsequently, the welfare state had the objective of modernizing and improving the role of French Canadians in the Québec economy. Between the 1960s and the 1980s, the number of jobs in this sector tripled and francophone control of the economy grew from 47% to 60%. This increase in the region's public sector also had important repercussions on the region's economy since, on average, one job in the public service brings on the creation of another job in the private sector.

During the 1980s, and more particularly in the 1990s, the government attempted to reverse the situation. The welfare state and its numerous expenditures has made Canada one of the most indebted countries of all the industrialized nations. The solution seemed quite simple: cut expenses. This means that the public service has to limit its spending as much as possible by slashing employment and subsidies, then by privatizing and decentralizing the administration.

Even though Québec City has one of the lowest unemployment rates in the province, the general transformations that the province's economy has gone through have affected Québec City and its region's employment stability. The reduction and decentralization of the Québec government has therefore forced Québec City to turn to other directions.

To cope with government decentralization in favour of Montréal and the regions and to compensate for job losses, Québec City has had to diversify its economy. Provided with rich energy resources, a port deep enough to stay open all year and a solid road and railway network, Québec City is an ideal link between the major agricultural and economic centres of North America.

During the past few years, the Québec City region has put a great deal of effort into attracting new industries. Its qualified workforce, quality of life and accessibility have tipped the scale in its favour for several businesses that are now established here, such as manufacturers, telecommunications companies and high-tech businesses. However, despite the number of new jobs they have created, these big businesses haven't been popular with all of Québec City's residents; many are concerned with the pollution problems that come with such large industries, while others fear that a badly planned industrial configuration might one day disfigure their city.

Université Laval (Laval University) also plays an important role in the region's economic development by providing a qualified work force. It features a research and development department whose primary task is promoting and managing the transfer of technology from the university to various companies in the area. The creation of a technological park, an initiative of Université Laval and the Groupe d'Action Pour l'Avancement Technolo-gique et Industriel de la Région de Québec (the group working for technological and industrial advancement in the Québec City Region) is a good example of the influence this institution has on the region's economic vitality.

The capital has succeeded in revitalizing its economy with its specialized work force and the possibilities for research and development offered by the university and leading industries. In addition, Québec City is the seat of the provincial government and despite the reductions imposed on the public service, it will continue to be a driving force in the region.

Tourism also occupies an important place in the region's economy, generating approximately the same number of jobs as the manufacturing sector. Tourism is thus an important ever growing economic sector in the region. Cruise ships from Europe and the United States stop in Québec City more and more often, especially since Pointe-à-Carcy was renovated. With Mont-Sainte-Anne close by, Montmorency Falls just a few minutes from downtown, a carnival in the winter and numerous festivals in the summer, tourism is booming all year long.

Culture

Québec City has always enjoyed a very impressive and varied cultural life. Numerous artists such as Cornelius Krieghoff, Maurice Cullen, James Wilson Morrice, Clarence Gagnon, Adrien Hébert, Jean-Paul Lemieux, Jean-Guy Desrosiers and others have been influenced by this city and at the same time have enriched the city's image.

Several artists have found inspiration in the region and have chosen to settle in Québec City or its surroundings. For example, Félix Leclerc (1914-1988), composer, poet and performer, was the first Québec singer to gain success in Europe, opening the way for many other Québec artists. Leclerc liked to spend his free time on Île d'Orléans, a place that was close to his heart and that is prominently featured in his work.

Today, Québec City continues to be the birthplace of several interesting artistic projects. Performing-arts centres Méduse (see p 132) and Ex Machina (see p 101) are only two examples in a city where theatres and other artistic sites abound. The film industry is also quite rich.

The aforementioned Ex Machina was founded by Robert Lepage. Born in the Haute-Ville on December 12, 1957, this director and producer has had remarkable international success. Not unlike Félix Leclerc, it took his huge popularity in Europe to make Québec recognize Lepage's immense talent. This talent is particularly visible in his plays *Les Plaques Tectoniques*, *La Trilogie des Dragons* and *Les Aiguilles et l'Opium* as well as his films *Le Confessionnal*, *Le Polygraphe*, *Nô* and *Possible Worlds*. *Le Confessionnal* takes place in Québec City and draws a parallel with the movie *I Confess* filmed here by Alfred Hitchcock in the 1950s. Lepage's film presents magnificent images of Québec City. Opera, theatre, cinema, rock concerts… Robert Lepage is involved in everything.

Literature

During the 19th century, Québec City was the setting of many novels. Although the most popular genre at the time was European-style adventure stories, Québec literature was usually limited to glorifying the past and idealizing country life, and was clearly behind the times when compared to Western literature in general. In the beginning, the use of Québec City as a setting was hardly recognizable but has become increasingly evident over the years. As more novels have been published, from *Les Anciens Canadiens* by Philippe Aubert de Gaspé to Roger Lemelin's well known *Au Pied de la Pente Douce* (1944) and *Les Plouffe* (1948), Québec City's image has transformed from that of a vague, undefined place to a very lively, bustling French Canadian city. Even though it was once conquered by the British and is not as commercially significant as other cities, Québec remains the intellectual capital of French Canada and a symbol of resistance for French Canadians.

Roger Lemelin (1919-1994), a successful writer who described the colourful poor neighbourhoods of Québec City in his novels *Au Pied de la Pente Douce*, *Les Plouffe* and *Le Crime d'Ovide Plouffe* (1982), was born in Québec City. These last two works became very popular and were adapted for radio and television, then for the movies. In 1974, Lemelin was elected as a foreign member to France's Académie Goncourt.

Famed novelist Anne Hébert (1916-2000) was born in Sainte-Catherine-de-la-Jacques-Cartier, in the Québec City region. Her novel *L'Enfant chargé de songes* brings the city to life as though it were an actual character.

Québec's Emblems

In 1999, the Québec government adopted the iris versicolor as its floral emblem. Until then, the province's official flower had been the white lily (*fleur-de-lys*) that adorns its flag, commemorating the French origins of the founders of Québec. But because the white lily doesn't actually grow here, the iris was chosen. Indeed, not only is the iris indigenous to the province, it symbolizes its people in several ways: it grows in wet environments, which are omnipresent in Québec; it blossoms in late June, at the time of St. Jean Baptiste Day, Québec's national holiday; and it is usually blue, the colour of the Québec flag, but it also comes in many different varieties, just like the province's various cultural communities. Québec's official tree is the yellow birch, while its aviary emblem is the beautiful snowy owl.

Portrait

Several contemporary writers also originate from this region, such as Chrystine Brouillet, whose forte is detective novels, novelists Yves Thériault, Monique Proulx and Marie-Claire Blais, as well as poet Pierre Morency.

Architecture

Québec City is first and foremost the only walled city on the North American continent. The city was fortified for security reasons and its position on top of Cap Diamant was also strategic. Champlain had Fort Saint-Louis built at the beginning of the 17th century. Originally, the walls served to face British threats and ward off Aboriginal attacks. Very early on, major fortification work transformed Québec City into a veritable stronghold: the construction of the Batterie Royale in 1691, the Dauphine Redoubt in 1712, and in 1720, the walls that more or less correspond to the ramparts we see today. The buildings inside the walls and Vieux-Québec give the city its Old French Regime look.

Québec City has one of the richest architectural heritages in North America. As the cradle of New France, it is especially evocative of Europe in its architecture and atmosphere. But its architecture had to be adapted, particularly because of the harsh winters and lack of specialized workers and materials. The buildings here are simple and efficient without extravagance. A typical house of this period was rectangular in shape with a two-sided sloping roof covered with cedar shingles. To combat the cold Québec City winters, this type of habitation was fitted with only a few windows and one or two fireplaces. The interior was quite rustic since the main preoccupation was to keep warm at all times.

Although this type of dwelling was found mainly in the countryside, the same kind of architecture could also be seen in the city itself. As well as having to think about the cold, the city's inhabitants had to be careful about fires. The proximity of the buildings and the wood used in their construction meant that fire could spread very quickly. Following the great fire of 1682 which almost completely destroyed the Basse-Ville, the Intendents of New France issued two edicts in 1721 and in 1727 regulating construction in order to reduce the risk of fire inside the city walls. From then on, the use of wood and the construction of mansard roofs — their structure was complex and compact, presenting a great danger for fire – were both prohibited. All buildings had to be constructed of stone and equipped with firebreaking walls. In addition, the floors that separated a house's various storeys had to be covered with terra cotta tiles. All of these changes then allowed the realignment of Basse-Ville streets and the creation of Place Royale.

In neighbourhoods like Petit-Champlain you will find stone houses dating from this era, such as the Louis-Jolliet House (16 Rue du Petit-Champlain) or the Demers House (28 Boulevard Champlain). The decision to forbid the use of wood also resulted in the creation of the first suburbs outside city walls since the poorer settlers were forced to move out of town, unable to meet the costly building requirements.

Following the British victory on the Plains of Abraham, New France became part of the British Empire and the face of Québec City gradually changed as the anglophone population increased. For instance, on Grande Allée, a previously simple tree-lined country road, large domains appeared where the English built Second Empire and, later on, Victorian mansions. Today these buildings have been transformed into bars or restaurants with terraces overlooking Grande Allée.

Iris versicolor

Practical Information

Information in this chapter will help you to better plan your trip, not only well in advance, but once you've arrived in Québec City.

Important details on entrance formalities and other procedures, as well as general information, have been compiled for visitors from other countries. We will also explain how to use this guide. All this said, we wish you a great trip to Québec City!

The area code for Québec City and region is 418.

Entrance Formalities

Passports

A valid passport is usually sufficient for most visitors planning to stay less than three months in Canada. U.S. citizens do not need a passport, but it is, however, a good form of identification. US citizens and citizens of Western Europe do not need a visa. For a complete list of countries whose citizens require a visa, see the **Canadian Citizenship and Immigration** Web site *(www.cic.gc.ca)* or contact the Canadian embassy or consulate nearest you.

Extended Visits

Visitors must submit a request to extend their visit **in writing before** the expiration of the first three months of their visit or of their visa (the date is usually written in your passport) to an Immigration Canada office. To make a request you must have a valid passport, a return ticket, proof of sufficient funds to cover the stay, as well as the $65 non-refundable filing fee. In some cases (work, study), however, the request must be made **before** arriving in Canada.

Extended Visits

Visitors must submit a request to extend their visit **in writing** and **before** the expiration of their visa (the date is usually written in your passport) to an Immigration Canada office. To make a request, you must have a valid passport, a return ticket, proof of sufficient funds to cover the stay, as well as the $65 non-refundable filing-fee. In some cases (work, study), however, the request must be made **before** arriving in Canada.

Customs

If you are bringing gifts into Canada, remember that certain restrictions apply:

Smokers (minimum age is 18, 19 in British Columbia, Ontario, New Brunswick, Nova Scotia, Prince Edward Island, and Newfoundland and Labrador) can bring in a maximum of 200 cigarettes, 50 cigars, 200g of tobacco, and 200 tobacco sticks.

For **wine,** the limit is 1.5 litres; for **liquor,** 1.14 litres. The limit for beer is 24 355ml cans or 341ml bottles. The minimum drinking age in Canada is 19 years, except in Quebec, Manitoba and Alberta, where it is 18 years.

For more information on Canadian customs regulations, contact the **Canada Customs and Revenue Agency** (☎800-461-9999 *within Canada,* ☎204-983-3500 *or 506-636-5067 outside Canada, www.ccra-adrc.gc. ca).*

There are very strict rules regarding the importation of **plants**, **flowers**, and other **vegetation**; it is therefore not advisable to bring any of these types of products into the country.

If you are travelling with your **pet**, you will need a rabies-vaccination certificate. For more information on travelling with animals, plants or food, contact the **Canadian Food Inspection Agency** *(www.cfia-acia.agr. ca)* or the Canadian embassy or consulate nearest you before your departure for Canada.

Embassies and Consulates

Abroad

DENMARK
Canadian Embassy
Kr. Bernikowsgade 1,
1105 Copenhagen K
☎*(45) 12.22.99*
≠*(45) 14.05.85*

GERMANY
Canadian Consulate General
Internationales Handelzentrum
Friedrichstrasse 95, 23rd floor
10117 Berlin
☎*(30) 261.11.61*
≠*(30) 262.92.06*

GREAT BRITAIN
Canada High Commission
Macdonald House
One Grosvenor Square
London, W1X 0AB
☎*(171) 258-6600*
≠*(171) 258-6384*

NETHERLANDS
Canadian Embassy
Parkstraat 25, 2514JD, The Hague
☎*(70) 361-4111*
≠*(70) 365-6283*

SWEDEN
Canadian Embassy
Tegelbacken 4, 7th floor, Stockholm
☎*(8) 613-9900*
≠*(8) 24.24.91*

UNITED STATES
Canadian Embassy
501 Pennsylvania Ave. NW
Washington, DC, 20001
☎*(202) 682-1740*
≠*(202) 682-7726*

Canadian Consulates General:

1175 Peachtree St. NE
100 Colony Square, Suite 1700,
Atlanta, Georgia, 30361-6205
☎*(404) 532-2000*
≠*(404) 532-2050*

Three Copley Place, Suite 400
Boston, Massachusetts, 02116
☎*(617) 262-3760*
≠*(617) 262-3415*

Two Prudential Plaza, 180 N
Stetson Ave., Suite 2400,
Chicago, Illinois, 60601
☎*(312) 616-1860*
≠*(312) 616-1877*

St. Paul Place, Suite 1700,
750 N. St. Paul St.,
Dallas, Texas, 75201-3247
☎*(214) 922-9806*
≠*(214) 922-9815*

Practical
Information

600 Renaissance Center, Suite 1100
Detroit, Michigan, 48234-1798
☎ *(313) 567-2085*
📠 *(313) 567-2164*

550 South Hope St., 9th floor
Los Angeles, California, 90071-2327
☎ *(213) 346-2700*
📠 *(213) 620-8827*

Suite 900, 701 Fourth Ave. S
Minneapolis, Minnesota,
55415-1899
☎ *(612) 333-4641*
📠 *(612) 332-4061*

1251 Avenue of the Americas,
Concourse Level,
New York, NY 10020-1175
☎ *(212) 596-1628*
📠 *(212) 596-1666/1790*

3000 HSBC Center,
Buffalo, NY 14203-2884.
☎ *(716) 858-9500*
📠 *(716) 852-4340*

412 Plaza 600, Sixth and Stewart sts.,
Seattle, Washington 98101-1286
☎ *(206) 442-1777*
📠 *(206) 443-9662*

In Montréal

DENMARK
1 Place-Ville-Marie, 35th floor
H3B 4M4
☎ *(514) 877-3060*

GERMANY
1250 Boulevard René-Lévesque Ouest,
Suite 4315, H3B 4X1
☎ *(514) 931-2277*

GREAT BRITAIN
1000 de la Gauchetière Ouest
Suite 901, H3B 3A7
☎ *(514) 866-5863*

NETHERLANDS
1002 Rue Sherbrooke Ouest
Suite 2201, H3A 3L6
☎ *(514) 849-4247*
📠 *(514) 849-8260*

SWEDEN
8400 Boulevard Décarie, H4P 2N2
☎ *(514) 345-2727*

UNITED STATES
Place Félix-Martin
1155 Rue Saint-Alexandre
☎ *(514) 398-9695*
📠 *(514) 398-9748*
Mailing address:
C.P. 65 Station Desjardins
Montréal, H5B 1G1

In Québec City

UNITED STATES
Consulate General
2 Place Terrasse Dufferin, G1R 4T9
☎ *(418) 692-2095*

Tourist Information

Tourist information is available from Tourisme Québec, the Délégations Générales du Québec abroad and the various offices of the Office du Tourisme et des Congrès de la région de Québec. A tourist information service is also available from people on mopeds in Vieux-Québec during the summer. The mopeds are painted green and have a flag with a question mark on it.

Tourisme Québec
P.O. Box 979, Montréal, H3C 2W3
☎ *(514) 873-2015*
or 800-363-7777
www.bonjourquebec.com

Canada and Abroad

BELGIUM
Délégation Générale du Québec
46 Avenue des Arts, 7e étage
1000 Bruxelles
(Métro Art-Loi)
☎ *(02) 512.00.36*
≈ *(02) 514.26.41*

CANADA
Bureau du Québec
20 Queen St. W, Suite 1504
Toronto, Ontario, M5H 3S3
☎ *(416) 977-6060*
≈ *(416) 596-1407*

GERMANY
Destination Québec
Possfatch 200 247
63469 Maintal 2
☎ *49 6181 45178*
≈ *49 6181 497758*

GREAT BRITAIN
Destination Québec
c/o Aurora Marketing, Suite 154
4th Floor, 35-37 Grosvenor Gardens
House, Grosvenor Gardens, Victoria
London, SW1W 0BS
☎ *(171) 233-8011*
≈ *(171) 233-7203*

SWITZERLAND
Welcome to Canada!
22, Freihofstrasse, 8700 Küsnacht
☎ *(1) 910 90 01*
≈ *(1) 910 38 24*

UNITED STATES
Tour & Travel
140W, 69th St.,
New York, NY 10023-5107
☎ *(718) 579-8401*

In Québec City

Centre Infotouriste
12 Rue Sainte-Anne, Québec G1R 3X2
☎ *694-1602 or 800-665-1528*
They give detailed information and supply road maps, travel brochures, and lodging guides for all of Québec's tourist regions.

Office du Tourisme et des Congrès de la région de Québec
835 Avenue Wildfrid Laurier, G1R 2L3
☎ *522-3511*
≈ *529-3121*
www.quebecregion.com

Sainte-Foy

Office du Tourisme et des Congrès de la région de Québec
3300 Avenue des Hôtels, G1R 2L3
☎ *649-2608*
≈ *522-0830*
www.quebecregion.com

Beauport

Bureau Touristique du Parc de la Chute-Montmorency
4300 Boulevard Sainte-Anne
(Route 138)
end Jun to early Sep

Practical Information

Sainte-Anne-de Beaupré

Bureau d'Information Touristique de la Côte-de-Beaupré
9310 Boulevard Sainte-Anne
☎827-5281

Île d'Orléans

Bureau Touristique de l'île d'Orléans
490 Côte du Pont, Saint-Pierre
☎828-9411

On the Internet

Here are some Web sites that will help you find out about Québec City online.

Tourisme Québec
www.bonjourquebec.com

Office du Tourisme et des Congrès de la région de Québec
www.quebecregion.com

Québec City
www.ville.quebec.qc.ca

Cultural information
www.quebecplus.ca
www.voir.ca/qc
www.telegraph.com

Getting There

If you are leaving from Montréal take the Jean-Lesage Autoroute (20 Est) as far as the Pierre-Laporte Bridge, cross the bridge and take Boulevard Laurier which will successively change its name to Chemin Saint-Louis and Grande Allée. This road leads you directly to the Haute-Ville. You can also arrive by Félix Leclerc Autoroute (40 Est) which will take you as far as Sainte-Foy and from there signs for Boulevard Charest will lead you to the centre of Basse-Ville. To get to the Haute-Ville just take Rue Dorchester and then Côte d'Abraham.

Arriving from Ottawa on Autoroute 417, take Félix Leclere Autoroute (40 Est) to Sainte-Foy and then follow the signs for Boulevard Charest Est. You will arrive in the Basse-Ville. From Toronto, take the Jean-Lesage Autoroute (20 Est) until the exit for the Pierre-Laporte Bridge. Cross the bridge and follow the signs for Boulevard Laurier which will eventually become Grande Allée.

From the United States, take Highway 55 then Autoroute 20 Est. You will enter Québec City by the Pierre-Laporte Bridge and then take Boulevard Laurier.

When arriving in Québec City by car, the most common route is via Grande Allée. After passing through a typical North American-style suburb, you come to a rather British-looking part

Table of Distances (in kilometres)
Via the shortest route

	Boston (Mass.)	Charlottetown (P.E.I.)	Chibougamau	Chicoutimi	Gaspé	Halifax (N.S.)	Hull / Ottawa	Montréal	New York (N.Y.)	Niagara Falls (Ont.)	Québec City	Rouyn-Noranda	Sherbrooke	Toronto (Ont.)	Trois-Rivières
Baie-Comeau	1040	724	679	316	337	807	869	676	1239	1334	422	1304	662	1224	545
Boston (Mass.)		1081	1152	849	1247	1165	701	512	352	767	648	1136	426	906	566
Charlottetown (P.E.I.)			1347	992	867	265	1404	1194	1421	1836	984	1833	1187	1746	1089
Chibougamau				363	1039	1430	725	700	1308	1298	515	493	724	1124	574
Chicoutimi					649	1076	662	464	1045	1126	211	831	451	1000	338
Gaspé						952	1124	930	1550	1590	700	1559	915	1476	808
Halifax (N.S.)							1488	1290	1508	1919	1056	1916	1271	1828	1173
Hull / Ottawa								207	814	543	451	536	347	399	331
Montréal									608	670	253	638	147	546	142
New York (N.Y.)										685	834	1246	657	823	750
Niagara Falls (Ont.)											925	858	827	141	814
Québec City												877	240	802	130
Rouyn-Noranda													782	606	747
Sherbrooke														693	158
Toronto (Ont.)															688
Trois-Rivières															

Example: the distance between Québec City and Montréal is 253 km.

of town with tree-lined streets. Next come the provincial capital's government buildings and finally the imposing medieval-looking gates and behind them the historic streets of the old city, Vieux-Québec.

Airport

Jean-Lesage Airport

Aéroport International Jean-Lesage is the only airport in the vicinity of Québec City. Despite its small size, it does have international flights to the United States and France and serves Québec and the other Canadian provinces.

500 Rue Principale, Sainte-Foy
☎640-2700
www.aeroportdequebec.com

Location

Situated in L'Ancienne-Lorette, the airport is about 20km northwest of Québec City. To get downtown, head south on Route de l'Aéroport to Autoroute 40 Est and then take Boulevard Charest Est. The trip takes about 20min.

Information

For information about airport services (arrivals, departures, etc.) call ☎640-

2600, 24hrs a day for a recorded message. Call the same number and choose option "0" to speak to an agent Monday to Friday from 8am to 4:30pm. There is no toll-free line for general information. Here are the telephone numbers of several airline companies that you might want to call:

Air Canada:
☎692-0770 or 800-361-8620

Air Transat:
☎877-872-8728

Inter Canadien:
☎692-1031 or 800-363-7530

Car Rentals

Various car rental agencies, such as Budget, Thrifty, Hertz and National, are located at the airport (see p 42).

Foreign Exchange

The **Thomas Cook** (☎877-5768) foreign exchange office is open every day from 9am to 9pm.

Getting Around

By Car

Québec City has a very good public transportation system and plenty of taxis, so it is not necessary to use your car; it is even preferable to visit on foot. Most of the tourist attractions are relatively close together and all the tours we suggest are within walking distance. However, for the surrounding areas (Île d'Orléans for example), a car or bicycle is needed to cover the distance.

It is easy to get around by car in Québec City. In Vieux-Québec, parking lots are numerous but expensive. You can park on the street but read the signs limiting parking times carefully and do not forget to feed the parking meters regularly. Inspectors check the streets often and fines are expensive. The signs to leave town are clearly marked.

Things to Consider

Driver's License: As a general rule, foreign driver's licenses are valid for six months from the arrival date in Canada.

Winter Driving: Although roads are generally in good condition, the dangers brought on by drastic climatic conditions must be taken into consideration.

Highway Code: Turning right on a red light is **forbidden** in Québec. Priority to the right is the law here; however, it is not always observed, so

pay attention. Red signs marked "Arrêt" or "Stop" must always be respected. Come to a complete stop even if there is no apparent danger.

Traffic lights are often located on the opposite side of the intersection, so make sure to stop on the stop line.

When a school bus (usually yellow) has stopped and has its signals flashing, you must come to a complete stop, no matter what direction you are travelling in. Failing to stop at the flashing signals is considered a serious offense and carries a heavy penalty.

Wearing seatbelts in the front and back seats is compulsory at all times.

Pay attention to reserved bus lanes! They are marked by a large white diamond and signs clearly indicating the hours you cannot drive in these lanes, except when making a right turn.

There are no tolls on Québec highways (*autoroutes*), and the speed limit on them is 100km/h. The speed limit on secondary highways is 90km/h, and 50km/h in urban areas.

Gas Stations: Gasoline prices are less expensive than in Europe. Some gas stations

Practical Information

(especially in the downtown areas) might ask for payment in advance as a security measure, especially after 11pm.

Accidents and Emergencies

In case of serious accident, fire or other emergency, dial **911** or **0**.

If you run into trouble on the highway, pull onto the shoulder of the road and turn on the hazard lights. If it is a rental car, contact the rental company as soon as possible. Always file an accident report. If a disagreement arises over who was at fault in an accident, ask for police help.

If you are planning a lengthy car trip, it is a good idea to become a member of the Canadian Automobile Association, or CAA, which can offer help throughout Canada. If you are a member in your home country of an equivalent association (U.S.A.: American Automobile Association; Great Britain: Automobile Association; Australia: Australian Automobile Association), you have the right to some free services. For further information, contact your association or the CAA in Québec City ☎*624-0708*

Car Rentals

Generally a package including airfare, hotel and car or just hotel and car is less expensive than renting a car once you get here. Many travel agencies have agreements with the major car-rental companies (Avis, Budget, Hertz, etc.) and offer good values; contracts often include added bonuses (reduced ticket prices for shows, etc.). Package deals are usually a good deal. However, if you cannot get a package, it is cheaper to rent your car here than it is from abroad. However, here are the addresses of the main car rental companies:

Budget
Jean-Lesage Airport
☎*872-9885*
Vieux-Québec
29 Côte du Palais
☎*692-3660*
Sainte-Foy
2481 Chemin Sainte-Foy
☎*651-6518*

Discount
Sainte-Foy
Centre Innovation
2360 Chemin Sainte-Foy
☎*652-7289*

Hertz
Jean-Lesage Airport
☎*871-1571*
Québec
580 Grande Allée
☎*647-4949*
Vieux-Québec
44 Côte du Palais
☎*694-1224*

National
Jean-Lesage Airport
☎*871-1224*
Québec
Rue St-Paul
☎*694-1727*

Via Route
2605 Boulevard Hamel Ouest
☎*682-2660*

When renting a car, find out if:
The contract includes un-limited kilometres and if the insurance offered provides full coverage (accident, property damage, hospital costs for you and passen-gers, theft).

Don't forget:
To rent a car in Québec, you must be at least 21 years of age and have had a driver's license for **at least** one year. If you are be-tween 21 and 25, certain companies will ask for a $500 deposit, and in some cases they will also charge an extra sum for each day you rent the car. These conditions do not apply for those over 25 years of age.

A credit card is extremely useful for the deposit to avoid tying up large sums of money.

Most rental cars have an automatic transmission; however, you can request a car with a manual shift.

Child-safety seats cost extra.

By Public Transportation

When visiting Québec City, we strongly advise you to use public transportation. Run by the Société de Transport de la Communauté Urbaine de Québec (STCUQ), the transit system has a network of bus routes covering the entire city. There is no subway in Québec City; however, a Métrobus ser-vice has recently been established which leaves Beauport or Charlesbourg and goes as far as Sainte-Foy and vice versa. The buses go through Vieux-Québec, along Rue Saint-Jean, Avenue Cartier and across the university cam-pus; they stop opposite the large Sainte-Foy shopping centres and near the Sainte-Foy bus terminal. Métrobuses no. 800 or 801 are fast because they run on reserved lanes (see p 41) and stop less often than other buses. Métrobuses also run often, about every 10min.

You will find the public transportation guide in the telephone book. This map of the bus routes also con-tains the main landmarks to help you get around.

For unlimited use of public transportation, a monthly bus pass costs $59 (on sale

Practical Information

at the beginning of each month). You can also buy tickets costing $1.90 each or pay a fare of $2.25 in exact change for each trip. You can also buy a day-pass for $5.10. Students and senior citizens have reduced rates. Children five years of age and under travel free of charge. Tickets can be bought at most pharmacies or corner stores. These outlets also have folders describing the individual bus routes. **Take note, bus drivers do not sell tickets and do not give change**.

When you want to change buses, you must ask the driver for a transfer.

For more information about public transportation:
☎627-2511
www.stcuq.qc.ca

From mid-November to the end of March, there is a shuttle service for people staying in the city, who would like to take a day trip to the surrounding countryside. L'**Hiver Express** *($22 return per person;* ☎525-5191) stops in front of the main hotels in Québec City and Sainte-Foy every morning. These taxis will take you to the region's main tourist recreational sites such as Mont Saint-Anne and pick you up at the end of the afternoon.

By Taxi

A taxi from the airport to downtown costs about $25.

Taxi Co-op
☎*525-5191*

Taxi Quebec
☎*525-8123*

By Bus

The Québec City bus terminal is located in the Gare du Palais. Buses leave for Montréal every hour from 6am to 11pm. There is also a shuttle-bus service that goes directly to Montréal's Dorval airports.

Terminus d'Autocars de Québec
320 Rue Abraham-Martin
☎*525-3000*

There is the same bus service in Sainte-Foy because buses coming from Montréal stop in Sainte-Foy before continuing on to the Gare du Palais.

Terminus d'Autocars Sainte-Foy
3001 Chemin des Quatre-Bourgeois
☎*650-0087*

By Train

Trains from Montréal arrive at the Gare du Palais in the Basse-Ville and those coming from the east stop at Lévis on the other side of the river where the ferry crosses.

Gare du Palais
450 Rue de la Gare-du-Palais
☎*800-835-3037*

Gare de Charny
2326 Rue de la Gare Est

Gare de Sainte-Foy
3255 Chemin de la Gare
☎*800-835-3037*
www.viarail.com

Hitchhiking

During the summer, "free" hitchhiking is common and is easier outside large centres. Hitchhiking is prohibited on major highways and expressways.

"Organized" hitchhiking, or ridesharing, with Allo-Stop, works very well in all seasons. This reputed company pairs drivers who want to share their car for a small payment with passengers needing a ride. A membership card is required and costs $6 for a passenger and $7 for a driver per year. The driver receives part (approximately 60%) of the fees paid by the passengers. Destinations include virtually everywhere in the province of Québec. For example, a one-way trip between Québec and Montréal costs $15.

Children under 5 years of age cannot travel with Allo-Stop because of a regulation requiring the use of child-safety seats. Not all drivers accept smokers, and not all passengers want to be exposed to smoke, so check on this ahead of time.

For registration and information:

Allo-Stop Québec
665 Rue Saint-Jean
☎*522-0056*

By Ferry

Even if you have no reason to go to Lévis on the south shore of the St. Lawrence River, you should take the ferry trip just for the view. The ferry dock is across from Place Royale; you should have no trouble finding it. The return trip from Lévis gives you a magnificent view of Québec City. A one-way trip costs $2 during winter and $2.50 in summer for an adult, and $8.50 for a car in winter and $9.85 during summer (maximum six passengers). The timetable varies from one season to the next so it is better to check directly for the times.

Société des Traversiers du Québec
10 Rue des Traversiers
☎644-3704
www.traversiers.gouv.qc.ca

By Bicycle

One of the best ways to get around in the summer is on a bicycle. Bicycle paths and shared road spaces have been laid out to give cyclists access to certain parts of the city. To help you get around, there is a brochure as well as a map showing the bicycle paths and shared road spaces in the city and surrounding area. Also, consult the Ulysses Travel Guide *Le Québec cyclable* to obtain maps of those trails.

Cars are not always attentive and cyclists must be careful. Cyclists must follow the rules of the road and although it is not obligatory in Québec, we strongly recommend that you wear a helmet.

Promo-Vélo can provide you with information on the different types of tours in the region.

Promo-Vélo
P.O. Box 700 Succ. Haute-Ville
Québec, G1R 4S9
☎522-0087

Bicycle Rentals

Some bicycle shops have a rental service. These shops are listed in the chapter on outdoor activities (p 63) For other addresses consult the yellow pages under "Bicyclettes-Location" or "Bicycle Rental." Insurance is a good idea. Some places include theft insurance in the rental fee, but be sure to check this when you rent the bicycle.

Guided Tours

Several tourist agencies organize tours that give visitors the opportunity to discover the city in various ways. A walking tour provides a more intimate perspective of a neighbourhood than a tour bus. Cruises also provide a unique perspective of the city – its outline from the water. Although there are many options, a few should be mentioned as they are particularly worthwhile.

On Foot

Located in the tourist information office on Rue Sainte-Anne, **CD Tour** *($10, $15 for* two people; *12 Rue Sainte-Anne*, ☎*654-1115*) rents out portable audio-tours for various parts of the city. These tours are recorded on laser disc, enabling visitors to stop where and when they please. In the lively recordings, historic figures are brought back to life to tell visitors about the major events that shaped Québec City.

Another option is to take a "Québec, Fortified City" walking tour, offered by the **Centre d'Initiation aux Fortifications de Québec** (*$10; 90 min; end June to early Sep 9am to 5pm, rest of the year 10am to 5pm;* ☎*648-7016*) (see p 66). These start at the kiosk on Terrasse Dufferin.

The **Société Historique de Québec** (*$12; 72 Côte de la Montagne,* ☎*692-0556 or 692-0614*), on Côte de la Montagne, offers guided tours of Vieux-Québec. There are a number of themes from which to choose. These visits last between 2 and 3hrs and allow you to discover many aspects of Quebec City.

Les Tours Adlard (*$14; duration: 2hrs 15min; end of Jun to mid-Sep every day 8:30am to 7:30pm, rest of the year 9am to 5pm; 12 Rue Ste-Anne,* ☎*692-2358*) offers tours that relive history while recounting short anecdotes about how

the city has evolved. They also organize bus and trolley tours in the city and surrounding region.

By Bus

Les Tours Adlard (see above)

Les Tours du Vieux-Québec
☎*664-0460 or 800-267-TOUR*
Guided tours of the city and its surroundings are given in the comfort of a small air-conditioned bus. Visits to the area around Québec City include Côte-de-Beaupré, Sainte-Anne-de-Beaupré and Île d'Orléans. Tours last about 2 hrs and cost $26 per person. They are given all year long.

Grayline Québec
☎*649-9226 or 888-558-7668*
This company gives classical tours of the city and excursions to the surrounding area in a luxury bus, an air-conditioned minibus or a trolley. The city tour lasts 2hrs and costs $26. These tours are given throughout the year.

By Calèche (Horse-Drawn Carriage)

Calèches du Vieux-Québec
☎*683-9222*
You can visit Vieux-Québec by *calèche* all year long. This original way of discov-

Practical Information

ering the city adds to its charm. *Calèches* can be found almost anywhere in the old town. A ride costs $60 for about 35min.

By Boat

The **Croisières AML** (☎692-1159 or 800-563-4643) and the **Croisières de la Famille Dufour** (☎827-5711 or 800-463-5250) both offer cruises on the St. Lawrence that allow you to discover Québec City from another point of view (see p 180).

Money and Banking

There are several banks and *caisses populaires* (credit unions) in Vieux-Québec that exchange foreign currency. In most cases these institutions charge a commission. The *bureau de change* (exchange bureau) may not charge a fee but their rates are less competitive. You should compare rates and ask about fees. Most banks will exchange U.S. dollars.

Caisse Populaire Desjardins du Vieux-Québec
19 Rue Desjardins
☎522-6806

Échange de Devises Montréal
12 Rue Sainte-Anne
☎694-1014
46, Rue Petit-Champlain
☎694-0011

Transchange International
Promenades du Vieux-Québec
43 Rue de Buade
☎694-6906

Traveller's Cheques

Traveller's cheques are usually accepted in most department stores and hotels but it is more convenient to change them at the above mentioned places. In Québec City you can buy traveller's cheques in Canadian or U.S. dollars at most banks.

Credit Cards

Most major credit cards are accepted at stores, restaurants and hotels. While the main advantage of credit cards is that they allow visitors to avoid carrying large sums of money, using a credit card makes leaving a deposit for car rental much easier. Also, some cards, gold cards for example, automatically insure you when you rent a car. In addition, the exchange rate with a credit card is generally better. The most commonly accepted credit cards are Visa, MasterCard, and American Express.

By using a credit card you can avoid service charges when exchanging money. By overpaying your credit card (to avoid interest

Exchange Rates*

$1 CAN = $0.62 US	$1 US = $1.61 CAN
$1 CAN = £0.44	£1 = $2.30 CAN
$1 CAN = 0.70 € (euro)	1 € (euro) = $1.43 CAN
$1 CAN = 5.23 DKK	1 DKK = $0.19 CAN

*Samples only—rates fluctuate

charges) you can then withdraw against it. You can thus avoid carrying large amounts of money or traveller's cheques. Withdrawals can be made directly from an automatic teller using the personal identification number for your card.

Banks

Most banks offer a standard service to tourists. Visitors who chose to stay for a long period should note that non-residents cannot open bank accounts. In this case, the best way to have ready money is to use traveller's cheques. Withdrawing money from foreign accounts can be expensive because of the commission. People who have resident status, permanent or not (landed-immigrants, students) can open a bank account. A passport and proof of resident status are required.

Money can be withdrawn from any automatic banking machine with the Interac and Cirrus systems. Most automatic tellers are open 24hrs and many will now accept European bank cards so you can withdraw money directly from your account (check that you have access before you leave). You can also get money from a credit card but this is considered a loan and interest rates are high. Another possibility is to buy money-orders on which you do not have to pay a commission but this takes longer.

Banks are open Monday to Friday from 10am to 3pm. Most of them are also open Thursday and Friday evenings to either 6pm or 8pm.

Practical Information

Some are even open on Saturday morning.

Caisse Populaire Desjardins du Vieux-Québec
19 Rue Desjardins
☎*522-6806*

Banque Royale
700 Place d'Youville
☎*692-6800*

Banque Nationale
150 Boulevard René-Lévesque Est
☎*647-6100*

Currency

The monetary unit in Québec is the Canadian dollar ($), which is divided into cents (¢). One dollar=100 cents.

Bills come in 5-, 10-, 20-, 50-, 100-, 500- and 1000-dollar denominations, and coins come in 1-, 5-, 10- and 25-cent pieces and in 1- and 2-dollar coins.

Insurance

Cancellation

Your travel agent will usually offer you cancellation insurance when you buy your airline ticket or vacation package. This insurance allows you to be reimbursed for the ticket or package deal if your trip must be cancelled due to serious illness or death.

Theft

Most residential insurance policies protect some of your goods from theft, even if the theft occurs in a foreign country. To make a claim, you must fill out a police report. It may not be necessary to take out further insurance, depending on the amount covered by your current home policy. As policies vary considerably, you are advised to check with your insurance company.

Health

This is the most useful kind of insurance for travellers and should be purchased before your departure. Your insurance plan should be as complete as possible because health-care costs add up quickly. When buying insurance, make sure it covers all types of medical costs, such as hospitalization, nursing services and doctor's fees. Make sure your limit is high enough, as these expenses can be costly. A repatriation clause is also vital in case the required care is not available on site. Furthermore, since you may have to pay immediately, check your policy to see what provisions it includes for such situations. To avoid any problems during your vacation, always keep proof of your insurance policy on you.

Health

Vaccinations are not necessary for people coming from Europe, the United States and Australia. On the other hand, it is strongly suggested, particularly for medium or long-term stays, that visitors take out health and accident insurance. There are different types, so it is best to shop around. Bring along all medication, especially prescription drugs. Unless otherwise stated, the water is drinkable throughout Québec.

In case of an emergency dial ☎*911*.

Time Difference

Québec is 6hrs behind continental Europe and 3hrs ahead of the North American west coast. The entire province of Québec (save for the Îles-de-la-Madeleine, which are an hour ahead) operates on Eastern Standard Time. Keep in mind that there are several time zones across Canada. Daylight Savings Time (+1hr) starts the first Sunday in

April and finishes the last Sunday in October (-1hr)

Business Hours and Holidays

Stores

The law respecting business hours allows stores to be open the following hours:

● Monday to Wednesday from 8am to 9pm; most stores open at 9:30am and close at 5:30pm

● Thursday and Friday from 8am to 9pm; most open at 9:30am

● Saturday from 8am to 5pm; most open at 9:30am

● Sunday from 8am to 5pm; most open at noon. Not all stores open on Sundays.

Dépanneurs (convenience stores that sell food) are found throughout Québec and are open later, sometimes 24hrs a day.

Holidays

January 1st and 2nd

Easter Monday

3rd Monday in May
(*Fête de Dollard and Victoria Day*)

Practical Information

June 24
(*Saint-Jean-Baptiste Day, Québec's national holiday*)

July 1st
(*Canada Day*)

1st Monday in September
(*Labour Day*)

2nd Monday in October
(*Thanksgiving*)

November 11
(*Remembrance Day; only
banks and federal government
services are closed*)

December 25 and 26
(*Christmas*)

Climate and Clothing

Québec's seasonal extremes
set the province apart from
much of the world. Tem-
peratures can rise above
30°C in summer and drop
to -25°C in winter. Visiting
Québec during the two
"main" seasons (summer
and winter) is like experi-
encing two totally different
countries, with the seasons
influencing not only the
scenery, but the lifestyles
and behaviour of the province's residents. Because of
the extremes in Québec
City's weather, you should
carefully choose clothing
appropriate to the season of
your visit

Winter

*"Mon pays ce n'est pas un
pays, c'est l'hiver..."*

("My country is not a country, it is winter")

– Gilles Vigneault

Mid-November to the end
of March is the best time for
skiing, snowmobiling, skating, snowshoeing and other
winter sports. In general,
there are five or six large
snowstorms each winter.
Howling wind often makes
the temperatures bitterly
cold, causing "drifting
snow" (very fine snow that
is blown by the wind). One
bright spot is that though
the weather may be freez-
ing cold Quebec still gets
more hours of sunshine
than most of Europe.

With sweaters, gloves a
scarf, a hat (called "a
tuque"), you will be ready
to confront winter. Well...
almost! Remember, don't
ignore the cold. Here are a
few tips:

Wear a coat, preferably a
long one with a hood. Otherwise be sure to buy yourself a hat or a good pair of
earmuffs.

If you are fond of your
shoes, buy a pair of ga-
loshes, (they are quite
harmless). They are a kind

of rubber overshoe that is very practical for avoiding the corrosive salts used to melt the ice. They are easy to find and do not cost very much.

Visitors usually find the stores and other public places are overheated. The trick is to remove your scarf and open your coat the moment you step indoors.

If you feel a sudden chill while window-shopping, do not hesitate to go into a store to get warm. This way you will avoid catching a cold.

If you are going to ski, do not forget your sunglasses.

Spring

Spring is short, lasting roughly from the end of March to the end of May, and heralded by the arrival of "slush," a mixture of melted snow and mud, and the break up of ice in the St. Lawrence River. As the snow disappears, long-buried plants and grass, yellowed by frost and mud, come to life again. Nature's welcomed reawakening is spectacular. One of the signs that announce spring is the return of the snow geese flying in long *V* formations. Their calls mingle with those of the Québécois shouting, "It's spring!"

Heavy sweaters, woolen clothes and scarves are recommended for the in-between seasons of spring and autumn. Do not forget your umbrella and raincoat.

Summer

Summer in Québec blossoms from the end of May to the end of August and may surprise some who think of Québec as a land of snow and igloos. The heat can be quite extreme and often seems much hotter because of the accompanying humidity. The vegetation becomes lush, and don't be surprised to see some rather exotic-looking red and green peppers growing in window boxes. City streets are decorated with flowers, and restaurant terraces are always full.

Bring T-shirts, light shirts and trousers, shorts and sunglasses; a sweater will also be useful in the evening.

Autumn

The autumn colours can last from September to November. Maple trees form one of the most beautiful living pictures on the North American continent. Leaves are transformed into a kaleidoscope of colours from

Practical Information

bright green to scarlet red, to golden yellow. Temperatures will stay warm for a while, but eventually the days and especially the nights will become quite cold.

Like in spring, heavy sweaters, wool clothing and scarves are recommended for autumn, as are a raincoat and umbrella.

Indian Summer

This relatively short period (only a few days) during the late fall is like summer's triumphant return! Referred to as "Indian Summer", it is in fact the result of warm air currents from the Gulf of Mexico. It is called Indian Summer because it represented the last hunt before winter. Aboriginals took advantage of the warm weather to stock up on provisions before the cold weather arrived.

Security

Québec City is not a violent place. The quality of life here is quite outstanding and you should feel perfectly safe.

If you take normal precautions you should not be overly worried about personal security. However, in case of an emergency dial **911**.

Telecommunications

You do not need to dial the area code for the Québec City region (**418**) if you make a local call. For long-distance calls, dial 1 followed by the area code you are calling then the telephone number. Telephone numbers preceded by 800, 866, 877 or 888 mean you can call without incurring long-distance charges if you are dialing from Canada and often even from the United States. To reach the telephone operator, dial 0.

Considerably less expensive than in Europe, public phones are scattered throughout the city, easy to use and some even accept credit cards. Local calls cost $0.25 for unlimited time. For long distance calls, equip yourselves with quarters ($0.25 coins), or purchase a $10, $15 or $20 Smart Card ("La Puce"), on sale at newsstands, in convenience stores, or at Bell Téléboutiques. For example, a call from Montréal to Québec City will cost $2.50 for the first 3min and $0.38 for every additional minute. Calling from a private residence will cost even less. Paying by credit card or with the prepaid "HELLO!" card is also possible, but be advised that they are considerably more expensive.

When calling abroad you can use a local operator and pay local phone rates. First dial **011** then the international country code and then the phone number:

AUSTRALIA 61
BELGIUM 32
GERMANY 49
IRELAND 353
ITALY 39
NETHERLANDS 31
NEW ZEALAND 64
SPAIN 34
SWITZERLAND 41
UNITED KINGDOM 44

To call Great Britian, dial **011** + **44** + the area code (London **171** or **181**) + the number you are trying to reach. The same goes for Australia, New Zealand and most European countries.

Another way to call abroad is by using the direct access numbers below to contact an operator in your home country.

UNITED STATES
AT&T
☎ *800-CALL-ATT*
MCI
☎ *800-888-8000*

British Telecom Direct
☎ *800-408-6420*
☎ *363-4144*

Australia Telstra Direct
☎ *800-663-0683*

New Zealand Telecom Direct
☎ *800-663-0684*

Post Offices

Major post offices are open from 8am to 5:45pm. However, smaller outlets can be found all over the city, either in shopping centres, in *"depanneurs"*, and even pharmacies. For example, offices in the Tabagie Saint-Jean-Baptiste (620 Rue St-Jean) and the Pharmacie Jean Coutu (corner of Avenue Cartier and Boulevard René-Lévesque) are open much later than the others.

Bureau de Poste Principal
300 Rue Saint-Paul
☎ *694-6176*

Station B
58 Rue Dalhousie
☎ *694-6190*

Succursale Haute-Ville
5 Rue du Fort
☎ *694-6102*

Taxes and Tipping

Taxes

The ticket price on items usually **does not include tax**. There are two taxes, the GST (federal Goods and Services Tax or TPS in French) of 7% and the PST (provincial sales tax or TVQ

Practical
Information

in French) at 7.5% on goods and on services. They are cumulative, therefore you must add 14.59% in taxes to the price of most items and to restaurant and hotel prices. There is an additional $2 per night tax on hotel rooms.

There are some exceptions to this taxation system, such as books, which are only taxed 7% and food (except for ready-made meals), which is not taxed at all.

Tax Refunds for Non-Residents

Non-residents can be refunded for GST, the federal tax, paid on their purchases made while in Québec. To obtain a refund, it is important to keep your receipts. For further information, call ☎800-668-4748.

Tipping

Tipping applies to all table services, in restaurants or other places where customers are served at their tables (fast-food service is therefore not included in this category). Tipping is also compulsory in bars, nightclubs and taxis.

Depending on the quality of the service, patrons must leave approximately **15%** of the bill before tax. Unlike in Europe, the tip is not included in the bill, and clients must calculate the amount themselves and give it to the server. "Service charges" and "tip" have the same meaning in North America; do not forget to leave it.

Québec Cuisine

Although many restaurant dishes are similar to those served in the rest of Canada or the United States, some of them are prepared in a typically Québécois way. These unique dishes should definitely be tasted:

La soupe aux pois
pea soup

La tourtière
meat pie

Le pâté chinois
(also known as shepherd's pie) layered pie consisting of ground beef, potatoes, and corn

Les cretons
a type of pâté of ground pork cooked with onions in fat

Le jambon au sirop d'érable
ham with maple syrup

Les fèves au lard
baked beans

Le ragoût de pattes de cochon
pigs'-feet stew

Le cipaille
layered pie with different types of meat

La tarte aux pacanes
pecan pie

La tarte au sucre
sugar pie

La tarte aux bleuets
blueberry pie

Le sucre à la crème
rich maple-syrup fudge

In the country, you may also have the opportunity to enjoy some exceptional regional specialties like venison, hare, beaver, Atlantic salmon, Arctic char and Abitibi caviar.

Wine, Beer and Alcohol

In Québec, the provincial government is responsible for regulating alcohol, sold in liquor stores known as Société des Alcool du Québec (SAQ). If you wish to purchase wine, imported beer or hard liquor, you must go to a branch of the SAQ. Some outlets, known as "Sélection," offer a more varied and specialized selection of wines and spirits. SAQ outlets can be found throughout the city, but their opening hours are fairly limited, with the exception of so-called "Ex-

press" branches, open later but offering a more limited choice. As a general rule, their opening hours are the same as those of stores. Convenience and grocery stores have authorization to sell Canadian beer and a few wines, but the choice is slim and the quality of wines mediocre.

You must be at least 18 years old to purchase alcohol, the sale of which is not permitted after 11pm.

A few SAQ addresses:
1059 Avenue Cartier
☎643-4334

888 Rue Saint-Jean, almost at the corner of Avenue Dufferin
☎643-4337

SAQ Sélection
400 Boul. Jean-Lesage,
near the Gare du Palais
☎643-4339

SAQ Signature
Château Frontenac

Beer

Two huge breweries share the largest part of the beer market in Québec: Labatt and Molson-O'Keefe. They each produce different types of beer, mostly light ales, with varying levels of alcohol. In bars, restaurants, and nightclubs, draft beer is cheaper than bottled beer.

Practical Information

Besides these large breweries, some interesting independent micro-breweries have developed in the past few years. The variety and taste of these beers make them quite popular in Québec. However, because they are microbrews, they are not available everywhere. Here are a few of the micro-brewery beers: Unibroue (Maudite, Blanche de Chambly and Fin du Monde), McAuslan (Griffon, St-Ambroise), Le Cheval Blanc (Cap Tourmente, Berlue), Les Brasseurs du Nord (Boréale) and GMT (Belle Gueule).

Advice for Smokers

Smoking is considered a problem that must be eliminated. It is prohibited to smoke in most public places.

Smoking sections in public places (restaurants, cafés) must be closed off. Cigarettes are still sold in most places though (bars, grocery and convenience stores, and newspaper and magazine shops). You must be 18 years old to buy cigarettes.

Senior Citizens

Older people who would like to meet people their age can do so through the organization listed below. It provides information about activities and local clubs throughout Québec:

Fédération de l'Âge d'Or du Québec
4545 Avenue Pierre-de-Coubertin
C.P. 1000, Succursale M, Montréal
H1V 3R2
☎*(514) 252-3017*

Reduced transportation fares and entertainment tickets are often made available to seniors. Do not hesitate to ask.

Gay and Lesbian Life

Québec City provides some services for the gay community, which is concentrated mainly in Faubourg Saint-Jean-Baptiste.

There is a telephone service called **Gai Écoute** *(☎888-505-1010)*. And several support groups have been set up to meet the community's various needs of as well. For information about these groups, call CLSC Haute-Ville *(☎641-0784)*.

Free magazines *Fugues* and *Être Québec* are published monthly and are available in bars. They include information on the gay community's favourite meeting places.

Travellers with Disabilities

Keroul, an association that specializes in tourism for people with disabilities, publishes a guide, *Accessible Québec* (\$10), which lists places accessible to people with disabilities throughout the province. These places are classified according to tourist regions. In most of Quebec's regions, there are associations that organize leisure and sports activities as well. For the addresses of these associations, contact the Association Québécoise de Loisir pour Personnes Handicapées.

KEROUL
4545 Avenue Pierre-de-Coubertin
C.P. 1000 Succursale M
Montreal H1V 3R2
☎(514) 252-3104
www.keroul.qc.ca

Association Régionale de Loisir pour Personnes Handicapées/Québec–Chaudière-Appalaches
525 Boulevard Hamel Est, suite A-22
Québec, G1M 2S8
☎529-6134

Children

Children in Québec are treated like royalty. Facilities are available almost everywhere you go, whether it be transportation or leisure activities. Generally, children under two years of age travel for free, and those under 12 are eligible for fare reductions. The same rules apply for various leisure activities and shows. Find out before you purchase tickets. High chairs and children's menus are available in most restaurants, while a few of the larger stores provide a babysitting service while parents shop.

Pets

As a rule, animals are not allowed in most public places. If you decide to travel with your dog, you will not be able to take a bus. It is also impossible to go shopping with a dog in most places (even shopping centres) and certain covered markets. However, some hotels accept pets; make sure to check before leaving home. Animals however, are not permitted in food stores or restaurants.

Practical Information

Miscellaneous

Barbers and Hairstylists: As in restaurants, it is customary to tip 10% to 15% of the bill before taxes.

Drugs: Recreational drugs are against the law and not tolerated (even "soft" drugs). Anyone caught with drugs in their possession risks severe consequences.

Économusées:
Economuseums are educational, working museum found almost everywhere in Québec. They are intended to present Québec's traditional arts and crafts and are located in forges, flour mills, sculpture studios and other places where you can watch people at their craft.

Electricity: Voltage is 110 volts throughout Canada, the same as in the United States. Electricity plugs have two parallel, flat pins. Adaptors are available here.

Laundromats: Laundromats and dry cleaners are found almost everywhere in urban areas. In most cases, detergent is sold on site. Although change machines are sometimes provided, it is best to bring plenty of quarters (25-cent coins) with you.

Museums: Most museums charge admission; however, permanent exhibits at some museums are free, while reductions are offered for temporary exhibits. Reduced prices are available for seniors, children, and students. Call the museum for further details.

Newspapers: International newspapers are readily available here. Québec City's major newspapers are *Le Soleil* and *Le Journal de Québec*.

Pharmacies: In addition to traditional pharmacies, there are huge chain stores (medical- and beauty- product supermarkets). Do not be surprised to find chocolates and detergent next to cough drops and headache medication.

Public Washrooms: Most shopping centres have public toilets. But if you cannot find one you may be able to use the facilities in a bar or a restaurant.

Religion: Almost all religions are represented. Unlike English Canada, the majority of the Québec population is Catholic, although most Quebecers are not practising.

Weather: For road conditions, call ☎*643-6830*; for weather forecasts, call ☎*648-7766*.

Exploring

Québec City comprises eight districts totalling about half a million people, the majority of whom speak French.

It is difficult to pinpoint a specific downtown area in this city since some of the nearby suburbs are attracting more and more people. In fact, two or three areas, such as Vieux-Québec or Grande Allée, could claim this title. On the other hand, it is easier to locate Haute-Ville (uppertown) and Basse-Ville (lowertown), as they are often called by the Québécois. It is not difficult to distinguish them because the former, more bourgeois, is perched high on the promontory, while the latter is spread out at the foot of the north side.

In the first nine tours of this chapter, you will discover Québec City and its nearby suburbs. The last two excursions will take you outside the city to the Basilica of Sainte-Anne-de-Beaupré and the beautiful Île d'Orléans, among other places. The city tours are designed to maximize walking and use of public transportation, since visiting the city this way will allow you to feel the life that flows through its arteries. If you prefer, you can visit the city by car, but a car will be necessary to follow the last three tours.

Each tour includes information about the main tourist attractions and provides a historical and cultural overview. The attractions are classified according to a system of stars so that you can set your priorities, depending on your schedule.

★   Interesting
★★   Worth a visit
★★★   Not to be missed

The address, opening hours and cost are featured in brackets with each attraction. The admission price given is for one adult. Keep in mind that some places offer discounts to children, students and seniors, as well as family rates. Many of these attractions are only open during the tourist season; this will be indicated in the above-mentioned brackets. However, during the off season, some will welcome you if you make an appointment,

especially if you are with a group.

Follow this guide and let yourself be enticed by one of the most beautiful cities in the world!

Tour A: Vieux-Québec

(two to three days)

Vieux-Québec is divided into two parts by Cap Diamant. The part that spreads out between the river and the cliff is featured in the next tour (see p 89). The section covering the plateau atop Cap Diamant is informally called Vieux-Québec. As the administrative and institutional centre, it is adorned with convents, chapels and public buildings whose construction dates back, in some cases, to the 17th century. The walls of Haute-Ville, dominated by the citadel, surround this section of Vieux-Québec and give it the characteristic look of a fortress. These same walls long contained the development of the town, resulting in a densely built-up bourgeois and aristocratic milieu. With time, the picturesque urban planning of the 19th century contributed

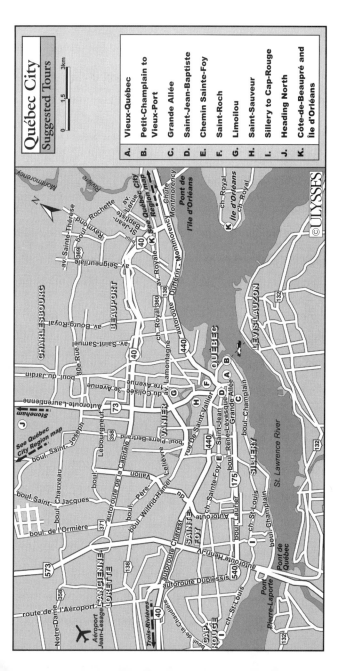

Québec City
Suggested Tours

0   1,5   3km

A. Vieux-Québec
B. Petit-Champlain to Vieux-Port
C. Grande Allée
D. Saint-Jean-Baptiste
E. Chemin Sainte-Foy
F. Saint-Roch
G. Limoilou
H. Saint-Sauveur
I. Sillery to Cap-Rouge
J. Heading North
K. Côte-de-Beaupré and île d'Orléans

© ULYSSES

to the present-day image of Québec City through the construction of such magnificent buildings as the Château Frontenac and the creation of such public spaces as Terrasse Dufferin, in the *belle époque* spirit.

The Haute-Ville walking tour begins at Porte Saint-Louis, near the parliament buildings.

Porte Saint-Louis *(at the beginning of the street of the same name)*, a gateway, is the result of Québec City merchants' pressuring the government between 1870 and 1875 to tear down the wall surrounding the city. The Governor General of Canada at the time, Lord Dufferin, was opposed to the idea and instead put forward a plan drafted by Irishman William H. Lynn to showcase the walls while improving traffic circulation. The design he submitted exhibits a Victorian romanticism in its use of grand gateways that bring to mind images of medieval castles and horsemen. The pepper-box tower of Porte Saint-Louis, built in

1878, makes for a striking first impression upon arriving in downtown Québec City.

Past Porte Saint-Louis, to the left and facing Parc de l'Esplanade, are the **busts** of British Prime Minister Winston Churchill and U.S. President Franklin D. Roosevelt. The two statues commemorate the Québec Conferences that were held by the Allies in 1943 and 1944.

On the right, on the opposite side of the street, is the **Club de la Garnison** *(97 Rue Saint-Louis)*, reserved for army officers, as well as the road leading to the citadel. As a visit to the citadel may require 2 to 3hrs, it is best to set aside extra time to take a tour of the premises (see p 87).

The **Fortifications of Québec National Historic Site ★** *($3; early May to mid-Oct every day 9am to 5pm, rest of the year 10am to 5pm; 648-7016)* displays models and maps outlining the development of Québec City's defense system and you can visit **Poudrière de l'Esplanade**. Booklets are available with a com

Porte Saint-Louis

The beautiful Fresque des Québécois covers the wall of a historic house in Place-Royale.
- *Louise Leblanc/ Commission de la capitale nationale du Québec*

e of the most spectacular natural phenomena in Québec is without question the Montmorency lls, which can actually be viewed from bove. Quite a sight!
- *Perry Mastrovito*

Located on the shores of the St. Lawrence River, the Sainte-Anne-d
Beaupré Basilica attracts many pilgrims each year. - *Y. Tessier*

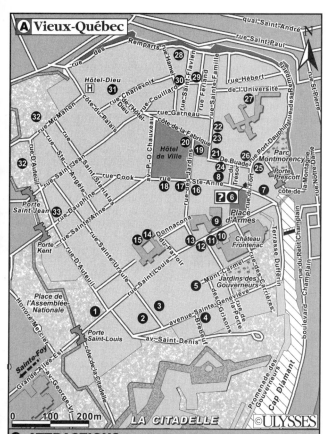

A Vieux-Québec

(map labels)

quai-Saint-André
rue-Saint-Paul
des Remparts
rue-Hamel
Hôtel-Dieu
rue-Hébert
de-l'Université
côte-du-Palais
rue-Charlevoix
côte-de-l'Hôtel-Dieu
rue-Saint-Flavien
rue-Saint-Famille
rue-Ferland
rue-McMahon
rue-Garneau
côte-de-la-Fabrique
rue-Sainte-Jean
rue-D'Auteuil
rue-Saint-Jean
rue-Sainte-Angèle
rue-Saint-Stanislas
rue-Cook
av.-P.-O.-Chauveau
Hôtel de Ville
rue-des-Jardins
De-Buade
Trésor
Parc Montmorency
rue-Port-Dauphin
rue-Sainte-Anne
Porte Prescott
côte-de
Porte Saint-Jean
rue-Dauphine
Porte Kent
rue-Sainte-Ursule
rue-Sainte-Anne
Donnacona
Place d'Armes
Château Frontenac
Terrasse Dufferin
rue-du-Parloir
rue-Saint-Louis
Mont-Carmel
Jardins des Gouverneurs
Place de l'Assemblée-Nationale
Honoré-Mercier
rue-des-Grisons
rue-de-la-Porte
avenue-Sainte-Geneviève
av.-Saint-Denis-E.
Porte Saint-Louis
côte-de-la-citadelle
Sainte-Foy
Grande-Allée-Est
rue-George-V.-E.
boulevard Champlain
rue-du-Petit-Champlain
rue-Notre-Dame
Promenade des Gouverneurs
Cap Diamant
LA CITADELLE
©ULYSSES
0   100   200m

● ATTRACTIONS

1. Fortifications of Québec National Historic Site
2. Chalmers-Wesley United Church
3. Sanctuaire Notre-Dame-du-Sacré-Cœur
4. Maison Cirice-Têtu
5. Cavalier du Moulin
6. Centre Infotouriste
7. Musée du Fort
8. Musée de Cire de Québec
9. Former courthouse
10. Maison Maillou
11. Maison Kent
12. Musée d'Art Inuit Brousseau
13. Maison Jacquet
14. Monastère des Ursulines
15. Musée des Ursulines
16. Holy Trinity Anglican Cathedral
17. Hôtel Clarendon
18. Édifice Price
19. Place de l'Hôtel-de-Ville

20. Hôtel de Ville et Centre d'Interprétation de la Vie Urbaine de la Ville de Québec
21. Cathédrale Catholique Notre-Dame-de-Québec
22. Séminaire de Québec
23. Musée de l'Amérique Française
24. Québec Expérience
25. Post Office and Parks Canada Exhibition Hall
26. Palais Archiépiscopal
27. Université Laval
28. Maison Montcalm
29. Musée Bon-Pasteur
30. Maison François-Xavier-Garneau
31. Chapelle and Musée de l'Hôtel-Dieu
32. Artillery Park National Historic Site
33. Église des Jésuites

plete tour of the city's fortifications, and the **Centre
d'Initiation aux Fortifications**
offers guided tours *($10)*.
Information plaques have
been placed along the wall,
providing another means of
discovering the city's history. The walkway on top
of the wall can be reached
by using the stairs next to
the city gates.

Baillargé or Baillairgé

Recent historical studies
have prompted us to use
the name Baillairgé to de-
signate this famous family
of Québec architects.
However, documents
signed by members of the
family reveal that they
themselves used both
Baillargé and Baillairgé.
Don't be surprised, therefore, if you see both; the
reference is always to the
same family.

Québec City's first wall was
built of earth and wooden
posts. It was erected on the
west side of the city in
1693, according to the plans
of engineer Dubois
Berthelot de Beaucours, to
protect Québec City from

the Iroquois. Work on
much stronger stone fortifications began in 1745, designed by engineer
Chaussegros de Léry, when
England and France entered
a new era of conflict. However, the wall was unfin-
ished when the city was
seized by the British in
1759. The British saw to the
completion of the project at
the end of the 18th century.
Some work on the citadel
began in 1693; however,
the structure as we know it
today was essentially built
between 1820 and 1832.
Nevertheless, the citadel is
largely designed along the
principles advanced by
Vauban in the 17th cen-
tury—principles that suit
the location admirably.

*Continue along Rue Saint-
Louis and turn right on Rue
Sainte-Ursule.*

Until the end of the 19th
century, Québec City had a
small but influential community of Scottish
Presbyterians, most of
whom were involved in
shipping and the lumber
trade. The **Chalmers-Wesley
United Church** *(78 Rue Sainte-
Ursule, ☎692-2640)*, an attractive Gothic Revival
structure, is presently used
by a variety of groups, testi-
mony to the decline in the
Scottish Presbyterian community. The church was
built in 1852, and designed
by John Wells, an architect

known for a number of famous buildings, including the Bank of Montreal headquarters. The elegant Gothic Revival spire of the church contributes to the picturesque aspect of the city. The church's organ was restored in 1985. Concerts are presented at the church every Sunday night from the beginning of July until the middle of August. Donations are appreciated.

The **Sanctuaire Notre-Dame-du-Sacré-Coeur** *(free admission; open every day 7am to 8pm; 71 Rue Sainte-Ursule,* ☎*692-3787)* faces Chalmers-Wesley United Church. The sanctuary was originally built for the Sacré Cœur missionaries. This place of worship, erected in 1910 and designed by François-Xavier Berlinguet, is now open to everyone. The sanctuary has a Gothic Revival facade. Its two rather narrow steeples seem dwarfed by the size of the building. The interior of the structure, with its stained glass windows and murals, is more attractive.

Return to Avenue Sainte-Geneviève and then turn left.

In addition to the city's major historical landmarks, Québec's appeal lies with its smaller, less imposing buildings, each of which has its own separate history. It is enjoyable to sim-ply wander the narrow streets of the old city, taking in the subtleties of architecture so atypical of North America. The **Maison Cirice-Têtu** ★ *(25 Avenue Sainte-Geneviève)* (house) was built in 1852. It was designed by Charles Baillargé, a member of a celebrated family of architects who, beginning in the 18th century, left an important mark on the architecture of Québec City and its surroundings. The Greek Revival facade of the house, a masterpiece of the genre, is tastefully decorated with palmettes and the discreet use of laurel. The main floor has huge bay windows that open onto a single expansive living room in the London style. From the time of its construction, the house incorporated all the modern amenities: central heating, hot running water and multiple bathrooms.

A short detour down Rue Mont-Carmel (to the left) brings you to one of the remnants of Québec City's earliest fortifications, located in an out-of-the-way spot behind a row of houses. The **Cavalier du Moulin** was built in 1693 by engineer Dubois Bertholot de Beaucours. It is a redoubt set within the city walls from which it would be possible to destroy them in the event of a successful enemy invasion. The fortification is named for the windmill, or *moulin*, that used to sit on top of it.

Terrasse Dufferin

than the pavement we are used to. It was built in 1879 at the request of the governor general of the time, Lord Dufferin. The boardwalk's open-air pavilions and ornate streetlamps were designed by Charles Baillargé and were inspired by the style of French urban architecture common under Napoleon III. Terrasse Dufferin is one of Québec City's most popular sights and is the preferred meeting place for young people. The view of the river, the south shore and Île d'Orléans is magnificent. During the winter months, a huge ice slide is set up at the western end of the boardwalk.

The charming square known as **Jardin des Gouverneurs ★** was originally the private garden of the governor of New France. The square was laid out in 1647 for Charles Huault de Montmagny to the west of Château Saint-Louis, the residence of the governor, which is no longer standing. A monument to opposing military leaders Wolfe and Montcalm, both of whom died on the battlefields of the Plains of Abraham, was erected during the restoration of the garden in 1827.

A walk on the wooden planks of the **Terrasse Dufferin ★★★**, overlooking the St. Lawrence, provides a different sensation

Terrasse Dufferin is located where the Château Saint-Louis, the long-destroyed elaborate residence of the governor of New France, used to stand. Built at the very edge of the escarpment, this three-storey building had a long, private stone terrace on the river side, while the main entrance, consisting of a fortified facade, opened onto Place d'Armes and featured pavilions with imperial-type roofs. The château was built in the 17th century by architect François de la Joue and was enlarged in 1719 by engineer Chausegros de Léry. Its rooms, linked one to the other, were the scene of elegant receptions given for French nobility. Plans for the future of the entire continent were drawn up in this building. Château Saint-Louis was badly damaged in the British invasion of the city at the time of the Conquest and was later remodelled according to British tastes before being destroyed by fire in 1834.

Château Frontenac

There are two **monuments** at the far end of Terrasse Dufferin. One is dedicated to the memory of Samuel de Champlain, the founder of Québec City and father of New France. It was designed by Parisian sculptor Paul Chevré and erected in 1898. The second monument informs visitors that Vieux-Québec was recog-

nized as a World Heritage Site by Unesco in 1985. Québec City is the first city in North America to be included on this list. A staircase just to the left of the Champlain monument leads to the Place-Royale quarter in Basse-Ville (Tour B). At the other end of the Terrasse, you'll find another staircase leading to the **Promenade des Gouverneurs** (see p 118).

The first half of the 19th century saw the emergence of Québec City's tourism industry when the romantic European nature of the city began to attract growing numbers of American visitors. In 1890, the Canadian Pacific Railway company, under Cornelius Van Horne, decided to create a chain of distinguished hotels across Canada. The first of these hotels (see p 197) was the **Château Frontenac ★ ★ ★** *(1 Rue des Carrières)*, named in honour of one of the best-known governors of New France, Louis de Buade, Comte de Frontenac (1622-1698).

The magnificent Château Frontenac, symbol of the province's capital city, is probably the most famous sight in Québec. Ironically,

Exploring

the hotel was designed by an American architect, Bruce Price (1845-1903), known for his New York skyscrapers. The look of the hotel, which combines certain elements of the Scottish manors and the châteaux of the Loire Valley in France, has come to be considered a national archetype style called "Château Style." Bruce Price, who also designed Montréal's Windsor train station and the famous Tuxedo Park development near New York, was inspired by the picturesque location chosen for the hotel and by the mix of French and English cultures in Canada.

The Château Frontenac was built in stages. Price's initial wing overlooked Terrasse Dufferin and was completed in 1893. Three sections were later added, the most important of these being the central tower (1923), the work of architects Edward and William Sutherland Maxwell. To fully appreciate the château, one must go inside to explore the main hall, decorated in a style popular in 18th-century Parisian *hôtels particuliers*, and visit the Bar Maritime in the large main tower overlooking the river.

The Château Frontenac has been the site of a number of important events in history. In 1944, the Québec Conference was held here. At this historic meeting, U.S. President Franklin D. Roosevelt, British Prime Minister Winston Churchill and Canadian Prime Minister Mackenzie King met to discuss the future of post-war Europe. On the way out of the courtyard is a stone with the inscription of the Order of Malta, dated 1647, the only remaining piece of Château Saint-Louis. **Tours** *($6.50; May to mid-Oct every day 10am to 6pm; mid-Oct to end of Apr Sat and Sun 1pm to 5pm; ☎691-2166)* of Château Frontenac are given by guides dressed in period costume.

Until the construction of the citadel, **Place d'Armes** ★ was a military parade ground. It became a public square in 1832. In 1916, the *Monument de la Foi* (Monument of Faith) was erected in Place d'Armes to mark the tricentennial of the arrival of the Récollet religious order in Québec. Abbot Adolphe Garneau's statue rests on a base designed by David Ouellet.

At the other end of the square are the Centre Infotouriste (a tourist information centre) and two museums. The back of the Holy Trinity Anglican Cathedral (see p 74) is also visible from here.

The **Centre Infotouriste** *(12 Rue Sainte-Anne)* is located in the former Union Hotel, a white building with a copper roof. A group of wealthy Quebecers saw the need for a luxury hotel in Québec City and commissioned British architect Edward Cannon to head the project which was completed in 1803.

On either side of the Centre Infotouriste are two popular tourist attractions. Using an elaborate model of the city along with a sound and light show, the **Musée du Fort** *($6.75; Jul to mid-Sep every day 10am to 7pm; mid-Sep to end Oct and Apr to end Jun every day 10am to 5pm; Feb and Mar Thu to Sun 10pm to 4pm; 10 Rue Sainte-Anne, ☎692-1759)* recreates the six sieges of Québec City, starting with the capture of the town by the Kirke brothers in 1629 and ending with the American invasion of 1775.

Musée de Cire de Québec *($3; May to Oct every day 9am to 10pm, rest of the year every day 10am to 5pm; 22 Rue Sainte-Anne, ☎692-2289)* displays wax likenesses of about 60 individuals grouped in 16 settings that depict Québec City's history or recent events. You will see Lara Fabian and Roch Voisine (contemporary pop-music stars) alongside Churchill, Champlain and Wolfe.

Return to Rue St-Louis.

Ancien Palais de Justice (Former Couthouse) ★ *(12 Rue Saint-Louis)* is the city's original courthouse, built in 1883 by Eugène-Étienne Taché, architect of the parliament buildings. The courthouse resembles the parliament in a number of ways. Its French Renaissance Revival design preceded the Château style as the "official" style of the city's major building projects. The interior of the building was renovated between 1922 and 1930; it has several large rooms with attractive woodwork. Since 1987, the Ancien Palais de Justice building has been used by Québec's Ministry of Finance.

Maison Maillou *(17 Rue Saint-Louis)* is the location of the seat of Québec's chamber of commerce. This attractive French Regime house was built in 1736 by architect Jean Maillou. It was saved from destruction after the stock market crash of 1929 led to the abandonment of plans to expand the Château Frontenac.

The history of **Maison Kent** *(24 Rue Saint-Louis)*, once a residence of Queen Victoria's father, the Duke of Kent, is somewhat cloudy. There is some disagreement as to whether the house was built in the 17th or 18th century. It is clear, however, from its English sash

Exploring

windows and low-pitched roof, that the house underwent major renovations during the 19th century. The agreement that handed Québec over to the British in 1759 was signed in this house. Ironically, it is now occupied by the Consulate General of France.

Continue on Rue Saint-Louis.

The Galerie d'Art Inuit Brousseau is well known for the quality of its works of art and now includes a small museum to house the owner's private collection: **Musée d'Art Inuit Brousseau** ★ *($6; every day 9:30am to 5:30pm; 39 Rue St-Louis, ☎694-1828).* Each of the five exhibition rooms has its own theme such as history, materials used, etc. The works are well placed and it is a pleasure to visit the bright, airy and modern display rooms. The historical and cultural notes are interesting and quite complete. At the end of the tour you can watch a documentary video on the artists whose works are presented or return to the adjoining shop to purchase some for yourself.

Maison Jacquet ★ *(34 Rue Saint-Louis)*, a small, red-roofed building covered in white roughcast dating from 1690, is the oldest house in Haute-Ville; it is the only house in Vieux-Québec that still looks just as it did in the 17th century. The house is distinguished from those built during the following century by its high, steep roof covering a living area with a very low ceiling. The house is named for François Jacquet, who once owned the land on which it stands. It was built by architect François de la Joue in 1690, for his own use. In 1815, the house was acquired by Philippe Aubert de Gaspé, author of the famous novel *Les Anciens Canadiens* (The Canadians of Old). The restaurant that now occupies the house takes its name from this book.

Turn right on Rue du Parloir.

At the corner of rue Donnacona, you will find the **Monastère des Ursulines** ★★★ *(18 Rue Donnacona; ☎694-0413).* In 1535, Sainte Angèle Merici founded the first Ursuline community in Brescia, Italy. After the community had established itself in France, it became a cloistered order dedicated to teaching (1620). With the help of a benefactor, Madame de la Peltrie, the Ursulines arrived in Québec City in 1639 and, in 1641, founded a monastery and convent where generations of young girls have received a good education. The Ursulines convent is the longest running girls' school in North America.

Maison Jacquet

Only the museum and chapel, a small part of the huge Ursulines complex, where several dozen nuns still live, are open to the public.

The Sainte-Ursuline chapel was rebuilt in 1901 on the site of the original 1722 chapel. Part of the magnificent interior decoration of the first chapel, created by Pierre-Nöel Levasseur between 1726 and 1736, survived and is present in the newer structure. The work includes a pulpit surmounted by a trumpeting angel and a beautiful altarpiece in the Louis XIV style. The tabernacle of the high altar is embellished with fine gilding applied by the Ursulinesé. The Sacred Heart tabernacle, a masterpiece of the genre, is attributed to Jaques Leblond,

also known as Latour, and dates from around 1770. Some of the paintings decorating the church come from the collection of Father Jean-Louis Desjardins, a former chaplain of the Ursulines. In 1820, Desjardins bought several dozen paintings from an art dealer in Paris. The paintings had previously hung in Paris churches but were removed during the French Revolution. Works from this collection can still be seen in churches all over Québec. At the entrance hangs *Jésus chez Simon le Pharisien* (Jesus with Simon the Pharisee) by Philippe de Champaigne, and to the right of the nave hangs *La Parabole des Dix Vierges* (The Parable of the Ten Virgins), by Pierre de Cortone.

The chapel was the burial site of the Marquis de

Exploring

Montcalm until 2001, when his remains were transferred to the Hôpital Général cemetery (see p 146). General of the French troops during the decisive Battle of the Plains of Abraham, he was fatally wounded during the conflict, as was his rival General Wolfe. The tomb of blessed Mère Marie de l'Incarnation, the founder of the Ursulines monastery in Québec is still there. An opening provides a view of the nuns' chancel, rebuilt in 1902 by David Ouellet who outfitted it with a cupola-shaped skylight. An interesting painting by an unknown artist, *La France Apportant la Foi aux Indiens de la Nouvelle-France* (France Bringing the Faith to the Indians of New France), also hangs in this section of the chapel.

The entrance to **Musée des Ursulines** *($5; May to Sep, Tue to Sat 10am to noon and 1pm to 5pm, Sun 1pm to 5pm; Oct to Dec and Feb to Apr Tue to Sun 1pm to 4:30pm 12 Rue Donnacona,* ☎*694-0694)* is across from the chapel. The museum outlines nearly four centuries of Ursuline history. On view are various works of art, Louis XIII furniture, impressive embroideries made of gold thread, and 18th-century altar cloths and church robes.

Continue on Rue Donnacona, and turn left on Rue des Jardins. Note the tiny little house on your left!

After the British Conquest of Québec, a small group of British administrators and military officers established themselves in Québec City. These men wanted to mark their presence through the construction of prestigious buildings with typically British designs. However, their small numbers resulted in the slow progress of this vision until the beginning of the 19th century when work began on The **Holy Trinity Anglican Cathedral** ★ ★ *(31 Rue des Jardins)* by Majors Robe and Hall, two military engineers inspired by St. Martin's Church in London Fields. The Palladian-style church was completed in 1804. This significant example of non-French architecture changed the look of the city. The church was the first Anglican cathedral built outside Britain and, in its elegant simplicity, is a good example of British colonial architecture. The roof was made steeper in 1815 so that it would not be weighted down by snow.

The cathedral's interior, more sober than that of most Catholic churches, is adorned with various generous gifts from King George III, including several pieces of silverware and pews made of English oak from the forests of Windsor. The bishop's chair is said to have been carved from an elm tree under which Samuel de Champlain liked to sit. There are stained-glass windows and commemorative plaques which were added over the years. There is also a Casavant organ dating from 1909 that was restored in 1959. Its set of eight bells is one of the oldest in Canada.

*Continue along Rue des Jardins. To the right is a cobblestone section of **Rue Sainte-Anne** and on the left is the Hôtel Clarendon and the Price building.*

The **Hôtel Clarendon** *(57 Rue Sainte-Anne)* began receiving guests in 1870 in the former Desbarats print shop (1858). It is the oldest hotel still operating in Québec (see p 196) The Charles Baillargé-designed restaurant on the main floor is also the oldest restaurant in Canada (see p 225) The Victorian charm of the somber woodwork evokes the *belle époque*. The Hôtel Clarendon was expanded in 1929 by the addition of a brick tower featuring an Art Deco entrance hall designed by Raoul Chênevert.

The design of **Édifice Price** ★ *(65 Rue Sainte-Anne)* manages to adhere to that of traditional North American skyscraper architecture and yet does not look out of place among the historic buildings of Haute-Ville. Architects Ross and MacDonald of Montréal gave the building a tall yet discreet silhouette when they designed it in 1929. It features a copper roof typical of Château-style architecture. The main hall of the building, a fine example of Art Deco design, is covered in polished travertine and bronze bas-reliefs depicting the various activities of the Price company, which specialized in the production of paper.

Walk back up to Rue des Jardins, that you take on the left.

The next stop is quaint **Maison Antoine-Vanfelson** at 17 Rue des Jardins, built in 1780. A talented silversmith by the name of Laurent Amiot had a workshop here in the 19th century. The rooms on the second floor of this building feature wonderful Louis XV woodwork.

Place de l'Hôtel-de-Ville ★, a small square, was the location of the Notre-Dame market in the 18th century. A monument in honour of Cardinal Taschereau, created by André Vermare, was erected here in 1923.

Exploring

The American Romanesque Revival influence seen in the **Hôtel de Ville** *(2 Rue des Jardins)* stands out in a city where French and British traditions have always dominated the construction of public buildings. The building was completed in 1895 following disagreements among the mayor and the city councillors as to a building plan. Sadly, a Jesuit college dating from 1666 was demolished to make room for the city hall. Under the pleasant **jardins de l'Hôtel de Ville**, gardens outside the building, where popular events are held in the summer, is an underground parking lot, a much needed addition in this city of narrow streets.

The **Centre d'Interprétation de la Vie Urbaine de la Ville de Québec** *($2; end Jun to early Sep every day 10am to 5pm; rest of the year Tue-Sun 10am to 5pm; 43 Côte de la Fabrique, ☎691-4606)*, an information centre on urban life in Québec City, is located in the basement of city hall. It addresses questions of urban development and planning. An interesting model of the city provides an understanding of the layout of the area.

The history of Québec City's cathedral underscores the problems faced by builders in New France and the determination of the Québécois in the face of the worst circumstances. The **Basilique-Cathédrale Notre-Dame-de-Québec** ★★★ *(at the other end of Place de l'Hôtel-de-Ville)* as it stands today is the result of numerous phases of construction and a number of tragedies that left the church in ruins on two occasions. The first church on this site was built in 1632 under the orders of Samuel de Champlain, who was buried nearby four years later. This wooden church was replaced in 1647 by Église Notre-Dame-de-la-Paix, a stone church in the shape of a Roman cross that would later serve as the model for many rural parish churches. In 1674, New France was assigned its first bishop in residence. Monseigneur François-Xavier de Montmorency-Laval (1623-1708) decided that this small church, after renovations befitting its status as the heart of such an enormous ministry, would become the seat of the Catholic Church in Québec. A grandiose plan was commissioned from architect Claude Baillif, which, despite personal financial contributions from Louis XIV, was eventually scaled down. Only the base of the west tower survives from this period. In 1742, the bishop had the church remodelled by engineer Gaspard Chaussegros de

Léry, who is responsible for its present layout, featuring an extended nave illuminated from above. The cathedral resembles many urban churches built in France during the same period.

During the siege of Québec in 1759, the cathedral was bombarded and reduced to ruins. It was not rebuilt until the status of Catholics in Québec was settled by the British crown. The oldest Catholic parish north of Mexico was finally allowed to begin the reconstruction of its church in 1770, using the 1742 plans. The work was directed by Jean Baillargé (1726-1805), a member of the well-known family of architects

and craftsmen. This marked the beginning of the Baillargé family's extended, fervent involvement with the reconstruction and renovation of the church. In 1789, the decoration of the church interior was entrusted to Jean Baillargé's son François (1759-1830), who had recently returned from three years of studying architecture in Paris at the Académie Royale. He designed the chancel's beautiful gilt baldaquin with winged caryatids four years later. The high altar, the first in Québec to be designed to look like the facade of a Basilica, was put into place in 1797. The addition of baroque pews and a plaster vault created an interesting contrast. Thus completed, the spectacular interior emphasized the use of gilding, wood and white plasterwork according to typically Québécois traditions.

In 1843, Thomas Baillargé (1791-1859), the son of François, created the present neoclassical fa-

Basilique-Cathédrale Notre-Dame-de-Québec

Exploring

cade and attempted to erect a steeple on the east side of the church. Work on the steeple was halted at the halfway point when it was discovered that the 17th-century foundations were not strong enough. Charles Baillargé (1826-1906), Thomas Baillargé's cousin, designed the wrought-iron gate around the front square in 1858. Between 1920 and 1922, the church was carefully restored, but just a few weeks after the work was completed a fire seriously damaged the building. Raoul Chênevert and Maxime Roisin, who had already come to Québec from Paris to take on the reconstruction of the Basilica in Sainte-Anne-de-Beaupré, were put in charge of yet another restoration of the cathedral. In 1959, a mausoleum was put into place in the basement of the church. It holds the remains of Québec bishops and various governors (Frontenac, Vaudreuil, de Callière). In recent years, several masterpieces that were hanging in the church have been stolen, leaving bare walls and increasing the need to safeguard the remaining paintings, including the beautiful *Saint-Jérôme*, by Jacques-Louis David (1780), now at the Musée de l'Amérique Française.

Feux Sacrés *($7.50; early May to mid-Oct every day 1pm to 9pm; 20 Rue Buade, ☎694-4000)*, a sound and light show, is set up inside the cathedral. It illustrates a page of Québec's history with the aid of three-dimensional effects on three screens. Shows are in French and English simultaneously.

During the 17th century, the **Séminaire de Québec ★★★** *(late Jun to late Aug; 2 Côte de la Fabrique, ☎692-3981)*, a religious complex, was an oasis of European civilization in a rugged and hostile territory. To get an idea of how it must have appeared to students of the day, go through the old gate (decorated with the seminary's coat of arms) and into the courtyard before proceeding through the opposite entryway to the reception desk.

The seminary was founded in 1663 by Monseigneur Francois de Laval, on orders from the Séminaire des Missions Étrangères de Paris (seminary of foreign missions), with which it remained affiliated until 1763. As headquarters of the clergy throughout the colony, it was at the seminary that future priests studied, that parochial funds were administered, and that ministerial appointments were made. Louis XIV's Minister,

Colbert, further required the seminary to establish a smaller school devoted to the conversion and education of native people. Following the British Conquest and the subsequent banishing of the Jesuits, the seminary became a college devoted to classical education. It also served as housing for the bishop of Québec after his palace was destroyed during the invasion. In 1852, the seminary founded the Université Laval, the first French-language university in North America. The Séminaire's vast ensemble of buildings now includes the priests' residence, a private school for boys and girls, the faculty of architecture of Université Laval, and the Musée de l'Amérique Française (see below), which manages these historic buildings.

Today's seminary is the result of rebuilding efforts following numerous fires and bombardments. Across from the old gate the wing devoted to the offices of the Procurator can be seen, complete with sundial. During the 1690 attack of Admiral Phipps, it was in the vaulted cellars of this wing that the citizens of Québec City took refuge.

It also contains the private chapel of Monseigneur Briand (1785), decorated with sculpted olive branches by Pierre Emond. Forming a right angle with the chapel is the beautiful parlor wing, constructed in 1696. The use of segmented arch windows in this attractive building betrays the direct influence of French models, which were used prior to making adaptations to Québec climate. Guided tours leave from the Musée de l'Amérique Française.

The exterior chapel was built in 1890 to replace the original, which dated from 1752 and burned down in 1888. In order to avoid any such recurrence, the interior, which is similar to that of Église de la Trinité in Paris, was covered over in tin and zinc and painted in *trompe l'oeil*, following the design of Paul Alexandre de Cardonnel and Joseph-Ferdinand Peachy. The chapel contains the most significant collection of relics in North America, including these of Saint-Augustine and Saint-Anselm, the martyrs of Tonkin, Saint Charles Borromé and Ignatius of Loyola. Some religious relics are both large and authentic while others are rather small and dubious. On the left is a funeral chapel housing a tomb containing the remains of Monseigneur de Laval, the first bishop of North America.

Musée de l'Amérique Française ★★ *($4, $8.50*

Exploring

package with Musée de la Civilisation and Centre d'Interprétation de la Place-Royale; late Jun to early Sep every day 10am to 5:30pm; early Sep to late Jun Tue-Sun 10am to 5pm; 2 Côte de la Fabrique, ☎692-2843, www.mcq.org) is dedicated to the seven North American communities that were formed by French immigration. Other than the Québécois, they are the Acadians, Franco-Ontarians, francophones from the West, Metis and francophones from Louisiana and New England. It contains over 450,000 artifacts including silverware, paintings, oriental art and numismatics, as well as scientific instruments, collected for educational purposes over the course of the last three centuries by the priests of the seminary. The museum occupies five floors of what used to be the residences of the Université Laval. The first Egyptian mummy brought to America is on view, as are several items that belonged to Monseigneur de Laval. Temporary exhibitions are also held presenting figures from history as well.

On returning to Place de l'Hôtel-de-Ville, turn left on Rue Buade.

The old **Holt Renfrew** store *(43 Rue Buade)*, which opened in 1837, faces the cathedral. The store originally sold furs, which it supplied by appointment to Her Majesty the Queen, and for many years Holt's held the exclusive rights for the Canadian distribution of Dior and Saint-Laurent creations. Holt's is now closed, having given way to the boutiques of the **Promenades du Vieux-Québec**.

A little further on is the entrance to **Rue du Trésor,** which also leads to Place d'Armes and Rue Sainte-Anne. Artists come here to sell paintings, drawings and silkscreens, many of which depict views of Québec City.

Québec Expérience *($7.50; mid-May to mid-Oct every day 10am to 10pm; mid-Oct to mid-May every day 10am to 5pm; 8 Rue du Trésor, 3rd floor, ☎694-4000)*, is an elaborate show depicting the history of Québec City. This lively three-dimensional multimedia presentation takes viewers back in time to relive the great moments in the city's history through its important historical figures. A wonderful way to learn about Québec City's past, these half-hour shows are a big hit with the kids. Presented in both French and English.

The **Bureau de Poste** ★ *(3 Rue Buade)*, Canada's first

Rue du Trésor

This pretty little street where artists work during the summer has been called Rue du Trésor since the time of the French regime. In fact, the colonists passed through this street on the way to pay their taxes to the treasury, which was situated where Maison Maillou now stands. Strangely enough, this building now houses the Chambre de Commerce de Québec. One could say that true callings are not always lost with time!

post office, opened in Québec City in 1837. For a long time it was housed in the old Hôtel du Chien d'Or, a solid dwelling built around 1753 for a wealthy Bordeaux merchant, who ordered a bas-relief depicting a dog gnawing a bone executed above the doorway. The following inscription appeared underneath the bas-relief, which was relocated to the pediment of the present post office in 1872: *"Je suis un chien qui ronge l'os, en le rongeant je prends mon repos. Un temps viendra qui n'est pas venu où je mordrai qui m'aura mordu."* (I am a dog gnawing a bone, as I gnaw, I rest at home. Though it's not yet here there'll come a time when those who bit me will be paid in kind.) It is said that the message was destined for Intendant Bigot, a man known for being a swindler, who was so outraged he had the Bordeaux merchant killed.

The dome of the post office and the facade overlooking the river were added at the beginning of the 20th century. The building was renamed **Édifice Louis-Saint-Laurent**, in honour of the former prime minister of Canada. Besides the traditional post and philatelic services, a **Parks Canada Exhibition Hall** *(free admission; Mon-Fri 8am to 4:30pm, Sat and Sun 10am to 5pm; 3 Rue Buade, ☎648-4177)* was added to illustrate Canada's natural and historical heritage. Note that the hall will be closed in 2002 for renovations.

Facing the post office stands a monument to Monseigneur François de Montmorency Laval (1623-1708), the first bishop of Québec, whose diocese covered two thirds of the North American continent. Designed by Philippe Hébert and erected in 1908,

Exploring

the monument features an attractive staircase leading to Côte de la Montagne and from there to Basse-Ville.

The Laval Bishop's monument is located directly in front of **Palais Archiépiscopal** *(2 Rue Port-Dauphin)* or archbishopric, which was rebuilt by Thomas Baillargé in 1844. The first archbishopric stood in what is now Parc Montmorency. Designed by Claude Baillif and built between 1692 and 1700, the original palace was, by all accounts, one of the most gorgeous of its kind in New France. Drawings show an impressive building, complete with a recessed chapel whose interior was reminiscent of Paris's Val de Grace. Though the chapel was destroyed in 1759, the rest of the building was restored and then occupied by the Legislative Assembly of Lower Canada from 1792 to 1840. It was demolished in 1848 to make room for the new parliamentary buildings, which went up in flames only four years later.

Parc Montmorency ★ was laid out in 1875 after the city walls were lowered along Rue des Remparts and the governor general of Canada, Lord Dufferin, discovered the magnificent view from the promontory. George-Etienne Cartier, prime minister of the Do-

minion of Canada and one of the Fathers of Confederation, is honoured with a statue here, as are Louis Hébert, Guillaume Couillard and Marie Rollet, some of the original farmers of New France. These last three disembarked in 1617 and were granted the fiefdom of Sault-au-Matelot, on the future site of the seminary, in 1623. These attractive bronzes are the work of Montréal sculptor Alfred Laliberté.

Continue along rue des Remparts.

The halls of the old **Université Laval ★** can be seen through a gap in the wall of the ramparts. Built in 1856 in the gardens of the seminary, they were completed in 1875 with the addition of an impressive mansard roof surmounted by three silver lanterns. When the spotlights shine on them at night, it creates the atmosphere of a royal gala. Note that Université Laval is now located on a large campus in Sainte-Foy (see p 127).

Following **Rue des Remparts**, Basse-Ville (lower town) comes into view and you'll see a lot of old cannons. The patrician manors on the street along the ramparts provide a picturesque backdrop for the old Latin quarter which extends behind

Small Panes of Glass

Why do the windows of the old houses in Québec City and the rest of the province have many small panes instead of large panes of glass? You might think it is because of the cold and the snow. But the answer is even more down-to-earth. During colonial times, glass was imported from France.

Needless to say, much of it broke en route. As a result, the merchants decided to import smaller pieces of glass so there would be less risk of breakage. Even so, in order to protect the glass it was sometimes transported in large barrels of molasses!

them. The narrow streets and 18th-century houses in this neighbourhood are worth the detour.

Maison Montcalm *(45 to 51 Rue des Remparts)* was originally a very large residence constructed in 1727; it is now divided into three houses. Home of the Marquis de Montcalm at the time of the Battle of the Plains of Abraham, the building subsequently housed the officers of the British army before being subdivided and returned to private use. In the first half of the 19th century, many houses in Québec were covered in the sort of imitation stone boards that still

protect the masonry of the Montcalm house. Because of this example, it was believed that the covering lent a more refined look to the houses.

Take Rue Saint-Flavien.

At the corner of Rue Couillard is **Maison François-Xavier-Garneau** *($5; Fri-Sun 1pm to 5pm, tours on the hour; 14 Rue St-Flavien, ☎692-2240)*. Québec City businessman Louis Garneau recently bought this neoclassical house (1862) where historian and poet François-Xavier-Garneau lived during the last years of his life. Throughout the summer, an actor dressed in

Exploring

period costume is on site to make the past come alive as you visit the rooms and admire the objects on display.

Nearby, on Rue Couillard, is the **Musée Bon-Pasteur ★** *($2; year-round 1pm to 5pm, closed Mon; 14 Rue Couillard,* ☎*694-0243)*, founded in 1993, tells the story of the Bon Pasteur (Good Shepherd) community of nuns, which has been serving the poor of Québec City since 1850. The museum is located in the Béthanie house, an eclectic brick structure built around 1887 to shelter unwed mothers and their children. The museum occupies three floors of an 1878 addition and houses furniture as well as sacred objects manufactured or collected by the nuns, as well as a video documentary that recounts an adoption.

Walk back on Rue Couillard. Go down Rue Hamel until Rue Charlevoix where you turn left.

The Augustinian nurses founded their first convent in Québec in Sillery. Uneasy about the Iroquois, they relocated to Québec City in 1642 and began construction of the present complex, the **Chapelle** and **Musée de l'Hôtel-Dieu ★★** *(32 Rue Charlevoix)*, which includes a convent, a hospital and a chapel. Rebuilt

several times, today's buildings mostly date from the 20th century. The oldest remaining part is the 1756 convent, built on the vaulted foundations from 1695, hidden behind the 1800 chapel. This chapel was erected using material from various French buildings destroyed during the Seven Years' War. The stone was taken from the palace of the intendant, while its first ornaments came from the 17th-century Jesuit church. Today, only the iron balustrade of the bell tower bears witness to the original chapel. The present neoclassical facade was designed by Thomas Baillargé in 1839 after he completed the new interior in 1835. The nun's chancel can be seen to the right. Abbot Louis-Joseph Desjardins used the chapel as an auction house in 1817 and again in 1821, after he purchased the collection of a bankrupt Parisian banker who had amassed works confiscated from Paris churches during the French Revolution. *La Vision de Sainte-Thérèse d'Avila* (Saint Theresa of Avila's Vision), a work by François-Guillaume Ménageot which originally hung in the Carmel de Saint-Denis near Paris, can be seen in one of the side altars.

Musée des Augustines de l'Hôtel-Dieu *($3; Tue-Sat,*

9:30am to noon and 1:30pm to 5pm; Sun 1:30pm to 5pm; 32 Rue Charlevoix, ☎692-2492), is a museum which traces the history of the Augustinian community in New France through pieces of furniture, paintings, and medical instruments. On display is the chest that contained the meagre belongings of the founders (pre-1639), as well as pieces from the Château Saint-Louis, the residence of the first governors under the French Regime, including portraits of Louis XIV and of Cardinal Richelieu. Upon request, visitors can see the chapel and the vaulted cellars. The remains of Blessed Marie-Catherine de Saint-Augustin, the founder of the community in New France, are kept in an adjoining chapel, as is a beautiful gilded reliquary in the Louis XIV style, sculpted in 1717 by Noël Levasseur.

Follow the small street opposite the chapel (Rue Collins). At the corner of Rue Saint-Jean is a pleasant view of Côte de la Fabrique, with the Hôtel de Ville on the right and Cathédrale Notre-Dame in the background on the left. Turn right on Rue Saint-Jean, a lovely commercial street in the heart of Vieux-Québec.

A short detour to the left down Rue Saint-Stanislas gives a view of the old **Methodist Church** *(42 Rue Saint-Stanislas)*, a beautiful Gothic Revival building dating from 1850. Today it houses the **Institut Canadien**, a centre for literature and the arts. Before the Quiet Revolution of the 1960s, this centre was the focus of many a contentious dispute with the clergy over its "audacious" choice of books. The institute is home to a theatre and a branch of the municipal library.

The neighbouring building, number 44, is the **Ancienne Prison de Québec** (the old jail) built in 1808 by François Baillargé. In 1868, it was renovated to accommodate Morrin College, affiliated with Montréal's McGill University. This venerable institution of English-speaking Québec also houses the library of the **Québec Literary and Historical Society**, a learned society founded in 1824. The building on the corner of Rue Cook and Rue Dauphine surmounted by a palladian steeple is **St. Andrew's Presbyterian Church**, completed in 1811.

Return to Rue Saint-Jean which you'll cross. Turn left on Rue McMahon, and continue on to the reception and information centre at the Artillery Park.

Artillery Park National Historic Site ★★ *($4; early May to mid-Oct every day 10am to*

Exploring

5pm, end Mar to early May Wed-Sun, rest of the year hours vary; 2 Rue d'Auteuil, ☎648-4205), also called Lieu Historique National du Parc-de-l'Artillerie, takes up part of an enormous military installation running alongside the walls of the city. The reception and information centre is located in the old foundry where munitions were manufactured until 1964. On display is a fascinating model of Québec City, which was built between 1795 and 1810 by military engineer Jean-Baptiste Duberger for strategic planning. The model has only recently been returned to Québec City, after having been sent to England in 1813. It is an unparalleled source of information on the layout of the city in the years following the British Conquest.

The walk continues with a visit to the Dauphine Redoubt, a beautiful white roughcast building near Rue McMahon. In 1712, military engineer Dubois Berthelot de Beaucours drafted plans for the redoubt which was completed by Chaussegros de Léry in 1747. A redoubt is an independent fortified structure that serves as a retreat in case the troops are obliged to fall back. The redoubt was never really used for this purpose but rather as a military barracks.

Behind it can be seen several barracks and an old cartridge factory constructed by the British in the 19th century. The officers' barracks (1820), which has been converted into a children's centre for heritage interpretation, makes a nice end to the visit. You can take part in a 1hr guided tour led by characters in period costume or visit on your own with an audioguide. There are also two other exhibits on the site: the first is a collection of antique toys and the second features dolls in an economuseum named **Les Dames de Soie** ("the silk ladies").

Walk back up Rue d'Auteuil.

The newest of Québec City's gates, **Porte Saint-Jean** actually has rather ancient origins. As of 1693 it was one of only three entrances to the city. It was reinforced by Chaussegros de Léry in 1757, and then rebuilt by the British. To satisfy merchants who were clamouring for the total destruction of the walls, a "modern" gate equipped with tandem carriage tunnels and corresponding pedestrian passageways was erected in 1867. However, this structure did not fit in with Lord Dufferin's romantic vision of the city and was thus eliminated in 1898. The present gate did not replace it until 1936.

Number 29, on the left, is an **old Anglican orphanage** built for the Society for Promoting Christian Knowledge in 1824, and was the first Gothic Revival style building in Québec City. Its architecture was portentous, as it inaugurated the romantic current that would eventually permeate the city.

The last of Québec's Jesuits died in 1800, his community having been banished by the British and then, in 1774, by the Pope himself. The community was resuscitated in 1814, however, and returned to Québec City in 1840. Since its college and church on Place de l'Hôtel-de-Ville were no longer available, they were welcomed by the Congregationists, a brotherhood founded by the Jesuit Ponert in 1657 with a view to propagating the cult of the Virgin. These latter parishioners built the **Église des Jésuites** ★ *(Rue d'Auteuil, at the corner of Rue Dauphine)*. François Baillargé designed the plans for the church, which was completed in 1818. The facade was redone in 1930. The decoration of the interior began with the construction of the counterfeit vaulting. Its centrepiece is Pierre-Noël Levasseur's altar of 1770. Since 1925, the Jesuit

church has been Québec's sanctuary for the worship of Canada's martyred saints.

Porte Kent, like Porte Saint-Louis, is the result of Lord Dufferin's romantic vision of the city. The plans for this gate, Vieux-Québec's prettiest, were drawn up in 1878 by Charles Baillargé, following the ideas of Irishman William H. Lynn.

Climb the stairway to the top of Porte Kent and walk along the wall towards Porte Saint-Louis.

On the other side of the walls is the Hôtel du Parlement and inside, several patrician homes along the Rue d'Auteuil. Number 69, **Maison McGreevy** *(no visiting)* stands out by its sheer size. The house is the work of Thomas Fuller, the architect of the Parliament Buildings in Ottawa, as well as New York's State Capitol. It was built in 1868 by McGreevy, a construction entrepreneur who also built Canada's first parliament buildings. Behind the rather commercial-looking facade of yellow Nepean sandstone is a perfectly preserved Victorian interior.

Climb down the stairway from the wall at Porte Saint-Louis. Côte de la Citadelle is on the other side of Rue Saint-Louis.

Québec City's **Citadelle** ★ ★ ★ *(at the far*

Exploring

end of the Côte de la Citadelle; ☎*694-2815)* (citadel) represents three centuries of North American military history and is still in use. Since 1920, it has housed the Royal 22nd Regiment of the Canadian Army, a regiment distinguished for its bravery during World War II. Within the circumference of the enclosure are some 25 buildings, including the officers' mess, the hospital, the prison, and the official residence of the governor general of Canada, as well as the first observatory in Canada. The citadel's history began in 1693, when engineer Dubois Berthelot de Beaucours had the Cap Diamant redoubt built at the highest point of Québec City's defensive system, some 100m above the river. Today, this solid construction is included inside the King's bastion.

Throughout the 18th century, French and then British engineers developed projects for a citadel that remained unfulfilled. Chaussegros de Léry's powderhouse of 1750, which now houses the Museum of the Royal 22nd Regiment, and the temporary excavation works to the west (1783) are the only works of any scope accomplished during this period. The citadel that appears today was built between 1820 and 1832 by Colonel Elias Walker Durnford. Dubbed the "Gibraltar of America," and built according to principles expounded by Vauban in the 17th century, the citadel has never borne the brunt of a single cannonball, though it has acted as an important element of dissuasion.

Musée du Royal 22ᵉ Régiment *($6; Apr to mid-May every day 10am to 4pm, mid-May to mid-Jun every day 9am to 5pm, mid-Jun to early Sep every day 9am to 6pm, Sep 9am to 4pm, Oct 10am to 3pm;* ☎*694-2815)* is a museum that offers an interesting collection of arms, uniforms, insignia and military documents spanning almost 400 years. It is possible to take a guided tour of the whole installation, to witness the changing of the guard, the retreat, and the firing of the cannon. The changing of the guard lasts 30min and takes place every day from the end of June until the beginning of September at 6pm, weather permitting.

The retreat lasts 30min and can be seen through July and August, on Tuesday, Thursday, Saturday, and Sunday at 7pm, weather permitting.

Tour B: Petit-Champlain to Vieux-Port

(two days)

Québec's port and commercial area is a narrow *U*-shaped piece of land wedged near the waters of the St. Lawrence. This area is sometimes called Basse-Ville of Vieux-Québec because of its location just at the foot of the Cap Diamant escarpment. The cradle of New France, Place-Royale is where, in 1608, Samuel de Champlain (1567-1635) founded the settlement he called "Abitation," which would become Québec City. In the summer of 1759, three quarters of the city was badly damaged by British bombardment. It took 20 years to repair and rebuild the houses. In the 19th century, the construction of multiple embankments allowed the expansion of the town and enabled the area around Place-Royale to be linked by road with the area around the intendant's palace. The port's decline at the beginning of the 20th century led to the gradual abandonment of Place-Royale; restoration work began in 1959. The Petit-Champlain district has been reclaimed by artisans who have set up shop here, especially on the Rue du Petit-Champlain. This area now caters mostly to tourists, who visit the numerous studios to watch the craftspeople at work and to buy their wares.

This walking tour begins at Porte Prescott, which straddles Côte de la Montagne. Those who do not enjoy walking would be well advised to take the funicular from Terrasse Dufferin and to begin the tour at the start of Rue Petit-Champlain.

The **Funiculaire (Funicular)** *($1.50;* ☎*692-1132)* began operating in November 1879. It was put in place by entrepreneur W. A. Griffith in order to bring the lower and upper towns closer together. When the funicular was first built, water was transferred from one reservoir to another to make it function. It was converted to electricity in 1906, at the same time that Terrasse Dufferin was illuminated. The funicular is an outdoor elevator that eliminates the need to take the *Escalier Casse-Cou,* "break-neck stairway," or to go around Côte de la Montagne. The funicular was completely overhauled in 1998. It operated from 7:30am until at least 11pm.

Porte Prescott *(Côte de la Montagne)* can be reached

Exploring

from Côte de la Montagne or from Terrasse Dufferin by means of a stairway and a charming footbridge on the left of the funicular's entryway. This discreetly postmodern structure was built in 1983 by the architectural firm of Gauthier, Guité, Roy, which sought to evoke the 1797 gate by Gother Mann. It allows pedestrians to cross directly from Terrasse Dufferin to Parc Montmorency.

Descend Côte de la Montagne and take the Escalier Casse-Cou on the right.

The **Escalier Casse-Cou** *(Côte de la Montagne)*, which literally means "the break-neck strairway," has been here since 1682. Until the beginning of the 20th century, it had been made of planks that were in constant need of repair or replacement. It connects the various businesses situated on different levels. At the foot of the stairway is **Rue du Petit-Champlain**, a narrow pedestrian street flanked by charming craft shops and pleasant cafés located in 17th and 18th century houses. Some of the houses at the foot of the cape were

destroyed by rockslides prior to the cliff's reinforcement in the 19th century.

At the foot of the Escalier Casse-Cou, a small *économusée* (economuseum) unveils the secrets of glass-blowing. At **Atelier Verrerie La Mailloche** *(free admission; end Jun to early Nov every day 9am to 10pm, rest of the year 9:30am to 5:30pm; 58 Rue Sous-le-Fort, ☎694-0445)*, visitors can

Escalier Casse-Cou

observe the fascinating spectacle of artisans shaping molten glass according to traditional techniques. The finished products are sold in a shop on the second floor.

Maison Louis-Jolliet ★
(16 Rue du Petit-Champlain)

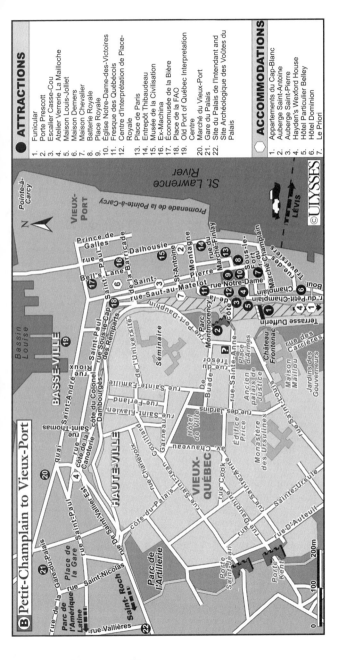

B Petit-Champlain to Vieux-Port

● ATTRACTIONS

1. Funicular
2. Porte Prescott
3. Escalier Casse-Cou
4. Atelier Verrerie La Mailloche
5. Maison Louis-Jolliet
6. Maison Demers
7. Maison Chevalier
8. Batterie Royale
9. Place Royale
10. Église Notre-Dame-des-Victoires
11. Fresque des Québécois
12. Centre d'Interprétation de Place-Royale
13. Place de Paris
14. Entrepôt Thibaudeau
15. Musée de la Civilisation
16. Ex-Machina
17. Économusée de la Bière
18. Place de la FAO
19. Old Port of Québec Interpretation Centre
20. Marché du Vieux-Port
21. Gare du Palais
22. Site du Palais de l'Intendant and Site Archéologique des Voûtes du Palais

⬡ ACCOMMODATIONS

1. Appartements du Cap-Blanc
2. Auberge Saint-Antoine
3. Auberge Saint-Pierre
4. Hayden's Wexford House
5. Hôtel Particulier Belley
6. Hôtel Dominion
7. Le Priori

© ULYSSES

is one of the earliest houses of Vieux-Québec (1683) and one of the few works of Claude Baillif still standing. The house was built after the great fire of 1682, which destroyed Basse-Ville. It was this tragedy that prompted the authorities to require that stone be used in all buildings. The fire also paved the way for some improvements in urban planning: roads were straightened and Place-Royale was created. Louis Jolliet (1645-1700) was the man who, along with Father Marquette, discovered the Mississippi and explored Hudson Bay. During the last years of his life, he taught hydrography at the Séminaire de Québec. The interior of the house was completely gutted and now contains the lower platform of the funicular (see above).

Follow Rue du Petit-Champlain until the end, where it meets Boulevard Champlain. You will see a colourful fresco on the facade of the last house.

You will probably need a few minutes to admire the many details that make up the beautiful **Fresque du Petit-Champlain** *(102 Rue du Petit-Champlain)*. Some 35 characters, both famous and unknown, who shaped the history of the province of Québec, and most particularly of Québec City and the Petit-Champlain district,

come to life in six rooms. From the first floor to the attic, they are presented in various settings, such as artisan workshops and an inn. You'll feel as though the walls suddenly open up on different chapters in history!

S-Shaped Linchpins

You have perhaps noticed the *S*-shaped pieces of iron that decorate the walls of some of this neighbourhood's old houses. These objects are linchpins that hold the stones in the walls on which the weight of the roof rests.

Retrace your steps and take the stairway that leads to Boulevard Champlain. At the foot of the stairway, make sure to turn around and admire the exceptional view from below of the Château Frontenac.

Maison Demers ★ *(28 Boulevard Champlain)* was built in 1689 by mason Jean Lerouge. This impressive residence is an example of the bourgeois style of Québec's Basse-Ville. A two-storey residential facade looks on to Rue du Petit-Champlain while the rear, which was used as a warehouse, extends down another two storeys to open directly onto l'Anse du Cul-de-Sac.

The cove called l'**Anse du Cul-de-Sac**, also known as the Anse aux Barques, was Québec City's first port. In 1745, Intendant Gilles Hocquart ordered the construction of a major shipyard in the western part of the cove. Several French battleships were built there using Canadian lumber. In 1854, the terminus of the Grand Trunk railway was built on the embankments, and in 1858 the Marché Champlain went up, only to be destroyed by fire in 1899. Although it is now filled in and built-up, one can still distinguish traces of this natural harbour by examining the older urban arrangement. The location is presently occupied by administrative buildings and by the **terminus of the Québec-Lévis ferry**. A short return trip on the ferry provides a spectacular view of the ensemble of Vieux-Québec. Taking the ferry in the winter affords a rare chance to come face to face with the ice floes of the St. Lawrence (see p 45).

Follow Boulevard Champlain east as far as Rue du Marché-Champlain. The ferry boards from the south end of this road.

Hôtel Jean-Baptiste-Chevalier ★ ★ *(60 Rue du Marché-Champlain)* is not a hotel but rather the townhouse of a wealthy family. The first building in the Place-Royale area to be restored, the hôtel is really three separate houses from three different periods: **Maison de l'Armateur Chevalier** (home of Chevalier the shipowner), built in a square in 1752; **Maison Frérot**, with a mansard roof (1683); and **Maison Dolbec**, dating from 1713. These houses were all repaired or partially rebuilt after the British Conquest. As a group, they were rescued from deterioration in 1955 by Gérard Morisset, the director of the Inventaire des Oeuvres d'Art, who suggested that they be purchased and restored by the government of Québec. This decision had a domino effect and prevented the demolition of Place-Royale.

Maison Chevalier *(free admission; end Jun to end Oct every day 10am to 5:30pm, May to end Jun Tue-Sun 10am to 5:30pm, Nov to May Sat and Sun 10am to 5pm; 60 Rue du Marché-Champlain, ☎643-2158)* harbours an annex of the Musée de la Civilisation, where an interesting exhibit, "Habiter au Passé"

(Living in the Past) portrays the daily lives of the merchants of New France. The exhibit features furniture as well as everyday items. The original, stately Louis XV woodwork (circa 1764) can also be seen.

Take Rue Notre-Dame, and turn right onto Rue Sous-le-Fort.

With no walls to protect Basse-Ville, other means of defending it from the cannon-fire of ships in the river had to be found. Following the attack by Admiral Phipps in 1690, it was decided to set up the **Batterie Royale** ★ *(at the far end of Rue Sous-le-Fort)*, according to a plan drawn up by Claude Baillif. The strategic position of the battery allowed for the bombardment of any enemy ships foolhardy enough to venture into the narrows in front of the city. The ruins of the battery, long hidden under storehouses, were discovered in 1974. The crenellations, removed in the 19th century, were reconstructed, as was the wooden portal, discernible in a sketch from 1699.

The two rough stone houses on Rue Saint-Pierre, next to the battery, were built for Charles Guillemin in the early 18th century. The narrowness of the house on the left shows just how precious land was in Basse-Ville during the French Regime. Each lot, irregular or not, had to be used. A little further along, at number 25 Rue Saint-Pierre, is the Louis-Fornel house, where a number of artefacts are on display in vaults. This vaulted basement was built in the 17th century from the ruins of Champlain's stronghold, and extends right under the square.

Continue along Rue Saint-Pierre, and turn left on Rue de la Place to go up to Place-Royale.

Place-Royale ★★★ is the most European quarter of any city in North America. It resembles a village in northwestern France. Place-Royale is laden with symbolism, as it was on this very spot that New France was founded in 1608. After many unsuccessful attempts, this became the official departure point of French exploits in America. Under the French Regime, Place-Royale was the only densely populated area in a vast, untamed colony. Today, it contains the most significant concentration of 17th- and 18th-century buildings in the Americas north of Mexico.

The square itself was laid out in 1673 by Governor Frontenac as a market. It

Place-Royale

replaced the garden of Champlain's Abitation, a stronghold that went up in flames in 1682, along with the rest of Basse-Ville. In 1686, Intendant Jean Bochart de Champigny erected a **bronze bust of Louis XIV** in the middle of the square, hence the name of the square, Place-Royale. In 1928, François Bokanowski, then the French Minister of Commerce and Communications, presented Québécois Athanase David with a bronze replica of the marble bust of Louis XIV in the Gallerie de Diane at Versailles to replace the missing statue. The bronze, by Alexis Rudier, was not set up until 1931, for fear of offending England.

Small, unpretentious **Église Notre-Dame-des-Victoires** ★★ *(free admission; May to mid-Oct Mon-Sat 9am to 4:30pm, closed Sat during weddings and christenings, Sun 9:30am to 4:30pm, mid-Oct to early May Tue-Sat 9am to noon, Sun 9am to 1pm; Place-Royale)* is the oldest church in Canada. Designed by Claude Baillif, it dates from 1688. It was built on the foundations of Champlain's *Abitation* and incorporates some of its walls. Beside the church, black granite marks the foundation remains from the second Abitation de Champlain. These vestiges were discovered in 1976.

Initially dedicated to the Baby Jesus, it was rechristened Notre-Dame-de-la-Victoire after Admiral Phipp's attack of 1690 failed. It was later renamed Notre-Dame-des-Victoires (the plural) in memory of the misfortune of British Admiral Walker, whose fleet ran aground on Île-aux-Oeufs during a storm in

Rue des Pain-Bénits

If you visit the city during the holidays, consider visiting Place-Royale, especially on January 3. This is the feast day of Sainte Geneviève, patron saint of the chapel adjoining Église Notre-Dame-des-Victoires. Every year since the colony was established, blessed bread rolls are distributed to the people to celebrate this event. The little street that runs along the east side of the church is called Rue des Pains-Bénits (blessed-bread street). While eating your bread, take a look at the nativity scene inside the church.

1711. The bombardments of the Conquest left nothing standing but the walls of the church, spoiling the Levasseur's lovely interior. The church was restored in 1766, but was not fully re-built until the current steeple was added in 1861. Raphaël Giroux is responsible for most of the present interior, which was undertaken between 1854 and 1857, but the strange "for-

tress" tabernacle of the main altar is a later work by David Ouellet (1878). Lastly, in 1888, Jean Tardivel painted the historical scenes on the vault and on the wall of the chancel. What are most striking, though, are the various pieces in the church: the *ex-voto* (an offering) that hangs from the centre of the vault depicting the *Brézé*, a ship that came to Canada in 1664 carrying soldiers of the Carignan Regiment; and the beautiful tabernacle in the Sainte-Geneviève chapel, attributed to Pierre-Noël Levasseur (circa 1730). Among the paintings are works by Boyermans and Van Loo, originally from the collection of Abbot Desjardins.

Under the French Regime, the square attracted many merchants and ship owners who commissioned the building of attractive residences. The tall house on the southwest corner of the square and on Rue de la Place, **Maison Barbel**, was built in 1754 for the formidable businesswoman Anne-Marie Barbel, widow of Louis Fornel. At the time, she owned a pottery factory on Rivière Saint-Charles and held the lease on the lucrative trading post at Tadoussac.

In the heart of Québec City, the Plains of Abraham form a sea of green grass, flowers and trees, making it an enchanting place for a stroll.
- Y. Tessier

Old multi-storeyed buildings such these, facing the Gare du Palais, have retained their charm, thanks to the loving care of their owners.
- P. Quittemelle

The houses on the sloping streets of Vieux-Québec are exceptionally charming with their flower-filled windows. - *R. Edgar*

Maison Dumont *(1 Place-Royale)* was designed in 1689 by the tireless Claude Baillif for the vintner Eustache Lambert Dumont. The house incorporated elements of the old store of the Compagnie des Habitants (1647). Visitors can see its huge vaulted basement now used, as it was in the past, to store casks and bottles of wine. Turned into an inn in the 19th century, the house was the favourite stopping place of U.S. President Howard Taft (1857-1930) on his way to his annual summer vacation in La Malbaie.

Maison Bruneau-Rageot-Drapeau, at number 3A, is a house built in 1763 using the walls of the old Nicolas Jérémie house. Jérémie was a Montagnais interpreter and a clerk at the fur-trading posts of Hudson Bay.

Maison Paradis, on Rue Notre-Dame, houses the **Atelier du Patrimoine Vivant** *(free admission; end Jun to mid-Oct every day 10am to 5pm; 42 Rue Notre-Dame, ☎647-1598)*. In these studios, various artisans hone their skills using traditional methods.

If you continue on Rue Notre-Dame towards Côte de la Montagne and then turn around, you will be surprised by the coloured spectacle. On the blind wall of Maison Soumande, in front of Parc de la Cetière, the colours of the **Fresque des Québécois** ★★ are displayed. In fact, if they're not careful, passersby may actually miss the fresco: it is a *trompe l'œil.* A team of French and Québec artists created this fresco with the guidance of specialists (historians, geographers, etc.) who made sure the painting was realistic and instructive. On a surface area of $420m^2$ they brought together Québec City's architecture and famous sites such as Cap Diamant, the ramparts, a bookshop, houses of Vieux-Québec—in short, different places that the town's inhabitants encounter every day. Just like the crowd of admiring onlookers that gathers rain or shine, you can amuse yourself for quite a while trying to identify the historical figures and the role they played. From top to bottom and from left to right, you will see Marie Guyart, Catherine de Longpré, François-Xavier Garneau, Louis-Joseph Papineau, Jean Talon, le Comte de Frontenac, Marie Fitzbach, Marcelle Mallet, Louis Jolliet, Alphonse Desjardins, Lord Dufferin, Félix Leclerc and finally, Samuel de Champlain, who started it all.

Return to Place-Royale and visit the **Centre**

Exploring

d'Interprétation de Place-Royale ★ ★ *($3, free admission early Nov to end Mar and Tue early Apr to end Jun, $8.50 package with Musée de la Civilisation and Musée de l'Amérique Française; end Oct to end Jun Tue-Sun 10am to 5pm, end Jun to end Oct every day 9:30am to 5pm; 27 Rue Notre-Dame, ☎646-3167, www.mcq.org)*, which was inaugurated in the fall of 1999. To accommodate the centre, both the Hazeur and Smith houses, which had burned down, were rebuilt in a modern style while using a large portion of the original materials. The omnipresent glass lets you admire the exposed rooms as well as the buildings' architecture from all angles. Along by the glass walls between the two houses, a stairway goes down Côte de la Montagne to Place-Royale. From the staircase, you can see some of the centre's treasures. On each of the three levels, an exhibition presents chapters of Place-Royale's history. There are also artifacts that were discovered during archaeological digs under the square. Whether they are whole objects or tiny pieces that are difficult to identify, they are all instructive. You can also watch a multimedia show and admire scale models such as the one representing the second Abitation de Champlain in 1635.

You will learn, among other things, that the first hotel to be established in Québec City was opened in 1648 by a Mr. Boidon. Coincidentally, his name in French (*Bois donc*) means "have a drink!". The hotel tradition continued on Place-Royale until the middle of the 20 century when the last hotel was destroyed by fire. Visitors had been welcomed, lodged and nourished there for 300 years. In the basement, the vaults of the house are transformed into a playroom where young and old can dress up as one of the former occupants. A great (and original) idea!

Continue along Rue de la Place until it opens onto Place de Paris.

Place de Paris ★ *(along Rue du Marché-Finlay)* is an elegant and sophisticated combination of contemporary art and traditional surroundings conceived by Québécois architect Jean Jobin in 1987. A large sculpture by French artist Jean-Pierre Raynault dominates the centre of the square. The work was presented by Jacques Chirac, who was then mayor of Paris, on behalf of his city, when he visited Québec City. Entitled *Dialogue avec l'Histoire* (Dialogue with History), the black granite and white marble work is said to evoke the first human presence in the area and forms a pair with the bust of Louis XIV, visible in the background. The Québécois have dubbed it the Colossus of Québec because of its imposing dimensions. From the square, which was once a market, there is a splendid view of the Batterie Royale, the Château Frontenac and the St. Lawrence River.

Entrepôt Thibaudeau *(215 Rue du Marché-Finlay)* is a huge building whose stone facade fronts onto Rue Dalhousie. It represents the last prosperous days of the area before its decline at the end of the 19th century. The Second Empire building is distinguished by its mansard roof and by its segmental arch openings. It was built in 1880, following the plans of Joseph-Ferdinand Peachy, for Isidore Thibaudeau, president and founder of the Banque Nationale and importer of European novelties.

Head back up the street towards Rue Saint-Pierre and turn right.

Further along at number 92 is yet another imposing merchant's house, **Maison Estèbe** (1752). It is now part of the Musée de la Civilisation, whose smooth stone walls

Vaults

The houses in Vieux-Québec often had vaulted cellars to support the building; because of their cool temperature, food and drink were often stored there. Some of these cellars have survived and can be visited. Maison Fornel, on Place-Royale, which houses the Association Québec-France, opens its vaults to visitors (9am to 4pm) and even presents small exhibitions. The entrances are at 25 Rue Saint-Pierre and 9 Place-Royale.

can be seen along the Rue Saint-Pierre. Guillaume Estèbe was a businessman and the director of the Saint-Maurice ironworks at Trois-Rivières. Having participated in a number of unsavoury schemes with Intendant Bigot during the Seven Years' War, he was locked-up in the Bastille for a few months on embezzlement charges. The house, where he lived for five years with his wife and 14 children, is built on an embankment that used to front

Exploring

onto a large private wharf which is now the courtyard of the museum. The courtyard is accessible through the gateway on the left. The 21-room interior escaped the bombardments of 1759. Some of the rooms feature handsome Louis XV woodwork. On the corner of Rue Saint-Jacques is the old **Banque de Québec** building (Edward Staveley, architect, 1861). Across the street, the old **Banque Molson** occupies an 18th-century house.

Turn right onto Rue Saint-Jacques. The entrance to the Musée de la Civilisation is on Rue Dalhousie, on the right.

The **Musée de la Civilisation** ★ ★ *($7, Tue free admission, except in summer, $8.50 package with Musée de l'Amérique Française and Centre d'Interprétation de la Place-Royale; end Jun to early Sep every day 10am to 7pm, early Sep to end Jun every day 10am to 5pm; 85 Rue Dalhousie,* ☎*643-2158, www.mcq.org)* is housed in a building, completed in 1988, in the traditional architectural style of Québec City, with its stylized roof, dormer windows and a belltower like those common to the area. Architect Moshe Safdie, who also designed the revolutionary Habitat '67 in Montréal, Ottawa's National Gallery and Vancouver's Public Library, designed a sculptural building with a monumental exterior staircase at its centre. The lobby provides a charming view of Maison Estèbe and its wharf while preserving a contemporary look that is underlined by Astri Reuch's sculpture, **La Débâcle**.

The Musée de la Civilisation presents a great variety of temporary exhibitions. Themes such as humour, circus and song, for example, have been the object of very lively displays. Travelling exhibitions also recount the world's great civilizations, while permanent exhibitions provide a portrait of civilizations from the region. "Mémoires" recounts the history of the Québec people; "Nous les Premières Nations," developed in collaboration with First Nations peoples, is a large exhibition tracing the history of the 11 Aboriginal nations that originally inhabited Québec. You can view many objects as well as audiovisual materials such as the work of filmmaker Arthur Lamothe. Some of the more remarkable items are the Aboriginal artifacts, the large French Regime fishing craft unearthed during excavations for the museum itself, some highly ornate 19th-century horse-drawn hearses, and some Chinese *objets d'art* and pieces of furniture, including an imperial bed, from the collection of the Jesuits. You can also visit the museum's vaulted cellar, which dates from the 18th century.

Head northeast, towards the Vieux Port, through Rue Dalhousie.

Beside the Musée de la Civilisation is a lavish *beaux-arts* fire station dating from 1912 that now houses **Ex Machina** (103 rue Dalhousie), a multi-disciplinary artistic production centre founded by Robert Lepage. Note the high tower with a copper dome rising on the southeast corner like a church spire, which was inspired by the tower of the Hôtel du Parlement. Firefighters used to hang up their hoses in the tower to dry and to prevent them from damage since in those days hoses were made out of fabric. The building has been expanded and in order to keep its character, a false wall similar to the original stone wall – but made of plastic – has been erected in front of the new part.

The **Vieux-Port ★** *(160 Rue Dalhousie)* (old port) is often criticized for being overly American in a city with such a pronounced European sensibility. It was refurbished by the Canadian government on the occasion of the maritime celebration, "Québec 1534-1984." There are various metallic structures designed to enliven the promenade, at the end of which is the handsome **Édifice de la Douane** *(2 Quai St-André)* (customs house). With its dome and columns, it features lovely neoclassical architecture. At the time the structure was built (1856-1857), the river actually flowed right next to it.

The entire port area between Place-Royale and the entrance of **Bassin Louise** is known as **Pointe-à-Carcy**. At the beginning of the year 2000, the Commission du Vieux-Port started a new phase to completely renovate Pointe-à-Carcy and turn it into a veritable harbour for pleasure boats.

An **Économusée de la Bière** *(free admission; every day noon to 3pm; 37 Quai Saint-André, ☎692-2877)* (beer economuseum) has been set up in an established Vieux-Port bar, L'Inox. By reading the information panels on the walls, you will learn more about the long and glorious history of beer. You can also discover the secrets of beer-brewing by taking a guided tour. Since L'Inox is a microbrewery it is possible to have the master brewer take you behind the scenes which are visible from the bar through a glass wall (reservations are necessary).

Exploring

And not only will he explain how he makes the beer, he will offer you a taste of his work.

Take Rue Saint-Pierre on your left.

Place de la FAO is located at the intersection of Rue Saint-Pierre, Saint-Paul and Sault-au-Matelot. This square honours the United Nations Food and Agriculture Organisation whose first meeting was held at the Château Frontenac in 1945. The sculpture at the centre of the square represents the prow of a boat as it emerges from the waves, its female figurehead, *La Vivrière*, firmly grasping all kinds of fruit, vegetables and grains.

In the square at the corner of Rue Saint-Pierre stands an imposing building with a large round portico which formerly housed the **Imperial Bank of Commerce**.

Take Rue Sault-au-Matelot to Rue de la Barricade. This street is named in honour of the barricade set up against invading revolutionaries coming from what was to become the United States. They attempted to take Québec City on December 31, 1775.

On the right, Rue de la Barricade leads to **Rue Sous-le-Cap**. This narrow passage was once wedged between the St. Lawrence and the Cap Diamant escarpment. At the end of the 19th century, the street housed working-class families of Irish origin. Today's inhabitants, finding the houses too small, have renovated the little cottages on the side of the cliff and connected them to their houses by walkways crossing the street at clothesline height. One almost enters Rue Sous-le-Cap on tiptoe because of the feeling that you're walking into another world. At the end of the street is Côte du Colonel-Dambourgès and then Rue Saint-Paul.

Rue Saint-Paul is a most pleasant street, lined with antique shops overflowing with beautiful Québec heritage furniture.

To get to the Centre d'Interprétation du Vieux-Port-de-Québec, take Rue Rioux or Rue des Navigateurs, which both meet up with Rue Quai Saint-André.

In the days of sailboats, Québec City was one of the most important gateways to America, since many vessels could not make their way any farther against the current. Its bustling port was surrounded by shipyards that made great use of plentiful and high-quality Canadian lumber. The first royal shipyards appeared under the French Regime in the cove known as l'Anse du Cul-de-Sac. The Napoleonic blockade of 1806 forced the British to turn to their Canadian colony for wood and for the construction of battleships. This was a great boost for a number of shipyards and made fortunes for many of their owners. The **Old Port of Quebec Interpretation Centre** *($3; early May to early Sep every day 10am to 5pm, early Sep to mid-Oct 1pm to 5pm; 100 Rue Saint-André, ☎648-3300)* is a national historic site that concentrates on those flourishing days of navigation in Québec. You can also take part in guided tours *($8)* of the Vieux-Port accompanied by characters in period costume.

Take the promenade that runs along the basin to the Vieux-Port market.

Most of Québec City's public markets were shut down in the 1960s because they had become obsolete in an age of air-conditioned supermarkets and frozen food. However, people continued to want fruit and vegetables fresh from the farm as well as the contact with the farmers. Moreover, the market was one of the only non-aseptic places people could congregate. Thus, the markets gradually began to reappear at the beginning of the 80s.

Marché du Vieux-Port ★ *(corner of Rue Saint-Thomas and Rue Saint-André)* was built in 1987 by the architectural partners Belzile, Brassard, Galienne and Lavoie. It is the successor to two other markets, Finlay and Champlain, that no longer exist. In the summer, the market is a pleasant place to stroll and take in the view of the Marina Bassin Louise at the edge of the market.

Continue along Rue Saint-Paul. Turn right on Rue Abraham-Martin and then left on Rue de la Gare-du-Palais until you reach the train station.

For over 50 years, the citizens of Québec City clamoured for a train station worthy of their city. Canadian Pacific finally fulfilled their wish in 1915. Designed by New York architect Harry Edward Prindle in the same style as the Château Frontenac, the **Gare du Palais ★** *(Rue de la Gare-du-Palais)* gives visitors a taste of the romance and charm that await them in Québec City. The 18m-high arrival hall that extends behind the giant window of the facade is bathed in sunlight from the leaded glass skylight on the roof. The faïence tiles and multicoloured bricks in the walls lend a striking aspect to the entire ambiance. The station was closed for almost 10

Exploring

Gare du Palais

years (from 1976 to 1985) at the time when railway companies were imitating airlines and moving their stations to the suburbs. Fortunately, it was reopened, with great pomp, and now houses the bus and train stations. Across from it, **Place de la Gare** offers a lovely spot where you can relax and admire an impressive fountain designed by Charles Daudelin.

The building on the right is Raoul Chênevert's 1938 **post office**. It illustrates the persistence of the Château style of architecture that is so emblematic of the city.

A little further on Boulevard Jean-Lesage is **Parc de l'Amérique-Latine**. There, two monuments honour the memory of two of the most important figures in Latin American history. The monuments to great liberators Simón Bolívar and José Martí were offered by the governments of Venezuela and Cuba respectively.

Return to to Rue Saint-Paul by Boulevard Jean-Lesage, which becomes Rue Vallière. At the corner of Rue Saint-Nicolas and Rue Saint-Paul, you are in the heart of the Quartier du Palais, so named because it surrounds the Palais de l'Intendant. To reach it, head west on Rue De Saint-Vallier.

The block bordered by Ruelle de l'Ancien-Chantier, Rue Saint-Vallier Est, Rue Saint-Paul and Rue Saint-Nicolas is known as **L'Îlot Saint-Nicolas**. It was restored with verve by architects De Blois, Côté, Leahy.

The handsome stone building on the corner and the two others behind it on Rue Saint-Nicolas housed the famous **Cabaret Chez Gérard** from 1938 to 1978. It was here that Charles Trenet, Rina Ketty and many other famous French singers performed. Charles Aznavour actually got his start here. In the bohemian days of the 1950s, he sang here every night for many months for a mere pittance.

The big Scottish-brick building with the pinnacle inscribed "**Les Maisons Lecourt**" was erected across from l'Îlot Saint-Nicolas using the remnants of Intendant Bigot's "royal store." Nicknamed *La Fripone* (The Rogue's) because of the extortionary prices Bigot and his accomplices exacted from the miserable populace, the location was one of only two in the city during the French Regime where one could moor a boat (the other being l'Anse du Cul-de-Sac). In the 17th century, warehouses and wharfs were built along the estuary of the Saint-Charles, as was a shipyard with a drydock that bequeathed the street its name, Rue de l'Ancien-Chantier, meaning "old shipyard."

The **Site du Palais de l'Intendant ★** and the **Centre d'Interprétation Archéologique** are part of **l'Îlot des Palais** *($3; end Jun to early Sep every day 10am to 5pm, rest of the year with reservations only; 8 Rue Vallière, ☎691-6092)* and the **Site Archéologique des Voûtes du Palais**, (the palace vaults archaeological site). The intendant oversaw the day-to-day affairs of the colony. The royal stores, the few state enterprises and the prison were located near his residence. With so many opportunities to make himself rich, it was only natural that his should be the most splendid mansion in New France. The remains of one wing of the palace can still be seen in the shape of the segment of brown brick foundation wall that is now aboveground. The location was originally that of the brewery set up by the first intendant, Jean Talon (1625-1694). Talon took great effort to populate and develop the colony. For his trouble, he was made secretary of the king's cabinet upon his return to France. His brewery was replaced by a palace designed by engineer La Guer Morville in 1716. This elegant building had a classical entrance in cut stone that gave onto a horseshoe-shaped staircase. Twenty or so ceremonial rooms, arranged in a row one after the other, served for receptions and the meetings of the Conseil Supérieur.

The palace was spared British cannon-fire only to be burned to the ground during the American invasion of 1775-76. The arches of its cellars were used as the foundation of the Boswell brewery in 1872, bringing the site full circle. Visitors

Exploring

are free to inspect the cellars, where the archeological information centre is located. The centre displays artifacts and ruins of the site itself.

To return to Haute-Ville, climb Côte du Palais at the end of Rue Saint-Nicolas.

Tour C: Grande Allée

(one day)

Grande Allée appears on 17th-century maps, but it was not built up until the first half of the 19th century, when the city grew beyond its walls. Grande Allée was originally a country road linking the town to Chemin du Roi, and then to Montréal. At that time, it was bordered by the large agricultural properties of the nobility and clergy of the French Regime. After the British Conquest, many of the domains were turned into country estates by English merchants who set their manors well back from the road. The neoclassical town then spilled over into the area before the Victorian city had a chance to stamp the landscape with its distinctive style. Today's Grande Allée is the most pleasant route into the old city and the focus of extra-mural Haute-Ville. Although it links the capital's various ministries, a portion of it is a cheery street, as many of the bourgeois houses on it have been converted into restaurants and bars.

This walking tour starts at Porte Saint-Louis and gradually works its way from the walled city.

On the right is Paul Chevré's monument to historian François-Xavier Garneau. On the left is the *Croix du Sacrifice* where Remembrance Day services are held every year on November 11.

The **Hôtel du Parlement** ★★★ *(free admission; guided tours end Jun to early Sep Mon-Fri 9am and 4:30pm, Sat and Sun 10am to 4:30pm, early Sep to Jun Mon-Fri 9am to 4:30pm; at the corner of Honoré-Mercier and Grande Allée Est, ☎643-7239)* is known to the Québécois as l'Assemblée Nationale, the National Assembly. The seat of the government of Québec, this imposing building was erected between 1877 and 1886. It has a lavish French Renaissance Revival exterior intended to reflect the unique cultural status of Québec in the North American context. Eugène-Étienne Taché (1836-1912) looked to the Louvre for his inspiration in both the plan of the qua-

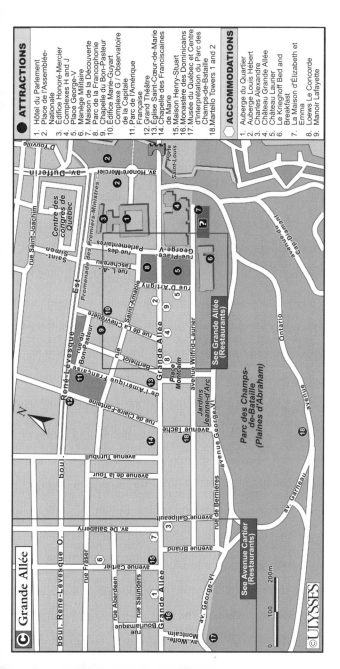

C Grande Allée

ATTRACTIONS

1. Hôtel du Parlement
2. Place de l'Assemblée-Nationale
3. Édifice Honoré-Mercier
4. Complexes H and J
5. Place George-V
6. Manège Militaire
7. Maison de la Découverte
8. Parc de la Francophonie
9. Chapelle du Bon-Pasteur
10. Édifice Marie-Guyart
    Complexe G / Observatoire de la Capitale
11. Parc de l'Amérique Française
12. Grand Théâtre
13. Église Saint-Cœur-de-Marie
14. Chapelle des Franciscaines de Marie
15. Maison Henry-Stuart
16. Monastère des Dominicains
17. Musée du Québec et Centre d'Interprétation du Parc des Champs-de-Bataille
18. Martello Towers 1 and 2

ACCOMMODATIONS

1. Auberge du Quartier
2. Auberge Louis Hébert
3. Charles Alexandre
4. Château Grande Allée
5. Château Laurier
6. Le Krieghoff Bed and Breakfast
7. La Maison d'Elizabeth et Emma
8. Loews Le Concorde
9. Manoir Lafayette

See Grande Allée (Restaurants)

See Avenue Cartier (Restaurants)

Parc des Champs-de-Bataille (Plaines d'Abraham)

© ULYSSES

0   100   200m

Hôtel du Parlement

drangular building and its decor. Originally destined to incorporate the two houses of parliament characteristic of the British system of government, as well as all of the ministries, it is today part of a group of buildings on either side of Grande Allée.

The numerous statues of the parliament's main facade constitute a sort of pantheon of Québec. The 22 bronzes of important figures in the history of Québec were cast by such well-known artists as Louis-Philippe Hébert and Alfred Laliberté. A raised inscription on the wall near the central passage identifies the statues. In front of the main entrance a bronze by Hébert entitled *La Halte dans la Forêt* (The Pause in the Forest) depicts an Aborigi-

nal family. The work, which is meant to honour the original inhabitants of Québec, was displayed at Paris's World's Fair in 1889. *Le Pêcheur à la Nigog* (Fisherman at the Nigog), by the same artist, hangs in the niche by the fountain.

The building's interior is a veritable compendium of the icons of Québec's history. The handsome woodwork is done in the tradition of religious architecture.

The members of parliament called *députés*, sit in the National Assembly, or Salon Bleu (Blue Chamber), where Charles Huot's painting, *La Première Séance de l'Assemblée Législative du Bas-Canada en 1792* (The First Session of the Legislative

Assembly of Lower Canada in 1792), hangs over the chair of the president of the Assembly. A large work by the same artist covers the ceiling and evokes the motto of Québec, *Je me souviens* (I remember). The Salon Rouge (Red Chamber), intended for the Conseil Législatif, an unelected body eliminated in 1968, is now used for parliamentary commissions. A painting entitled *Le Conseil Souverain* (The Sovereign Council), a reminder of the mode of government in the days of New France, graces this chamber.

La Halte dans la Forêt

Several of the windows of the parliament building boast gorgeous Art Nouveau stained glass by master glazier Henri Perdriau, a native of Saint-Pierre de Montélimar in Vendée, France. Undeniably, the most spectacular is the arch that adorns the entrance to the elegant Le Parlementaire restaurant (see p 234). This feature was designed by architect Omer Marchand in 1917. National Assembly debates are open to the public, but a pass is required.

In the Parc de l'Hôtel du Parlement, there are three important monuments: one in honour of Honoré Mercier, premier of Québec from 1887 to 1891; another in honour of Maurice Duplessis, premier during the *grande noirceur* or "great darkness" (1936-1939 and 1944-1959), as well as the one representing René Lévesque, who holds a special place in the hearts of the Québécois and who was the premier from 1976 to 1985. Also, the **Promenade des Premiers-Ministres**, informs us with signs about the premiers that have led Québec since 1867.

In front of the Assemblée Nationale notice the beautiful **Place de l'Assemblée-Nationale** divided in two by the handsome Avenue Honoré-Mercier. On the wall's side, many events are hosted throughout the year. In July, a stage is erected for the Summer Festival and in February, the Ice Palace,

Exploring

the focus of carnival festivities, is located here.

The dizzying growth of the civil service during the Quiet Revolution of the 1960s compelled the government to construct several modern buildings to house its various ministries. A row of beautiful Second Empire houses was demolished to make way for **Complexes H and J** (on Grande Allée opposite the Hôtel du Parlement). Dubbed "the bunker" by the Québécois, Pierre Saint-Gelais's 1970 building used to house the premier's office.

Since the spring of 2002, the offices of the Conseil Exécutif and the premier's cabinet have been located in the beautiful **Édifice Honoré-Mercier** (835 Boulevard René-Lévesque Est), on the north side of the Hôtel du Parlement. In fact, this is actually a homecoming since the building housed the premier's offices up until 1972. Before the move, the building was entirely renovated but the beauty of its architecture was preserved including its marble features, plaster mouldings and woodwork. It was built between 1922 and 1925 according to the designs of architect Chênevert.

Take Grande Allée westward, leaving Vieux-Québec. On the
left you will come to Rue Place-George-V, which runs along the square of the same name. Take this street to Avenue Wilfrid-Laurier.

Place George V and the **Manège Militaire** ★ (Avenue Wilfrid-Laurier), an expanse of lawn, is used as the training area and parade ground of the military's equestrians. There are cannons and a statue in memory of the two soldiers who perished attempting to douse the flames of the 1889 fire in the suburb of Saint-Sauveur. Otherwise, the grounds serve mainly to highlight the amusing Château-style facade of the Manège Militaire, (military riding academy) built in 1888 and designed by Eugène-Étienne Taché, who also designed the Hôtel du Parlement.

The Centre d'Interprétation du Parc des Champs-de-Bataille is on Avenue Wilfrid-Laurier behind the H and J Buildings, which border the Plains of Abraham. Hosted in one of the Citadelle buildings, **Maison de la Découverte** ★ (835 Avenue Wilfrid-Laurier, ☎649-6157) should please Québec City natives as much as visitors. Upstairs, at the Office du Tourisme de la région de Québec, travellers can get help finding their way around. And on the ground floor, questions are answered about the Parc des Champs-de-Bataille, its history and the many activities that go on here. There are also a few services and an entrance to the Plains of Abraham. Various guided tours leave from here. One of them takes place on board the "Bus d'Abraham" guided by Abraham Martin in person!

Go back towards Grande Allée.

Parc de la Francophonie *(between Rue Saint-Augustin and Rue d'Artigny)* and **Complexe G**, which appears in the background, both occupy the site of the old Saint-Louis quarter, today almost entirely vanished. Parc de la Francophonie was laid out for open-air shows. It also takes the name Le Pigeonnier, (dovecote) from the interesting concrete structure at its centre, based on an idea by landscape architects Schreiber and Williams, in 1973.

Continue west on Grande Allée, along the liveliest section.

A little further to the west, the fabric of the old city is again in evidence. **Terrasse Stadacona** *(numbers 640 to 664)*, on the right, is a neo-classical row of English-style townhouses: the multiple houses share a common facade. These houses date from 1847 and have been converted into bars and restaurants with terraces sheltered by multitudes of parasols. Opposite *(numbers 661 to 695)* is a group of Second Empire houses that dates from 1882, a period when Grande Allée was the most fashionable street in Québec City. These houses show the influence of the parliamentary buildings on the residential architecture of the quarter. Three other houses on Grande Allée are worth mentioning for the eclecticism of their facades: **Maison du Manufacturier de Chaussures W. A. Marsh** *(number 625)*, house of a prominent shoe manufacturer, designed in 1899 by Toronto architect Charles John Gibson; **Maison Garneau-Meredith** *(numbers 600 to 614)* of the same year; and **Maison William Price** *(number 575)*, a little Romeo-and-Juliet-style house which is, unfortunately, dwarfed by the hotel **Le Concorde**. The revolving restaurant (see p 239) of this hotel (see p 202) affords a magnificent view of Haute-Ville and the Plains of Abraham.

In little **Parc Montcalm**, next to the hotel, is a statue commemorating the general's death on September 13, 1759, at the Battle of the Plains of Abraham. The **statue of French General Charles de Gaulle** (1890-1970), which faces away

Exploring

from Montcalm, created quite a controversy when it was erected in the spring of 1997. Farther along, at the entrance to the Plains of Abraham, **Jardin Jeanne-d'Arc** boasts magnificent flower-beds and a statue of Joan of Arc astride a spirited charger. Note that you are now standing on a huge drinking-water reservoir located under this part of the Plains of Abraham!

Return to Grande Allée and go east, then turn left on Rue de La Chevrotière.

Behind the austere facade of the mother house of the Soeurs du Bon-Pasteur, a community devoted to the education of abandoned and delinquent girls, is the charming, Baroque Revival-style **Chapelle du Bon-Pasteur** ★★ *(free admission; Jul and Aug Tue-Sat, 1:30pm to 4:30pm; 1080 Rue de la Chevrotière)*. Designed by Charles Baillargé in 1866, this tall, narrow chapel houses an authentic baroque tabernacle dating from 1730. Pierre-Noël Levasseur's masterpiece of New France carving is surrounded by devotional miniatures hung on pilasters by the nuns.

Atop the 31 storeys of **Édifice Marie-Guyart** in Complexe G, the **Observatoire de la Capitale** *($4; end Jun to mid-Oct every day 10am to 7pm, mid-Oct to end Jun Tue-Sun 10am to 5pm; 1037 Rue De La Chevrotière, ☎644-9841)*, provides a splendid view of Québec City and the surrounding area. At 221m in altitude, it is the highest observation point in the city. For an even better view, use the telescopes.

Go back and turn right on Rue Saint-Amable. Walk as far as Parc de l'Amérique Française.

The **Parc de l'Amérique-Française** is centered around a collection of flags of the various francophone communities of America.

The **Grand Théâtre** *(269 Boulevard René-Lévesque Est, ☎643-8131)* is located at the far end of the park. Inaugurated in 1971, this theatre designed by Polish architect Victor Prus was to be a meeting place for members of Québec City's high society. There was quite a scandal, therefore, when Jordi Bonet's mural was unveiled and the assembled crowd read the lines from a poem by Claude Péloquin: *"Vous êtes pas tannés de mourir, bande de caves,"* (Aren't you suckers tired of dying?). The theatre has two halls (Louis-Fréchette and Octave-Crémazie) and presents symphony orchestra concerts as well as theatre, dance and variety shows.

Maison Henry-Stuart

Go back as far as Rue Scott where you turn right to return to Grande Allée.

Église Saint-Cœur de Marie *(530 Grande Allée Est)* was built for the Eudists in 1919 and designed by Ludger Robitaille. It looks more martial than devotional because of its bartizans, machicolations and towers. Its large archways are reminiscent of a Mediterranean fortress. Across the road is the most outlandish row of Second Empire houses still standing in Québec City *(455-555 Grande Allée Est)*, **Terrasse Frontenac**. The product of Joseph-Ferdinand Peachy's imagination (1895), its slender, fantastical peaks look like something from a fairy tale. **Chapelle des Franciscaines de Marie ★** is the chapel of a community of nuns devoted to serving God. They com-missioned the Sanctuaire de l'Adoration Perpétuelle (Sanctuary of Perpetual Adoration) in 1901. This exuberant Baroque Revival chapel invites the faithful to prayer and celebrates the everlasting presence of God. It features a small columned cupola supported by angels and a sumptuous marble baldaquin.

Several handsome, bourgeois houses dating from the early 20th century face the chapel. Among them, at numbers 433-435, is the residence of John Holt, proprietor of the Holt Renfrew stores. Both this and the neighbouring house, number 425, are designed like Scottish manors. Undeniably the most elegant, in its mild Flemish and Oriental eclecticism, is the house of Judge P. A. Choquette, designed by

Exploring

architect Georges-Émile Tanguay.

Continue in the same direction.

Maison Henry-Stuart *($5; end Jun to early Sep every day 11am to 5pm; 82 Grande Allée Ouest, ☎647-4347)*, on the corner of Cartier and Grande Allée, is one of the few remaining Regency-style Anglo-Norman cottages in Québec City. This type of colonial British architecture is distinguished by a large pavilion roof overhanging a low veranda surrounding the building. The house was built in 1849 and used to mark the border between the city and country; its original garden still surrounds it. The interior features several pieces of furniture from the Saint-Jean-Port-Joli manor and has been practically untouched since 1911. More or less closed to the public for a number of years, Maison Henry-Stuart and its garden, which belongs to the organisation "Jardins du Québec," now welcome visitors. The house is home to the Conseil des Monuments et Sites de Québec. Tea is now served here on summer afternoons.

Avenue Cartier is one of the most attractive shopping streets in town. The main artery in the Montcalm residential neighbourhood, it is lined with restaurants (see p 233), shops and specialty food stores that attract the yuppie clientele strolling around here.

In the area of the American-style **Maison Pollack** *(1 Grande Allée Ouest)* is the Renaissance Revival **Maison des Dames Protestantes** *(111 Grande Allée Ouest)*, built in 1862 by architect Michel Lecourt. Also nearby is **Maison Krieghoff** *(115 Grande-Allée Ouest)*, which was occupied in 1859 by the Dutch painter Cornelius Krieghoff.

Monastère des Dominicains ★ *(175 Grande Allée Ouest, closed to the public)* and its church are relatively recent testimonials to the persistence and historical exactitude of 20th century Gothic Revival architecture. This sober British-style building promotes reverence and meditation.

Turn left on Avenue Wolfe-Montcalm to the entrance to both Parc Champs-de-Bataille and the Musée du Québec.

Located at the roundabout is the **Monument to General Wolfe**, victor of the decisive Battle of the Plains of Abraham. It is said to stand on the exact spot where he fell. The 1832 monument has been the object of countless demonstrations and acts of vandalism. Toppled again in 1963, it was rebuilt, this time with an inscription in French.

The **Musée du Québec** ★ ★ ★ (*$10, free admission to permanent collection; early Jun to early Sep every day 10am to 6pm, Wed to 9pm; early Sep to end May Tue-Sun 11am to 5pm, Wed to 9pm; Parc des Champs de Bataille, ☎644-6460 or 866-220-2150, www.mdq.org*) was renovated and expanded in 1992. The older, west-facing 1933 Classical revival building is on the right. The entrance, parallel to Avenue Wolfe-Montcalm, is dominated by a glass tower similar to that of the Musée de la Civilisation. The first building is subterraneously linked with the old prison on the left. The latter has been cleverly restored to house exhibits and has

been rebaptized Édifice Ballairgé in honour of its architect. Some of the cells have been preserved.

A visit to this important museum allows one to become acquainted with the painting, sculpture and silverwork of Québec from the time of New France to today. In 2000, the museum inaugurated a gallery (Salle 3) in honour of painter Jean-Paul Riopelle, who died in 2002, in which his huge mural (42m) *Hommage à Rosa Luxembourg* is displayed. The collections of religious art gathered from Québec's rural parishes are particularly interesting. Also on display are official documents, including the original surrender of Québec (1759). The museum frequently hosts temporary exhibits from the United States and Europe. Many cultural activities are held here, such as conferences, films and concerts.

On the first floor of the museum's Édifice Baillargé is

Exploring

Jean-Paul Riopelle

Jean-Paul Riopelle was one of Québec's most renowned painters, and its best-known internationally. Many of the impressive number of paintings he created are exhibited throughout the world. This legendary character, an abstract painter famous for his huge paintings, left his mark on the world of contemporary art. He was born in Montréal in 1932, and his career took off with the Automatism movement in the 1940s. He was also a co-signatory of the Refus Global, a social manifesto. He lived in Paris for several years but returned to the province of Québec during the last years of his life. He died on March 12, 2002, in his manor on Île aux Grues, on the St. Lawrence River, in the migration path of the snow geese he held so dear to his heart.

the **Centre d'Interprétation du Parc des Champs-de-Bataille Nationaux (National Battlefield Park Interpretive Centre)** *($3.50; mid-May to early Sep every day 10am to 5:30pm, early Sep to mid-May Tue-Sun 10am to 5pm; Édifice Baillargé, level 1, ☎648-5641)*, which exhibits a reconstruction of the Battle of the Plains of Abraham and a model of the subsequent development of the area through a multi-media show.

Turn left on Avenue Georges VI and right on Avenue Garneau.

Parc des Champs-de-Bataille ★ ★ ★ *(free admission; ☎648-4071)* takes visitors back to July 1759: commanded by General Wolfe, the British fleet arrives in front of Québec City. The attack is launched almost immediately. Almost 40,000 cannonballs crash down on the besieged city. As the summer draws to a close, the British must make a decision before they are surprised by French reinforcements or trapped in the December freeze-up. On the 13th of September, under cover of night, British troops scale the Cap Diamant escarpment west of the fortifications. The ravines which here and there cut into the otherwise uniform mass of the escarpment allow them to climb and to remain concealed. By morning, the troops have taken position in the fields of Abraham Martin, hence the name also given to the park: **Plains of Abraham**. The French are surprised, as they had anticipated a direct attack on the citadel. Their troops, with the aid of a few hundred Aboriginal and (French) Canadians warriors, throw themselves against the British. The generals of both sides are slain, and the battle draws to a close in bloody chaos. New France is lost!

Parc des Champs-de-Bataille, where the battle took place, was created in 1908 to commemorate the event. With its 101ha, the park is a superb recreational space. Previously occupied by a military training ground, the Ursulines and a few farms, the park was laid out between 1929 and 1939 by landscape architect Frederick Todd. This project provided work for thousands of Québécois during the Depression. Today, the plains are a large green space crisscrossed by paths used for all kinds of winter and summer activities. You will find beautiful landscaping here as well as historical and cultural sites such as the **Kiosque Edwin-Bélanger**, which presents outdoor entertainment. At the park's eastern entrance, Maison de la Découverte (see p 110) presents a good introduction to the Plains, as various exhibitions and activities interpret its history and natural environment.

(see p 110)

Exploring

The **Tours Martello no.1 and no. 2** ★ (towers)

are characteristic of British defenses at the beginning of the 19th century. Tower number 1 (1808) is visible on the edge of Avenue Ontario; number 2 (1815) blends into the surrounding buildings on the corner of Avenue Laurier and Avenue Taché. Inside the first tower, an exhibition recounts some of the military strategies used in the 19th century (*$3.50; end Jun to early Sep every day 10am to 5:30pm*). Renovated and illuminated at night, a third tower stands further north. It is located at the other extremity of the cape, in the Saint-Jean-Baptiste district, on Rue Latourelle.

*This is the end of the Grande Allée walking tour. To return to the walled city, follow Avenue Ontario east to Avenue Georges VI or take Avenue du Cap-Diamant (in the hilly part of the park) to **Promenade des Gouverneurs**. The promenade follows the citadel and overlooks the Cap Diamant escarpment, winding up at Terrasse Dufferin. This route affords stunning views of the city, the St. Lawrence River and the south shore.*

Tour D: Saint-Jean-Baptiste

(two hours)

A hangout for young people, complete with bars, cafés and boutiques, the Saint-Jean-Baptiste quarter is perched on a hillside between Haute-Ville and Basse-Ville. The abundance of pitched and mansard roofs is reminiscent of parts of the old city, but the orthogonal layout of the streets is quintessentially North American. Despite a terrible fire in 1845, this old Québec City suburb retains several examples of wooden constructions, which were forbidden inside the city's walls.

The Saint-Jean-Baptiste tour begins at Porte Saint-Jean, on Place d'Youville. It threads along Rue Saint-Jean, the neighbourhood's main artery.

Place d'Youville, also called "carré d'Youville" (square), is the public space at the entrance of the old section of town. Formerly an important market square, it is today a bustling crossroads and cultural forum. A redevelopment has given the square a large promenade area with some trees and benches. The counterscarp

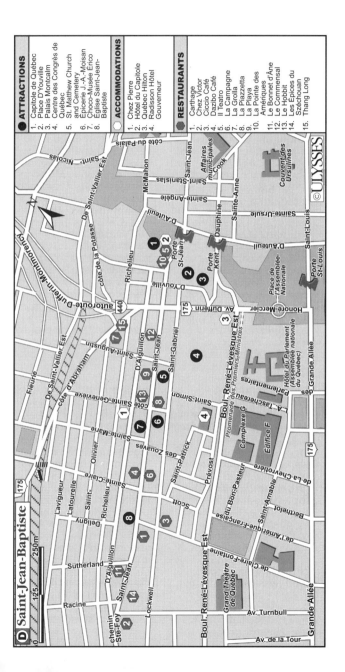

D Saint-Jean-Baptiste

● ATTRACTIONS
1. Capitole de Québec
2. Place D'Youville
3. Palais Montcalm
4. Centre des Congrès de Québec
5. St. Matthew Church and Cemetery
6. Épicerie J.-A.-Moisan
7. Choco-Musée Érico
8. Église Saint-Jean-Baptiste

○ ACCOMMODATIONS
1. Chez Pierre
2. Hôtel du Capitole
3. Québec Hilton
4. Radisson Hôtel Gouverneur

◆ RESTAURANTS
1. Carthage
2. Chez Victor
3. Ciccio Café
4. Dazibo Café
5. Il Teatro
6. La Campagne
7. La Grolla
8. La Piazzetta
9. La Playa
10. La Pointe des Amériques
11. Le Bonnet d'Âne
12. Le Commensal
13. Le Hobbit
14. Les Épices du Széchouan
15. Thang Long

© ULYSSES

wall, part of the fortifications removed in the 20th century, has been highlighted by the use of black granite blocks. In winter, part of the square is covered in ice, much to the delight of skaters who twirl around to the sound of cheerful tunes.

At the beginning of the 20th century, Québec City was in dire need of a new auditorium, its Académie de Musique having burnt to the ground in March 1900. With the help of private enterprise, the mayor undertook the search for a new location. The Canadian government, owner of the fortifications, offered to furnish a strip of land along the walls of the city. Although narrow, the lot grew wider toward the back, permitting the construction of a fitting hall, the **Capitole de Québec** ★ (972 Rue Saint-Jean). W. S. Painter, the ingenious Detroit architect already at work on the expansion of the Château Frontenac, devised a plan for a curved facade, giving the building a monumental air despite the limited size of the lot. Inaugurated in 1903 as the Auditorium de Québec, the building is one of the most impressive beaux-arts realizations in the country.

In 1927, the famous American cinema architect

Thomas W. Lamb converted the auditorium into a sumptuous 1,700-seat cinema. Renamed the Théâtre Capitole, the auditorium nevertheless served as a venue for shows until the construction of the Grand Théâtre in 1971. Abandoned for a few years, the Capitole was entirely refurbished in 1992 by architect Denis Saint-Louis. The building now houses a dinner-theatre in the hall, a luxury hotel (see p 203) and a restaurant (see p 243) in the curved facade. The Capitole has recently acquired the adjoining cinema, on front of which is an imposing round sign. The cinema has been converted into a nightclub.

The Montcalm Market was levelled in 1932 in order to build the multifunctional space called the **Palais Montcalm** (995 Place d'Youville). Also known as the Monument National, this is the venue of choice for political rallies and demonstrations of all kinds. The auditorium has a sparse architecture which draws on both neoclassical and Art Deco schools. Today, visitors come here to see concerts or exhibitions.

Chapelle du Couvent des Soeurs de la Charité (1856) is visible on leaving Place d'Youville. Its delicate Gothic Revival

Capitole de Québec

facade is dwarfed by two huge towers.

Cross Avenue Dufferin, which was recently well restored. Higher up at the corner of Rue Saint-Joachim is a large network of buildings that includes the Centre des Congrès, the Place Québec shopping centre and the Hilton and Radisson Gouverneur hotels.

Centre des Congrès de Québec *(900 Boulevard René-Lévesque Est, ☎644-4000 or 888-679-4000)* was inaugurated in 1996 and is situated north of the Hôtel du Parlement. This large, modern building features glass walls that let the daylight stream in. It has an exhibition hall, several conference rooms and even a ballroom, and is connected to the Place Québec shopping centre and the Hilton and Radisson Gouverneur hotels (see p 202). Its creation has revived this previously dreary part of Boulevard René-Lévesque. Between the Hilton Québec hotel and the Centre des Congrès is the **Promenade Desjardins**, which recalls the life and work of Alphonse Desjardins, founder of the Caisses Populaires Desjardins credit union. At the end of the promenade is a great view of the city and the faraway mountains. At the entrance to the Centre des Congrès is the lively sculpture *Le Quatuor d'airain*.

Exploring

From Rue Saint-Joachim, take Rue Saint-Augustin, which will lead you to Rue Saint-Jean, where you turn left.

There has been a cemetery on the site of the **Church and Cemetery of Saint Matthew** ★ *(755 Rue Saint-Jean)* since 1771, when Protestants, whether French Hugenot, English Anglican or Scottish Presbyterian, banded together to found a Protestant graveyard. Several 19th-century tombstones are still standing. The gravestones were carefully restored recently, and the cemetery is now a public garden.

Located in the cemetery, along Rue Saint-Jean, is a lovely Anglican church. Its Gothic Revival architecture was influenced by the Ecclesiologists, an influential school of Anglican thought that sought to re-establish ties with the traditions of the Middle Ages. In its design, and even in its materials, it looks more like an ancient village church than a Victorian church with a Gothic decor. The nave was first erected in 1848; then, in 1870, William Tutin Thomas, the Montréal architect who designed the Canadian Centre for Architecture's Shaughnessy House, drafted an enlargement, giving the church its present bell tower and interior. Québec's Anglican community dwindled in the 20th century, leading to the abandonment of the church. In 1980, it was cleverly converted into a branch of the municipal library. Several of the adornments crafted by British artists have been retained: Percy Bacon's handsome oak choir enclosure, Felix Morgan's alabaster pulpit, and Clutterbuck's beautiful stained glass. The sober vault with its exposed beams is also noteworthy.

Continue along Rue Saint-Jean.

At number 699, **Épicerie J.-A.-Moisan** *(699 Rue St-Jean)* was founded in 1871 and claims to be the "oldest grocery store in North America." It does in fact look like a general store from yesteryear, with its wooden floor and shelves, old advertisements and many tin cans.

The owner of the Érico chocolate shop, a favourite among "chocoholics," had the great idea of adding a small chocolate museum to his shop. If this interests you, stop by the **Choco-Musée Érico** *(free admission; 634 Rue Saint-Jean, ☎524-2122, www.chocomusee.com)* to learn how the Mayans used cocoa, find out how this fruit grows, discover different recipes and more. Thanks to a window on the kitchen, you can even observe chocolate "artists" at work. And don't forget to sample!

The **Église Saint-Jean-Baptiste** ★ *(Rue Saint-Jean on the corner of Rue de Ligny)* stands out as Joseph Ferdinand Peachy's masterpiece. A disciple of French eclecticism, Peachy was a whole hearted admirer of the Église de la Trinité in Paris. The resemblance here is striking, as much in the portico as in the interior. Completed in 1885, the building caused the bankruptcy of its architect, who was, unfortunately for him, held responsible for cracks that appeared in the facade during construction. In front of the church there is now an attractive little square.

For a beautiful view of the city, take the Rue Claire-Fontaine stairs up to the corner of Rue Lockwell on the right. The climb is steep but the view is worth the effort, especially in the evening when the Basse-Ville lights dance at your feet behind the imposing church. When strolling through this neighbourhood's attractive streets, you will have many opportunities to catch a glimpse of this great view. For example, you can go down Rue Sainte-Claire to the stairs leading to the Saint-Roch neighbourhood, which you will be able to see with the

Laurentian mountains in the background.

Tour E: Chemin Sainte-Foy

(half a day)

At the end of the 18th century, the Haute-Ville walls could no longer contain the expanding city. Suburbs were created around Saint-Jean-Baptiste church and Grande Allée. There was, however, an area that kept its pastoral charm up until the beginning of the 20th century: the farmland along an old country road, Chemin Sainte-Foy, leading to the village of the same name. Since 1950, **Sainte-Foy** has become Québec City's largest suburb. Sainte-Foy, like the other suburbs of Québec City, merged on January 1, 2002 to form the new mega-city of Québec. Because of its large shopping centres and exclusively low-rise housing, Sainte-Foy was known mainly as a dormitory suburb. But over the past few years, it has attempted to shed that reputation by creating civic and cultural facilities that could make more than one Québec town envious. Long described as a "progressive" city, it has conserved little of its past. This tour travels first through the Montcalm

Exploring

and Saint-Sacrement neighbourhoods, where the relatively well-to-do population lives on shaded streets that at times recall the outskirts of London. The tour then takes you to the modern campus of Université Laval.

The tour starts on Chemin Sainte-Foy at the corner of Avenue Cartier and heads west. Turn right on Avenue de l'Alverne.

The **Former Franciscan Monastery** *(on the northeast corner of Avenue Alverne and Rue des Franciscains)* today converted into a housing complex, was built in 1901 and was designed around a cloister inspired by the French Regime's monastery style. It is a remnant of one of several religious communities that settled along Chemin Sainte-Foy at the beginning of the 20th century. At that time, great stretches of land, far from the noise of the city, could be bought for a song.

Turn left on Rue des Franciscains, then left again on Avenue Désy. Turn right on Chemin Sainte-Foy, heading west.

The land along Chemin Sainte-Foy was granted to notable people and Québec religious communities in the early part of the 17th century, but, shortly after the Conquest, a number of

these huge properties were handed over to British dignitaries. Following the example of the domains in Sillery (see p 147), several of them would be turned into country gardens with villas. These domains were divided up in the 20th century and residential developments and institutional buildings replaced most of the villas. However, a few of these residences have survived. Such is the case of the **Villa Westfield** *(private, no visiting; 430 Chemin Sainte-Foy)*, built around 1825 for Charles Grey Stewart, a Lower Canada customs inspector. Its monumental-English-style architecture features neoclassical ornamentation. It was once surrounded by a magnificent English garden.

A little further west is the **Couvent des Sœurs de Saint-Joseph-de-Saint-Vallier** *(560 Chemin Sainte-Foy)*, which was formerly the residence of Andrew Thompson, at which time it was called "Bijou." The house, which forms the central part of the convent, was build in 1874 in the Second Empire style and can be recognized by its mansard roof and curved segmental openings. The wings added by the religious order fit admirably well with the architecture of the house. In 1927, a neo-Romanesque chapel was

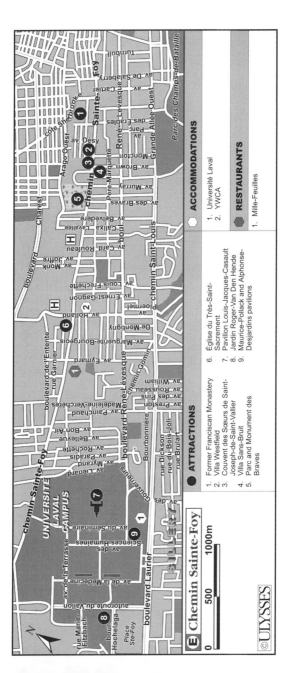

Chemin Sainte-Foy

E

0   500   1000m

● ATTRACTIONS

1. Former Franciscan Monastery
2. Villa Westfield
3. Couvent des Sœurs de Saint-Joseph-de-Saint-Vallier
4. Villa Sans-Bruit
5. Parc and Monument des Braves

6. Église du Très-Saint-Sacrement
7. Pavillon Louis-Jacques-Casault
8. Jardin Roger-Van Den Hende
9. Maurice-Pollack and Alphonse-Desjardins pavilions

ACCOMMODATIONS

1. Université Laval
2. YWCA

RESTAURANTS

1. Mille-Feuilles

© ULYSSES

built in the eastern part of the convent.

Turn left on Avenue Brown.

Here you can see the **Villa Sans-Bruit** *(874 Avenue Brown),* constructed around 1850. The mansard roof was added in 1880 at the time when the house belonged to the Laurie family. Until recently, this area of the Haute-Ville was considered the bastion of Québec City's small anglophone community.

Head south on Avenue Brown. Turn right on Rue du Père-Marquette where you will find the Église des Saints-Martyrs-Canadiens (1929), then turn right again on Avenue des Braves.

Avenue des Braves ★ is in line with the monument of the same name (see below). When the avenue was planned in 1912, it was to be Québec City's most prestigious residential street. Today, you can still see a few opulent stone and brick houses from the 1920s and 1930s. They were built for Québec City bourgeoisie who at the time were leaving their staid homes in the old city for the more open spaces of the suburbs.

The beautiful residence at number 1080 belonged to Roger Lemelin, author of *Les Plouffe,* from 1953 to 1972.

And briefly, between 1994 and 1996, it was the official residence of Québec's premier at the time, Jacques Parizeau.

Go back up Avenue des Braves to the monument at the corner of Chemin Sainte-Foy.

On April 27, 1760, the Chevalier de Lévis arrived from Montréal leading 3,800 men and tried to capture Québec City, which had fallen to the British Army the previous autumn. Although they failed to enter the city, they succeeded in defeating General Murray's troops in Sainte-Foy, making this battle one of the only French victories of the Seven Years' War in New France. **Parc des Braves** ★ was created on the exact site of the battle. Weapons have been found here as well as skeletons of soldiers killed in action. Its name pays tribute to the courage of these valiant young men who made this rash move while waiting for help from a fleet of French reinforcements that would never arrive. In 1855, a **monument** designed by Charles Baillairgé was erected in their memory in the park. The statue of Bellone, an ancient war goddess standing atop a cast-iron column, was a gift from Prince Jérôme-Napoléon Bonaparte.

In 1930, landscape architect Frederick Todd redesigned Parc des Braves and as a result, wealthy families from the old city moved to the surrounding area. The park has lovely views of Basse-Ville and the Laurentian mountains.

Continue west on Chemin Sainte-Foy.

At the corner of Chemin Sainte-Foy and Rue Belvédère is the **Emplacement de la Terre de Jean Bourdon**. Bourdon was an engineer in New France during the first half of the 17th century and also owned the Pointe-aux-Trembles (Neuville) Seigneury. Around 1645, Bourdon had a farm built on this land, which he fortified with stone. The farm had a small and a large dwelling, a chapel, two barns and three storehouses. Unfortunately, these buildings disappeared during the upheaval that followed the Conquest.

Large institutions such as the imposing Saint-Sacrement Hospital (number 1050) can be found along Chemin Sainte-Foy.

Église du Très-Saint-Sacrement *(1330 Chemin Sainte-Foy)* is a late neo-Romanesque work of the 1920s by architects Charles Bernier of Montréal and Oscar Beaulé of Qué-

bec City. Influenced by late medieval architecture, they gave the church a slender, rather austere nave. However, the stained-glass windows by Marius Plamondon, installed in 1954, add a bit of colour. The noviciate of the Très-Saint-Sacrement is in the back.

From here, take bus number 7 along Chemin Sainte-Foy to reach the university campus 2km further west. Get off at the corner of Avenue du Séminaire to reach the centre of campus.

Université Laval Campus *(south of Chemin Sainte-Foy and west of Avenue Myrand)*.
Université Laval was founded in 1852, making it the oldest French-speaking university in America. It was first established in the heart of the old city, near the seminary and Catholic cathedral before being moved to its current site 100 years later. The university was named in honour of Monseigneur de Laval, the first bishop of New France. Each year this vast campus welcomes some 40,000 students. It features good examples of modern and postmodern Québec architecture: one of the interesting buildings is the **PEPS** (sports and physical education building), built in 1971, on the right, at the corner of Chemin Sainte-

Exploring

Foy and Avenue du Séminaire.

A little further to the left, **Pavillon Louis-Jacques-Casault** closes off the symmetrical perspective of the campus *(1210 Avenue du Séminaire)*. This building was constructed from 1954-1958 according to the designs of Ernest Cormier, who also created the Université de Montréal's main building. In the beginning, Pavillon Louis-Jacques-Casault was to be the "Great Seminary" for training priests, which explains the presence of the central chapel adorned with medieval-inspired towers. However, with the approach of the Révolution Tranquille (Quiet Revolution), such a building was considered a dinosaur, reflecting the architecture of the past despite its recent construction. Since 1980, it has housed the **Direction Générale des Archives Nationales du Québec** *(☎643-8904)* as well as the interesting **Centre Muséographique de l'Université Laval** *(☎656-7111)*.

This institution's collections are grouped according to four themes: The Universe, Earth, Life and Man. The museum is now closed and its reopening date is not yet known. The nearby **Pavillon Alexandre-de-Sève** and **La Laurentienne** are clearly more modern.
Centre d'Accueil et de Renseignements de l'Université Laval (reception and information centre) *(closed weekends, mid-Jun to mid Aug 8:30am to noon, 1:30pm to 4:30pm, Fri 8:30am to noon, 1:30pm to 4pm, rest of the year 8am to 5:30pm; Pavillon Alphonse-Desjardins, room 1106, ☎656-3333)*. Here visitors can obtain information on campus activities. Finally, west of Avenue des Sciences-Humaines on Avenue de la Médecine is the **Musée de Géologie du Pavillon Adrien-Pouliot** *(free admission; every day 8:30am to 5pm; ☎656-2193)* exhibiting fossils and minerals from around the world.

Cross the Vallon Highway to reach the Roger-Van den Hende Botanical Gardens.

One of the most interesting gardens in Québec City is found on the university campus. **Jardin Roger-Van den Hende ★** *(free admission; early May to late Sep, every day*

9am to 8pm; 2480 Boulevard Hochelaga, ☎656-3410) is named after the Université Laval scientist who created it from scratch. Used for research and teaching, the garden is also open to visitors. The arboretum, herbacetum, rose garden and water garden are all worth a visit. Guided tours are also offered.

To return to the old part of Québec City, take Métrobus no. 800 or 801 in front of the **Maurice-Pollack** *and* **Alphonse-Desjardins** *pavilions in the southern part of the campus, on the east side of the Vallon Highway. Note that nearly all the university buildings are connected by a series of long underground passageways that may be worth a visit for those interested in this kind of subterranean architecture!*

★

Tour F: Saint-Roch

(four hours)

While Quebec City's wealthier classes lived on the promontory, the working class district lined both sides of the Rivière Saint-Charles. There are no tourist attractions as such here, but the neighbourhood bustles with people going about their daily business. Saint-Roch, Saint-Sauveur and Limoilou are familiar names to the Québécois but unknown to visitors who seldom venture down to Basse-Ville. However, the Saint-Roch district, which lies at the foot of the northern cliff of Cap Diamant, has gone through a major revitalization process over the past few years. Overlooked by most travellers for a long time, this part of the city is slowly getting back on its feet, with several interesting businesses and shops now established here.

Originally settled by potters and tanners at the end of the French Regime, Saint-Roch slowly developed along Rue Saint-Vallier. Then, when the Napoleonic blockade forced Great Britain to rely on its colonies for its wood supply, huge shipyards were created on the banks of Rivière Saint-Charles. This attracted a large working-class population to Saint-Roch. A cholera epidemic in 1832 ravaged the area and almost a quarter of its inhabitants died. Floods then devastated it in both 1845 and 1866. The neighbourhood saw its largest industry disappear in a few years after France and Britain returned to normal relations and ships began using metal hulls (1860-1870).

This marked the beginning of a complete transformation that would make Saint-

Exploring

Roch one of the main industrial quarters in French Canada. A number of factories were created to produce goods for popular consumption (tobacco, shoes, clothing, furniture), in keeping with the tradition of 18th-century potters and tanners. Next to them, department stores such as Paquet, Pollack and the Syndicat de Québec, all established themselves on Boulevard Charest, completing the district's commercial activities. Like the workers, factory and shop owners were French Canadians, a phenomenon that was rarely seen in Canada in those days.

However, in the early 20th century, the well-to-do who still lived here left Saint-Roch to settle in Haute-Ville, mainly on Grande Allée. Then, during the 1960s, commercial activity began to compete more and more with the suburbs and gradually declined; as a result, department stores and factories were forced to shut down and the neglected neighbourhood was all but forgotten for the next few decades.

In the mid-1990s, construction and revitalization projects began at a rather slow pace then took off at an unprecedented speed, completely transforming Saint-Roch. In 1992, the city launched a plan of action intended to give this former commercial centre a little of its old vitality, beginning with the creation of a lovely park on a site previously occupied by dilapidated buildings and weeds. The Jardin de Saint-Roch, an ideal place for a stroll, has caused residents and developers to regain an interest in the district. Several businesses (especially in the fields of multimedia), schools, such as the École des Arts Visuels de l'Université Laval and the École Nationale d'Administration Publique (ÉNAP), theatres and other cultural sites are now established in Saint-Roch. Today, the old neighbourhood is practically unrecognizable, making it a great place to explore.

From the Vieux-Québec, go down the Côte du Palais to leave the walled city, then turn left on Rue Saint-Vallier Est, which travels under the Dufferin-Montmorency Highway. This tour can easily be combined with the "Petit Champlain to Vieux-Port" tour, which ends at Rue De Saint-Vallier Est, as well as the nearby "Saint-Sauveur" and "Limoilou" tours.

Rue Saint-Vallier Est between Côte du Palais and Côte d'Abraham is a thoroughfare dating from the French Regime, located outside the

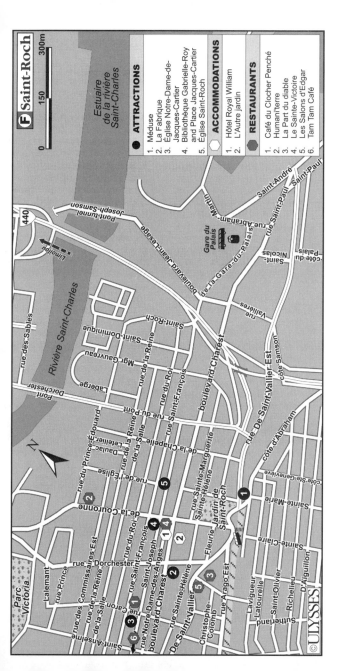

F Saint-Roch

Estuaire
de la rivière
Saint-Charles

● **ATTRACTIONS**

1. Méduse
2. La Fabrique
3. Église Notre-Dame-de-Jacques-Cartier
4. Bibliothèque Gabrielle-Roy and Place Jacques-Cartier
5. Église Saint-Roch

⬡ **ACCOMMODATIONS**

1. Hôtel Royal William
2. L'Autre jardin

⬢ **RESTAURANTS**

1. Café du Clocher Penché
2. Humani'terre
3. La Part du diable
4. Le Sainte-Victoire
5. Les Salons d'Edgar
6. Tam Tam Café

0 150 300m

© ULYSSES

boundaries of the historic quarter. It has been disfigured in many places, particularly by the construction of the Dufferin-Montmorency Highway ramps in 1970; nevertheless, it shows evidence of a very interesting past.

At number 870, you can see the ruins of the **Maison Blanche,** the secondary residence of Charles-Aubert de la Chesnaye, a wealthy merchant. The house was built in 1679 by architect Claude Baillif. In 1845, it was severely damaged by a fire and only half of it was salvaged. Today, only the arches and a few sections of wall remain from the original house.

A little further along are two cast-iron and wood staircases designed by Charles Baillairgé. One was constructed in 1883 and the other in 1889. Upon completion they connected the geographically and socially separate worlds of the city below and the city above. At number 715, a group of well-preserved buildings belongs to the Lépine-Cloutier Funeral Home,

which has been in operation since 1845.

Wedged between Rue Saint-Vallier Est and Côte d'Abraham, **Méduse** *(541 Rue Saint-Vallier Est,* ☎*640-9218)* houses various artists' associations that support and promote Québec culture. Comprised of restored houses and modern buildings that integrate the city's architecture, the complex is perched on the side of Cap Diamant, linking Haute-Ville and Basse-Ville. Associations in various fields such as photography, print-making and video are installed here, as well as studios and galleries. Radio Basse-Ville, a community radio station, and L'Abraham-Martin bistro are also located on the premises. Running along the east side is a stairway which links Côte d'Abraham to Rue Saint-Vallier Est.

At the foot of the stairway is **Îlot Fleuri**, a park where contemporary sculpture is

Squirrel

exhibited, adding a bit of spice to this green space.

At the corner of Côte d'Abraham and Rue de la Couronne, you will find a rock garden with a waterfall known as **Jardin de Saint-Roch**. The creation of this park seems to have launched the rejuvenation process of this neighbourhood. One could even say it marks the "entrance" to the neighbourhood.

Cross Côte d'Abraham. At the opposite corner of the garden is the Édifice du Soleil, so named because it housed the headquarters of Québec City's major newspaper, Le Soleil, for many years.

The section of Rue Saint-Vallier Est between Rue Dorchester and Boulevard Charest is livelier now that a few friendly bars, restaurants and stores have sprung up.

Turn right on Rue Dorchester.

La Fabrique ★ *(295 Boul. Charest Est at the corner of Rue Dorchester)* is located in the former Dominion Corset factory which, as its name indicates, was a manufacturer of corsets and brassieres. President Georges Amyot built this enormous factory between 1897 and 1911, creating jobs for the abundant workforce of young unmarried women.

Because Amyot believed a married woman's place was in the home and not the factory, marriage ment immediate dismissal.

The former Dominion Corset factory was restored and renamed "La Fabrique" in 1993. It now houses an interpretation centre recounting Québec City's rich industrial past, the **Centre de Développement Urbain de Québec**, as well as the **École des Arts Visuels de l'Université Laval**. Take a look at the facade's complex brickwork, the clocktower and the water tower, elements that are reminiscent of American factory architecture at the end of the 19th century.

Cross Boulevard Charest.

Boulevard Charest was created in 1928 to relieve this neighbourhood's congested narrow streets, since the roads built between 1790 and 1840 were no longer able to handle commercial and industrial traffic. There are a few prominent buildings on Boulevard Charest which once were Québec City's department stores. Today they are all closed. Number 740 is the former Pollack store, dating from 1950. The back of the old Paquet store can still be found at the corner of the Rue de l'Église, and at the corner of Rue de la

Exploring

Couronne, you can see the Syndicat de Québec, rebuilt in 1949 and shut down in 1981. The building was renovated and transformed into an office building in 2002.

Head west on Boulevard Charest, to your left, and turn right on Rue Caron.

Église Notre-Dame-de-Jacques-Cartier ★ *(corner of Rue Caron and Rue Saint-Joseph Est)* was originally the Saint-Roch Congregationalists' chapel. It was built in 1853 and expanded in 1875. In 1901, it brought together an entire parish. Its interior was richly decorated by Raphaël Giroux and includes lateral rood screens adorned with gold columns. At the back of the church is the stately embossed-stone presbytery constructed in 1902, but most noteworthy is its sloping steeple!

If you stroll around a bit, you'll see some of the **Saint-Roch workers' houses** ★, which are unique to Québec City's Basse-Ville. Compact and erected at the edge of the sidewalk, they are made of brownish brick or, occasionally, wood. They have sloping or mansard roofs and shuttered French windows. The architecture could be described as a kind of hybrid between North American working-class and French industrial-town architecture.

At the beginning of the 19th century, as Saint-Roch was rapidly developing, many wooden houses spring up, which were inspired by the French Regime's country houses. But the great fire of 1845 reduced the neighbourhood to ashes and changed the rules of the game. After the fire, brick or stone construction became mandatory and wood ornamentation was discouraged. These rules were softened at the end of the 19th century and several houses were then decorated with Victorian wood trim. But the face of Saint-Roch did not change significantly and has kept its quaint, old-time image to this day.

Take Rue Saint-Joseph Est to the corner of Rue de la Couronne.

This is the heart of Saint-Roch. In 1831, the creation of a marketplace was planned for this location but it was only in 1857 that two of its halls were actually built. One of them burned down in 1911 and the other was demolished around 1930 to create **Place Jacques-Cartier**. The statue of the famous explorer, which can be seen at the centre of the square, was a gift from the City of Saint-Malo, France.

At the far end, **Bibliothèque Gabrielle-Roy** *(Mon noon to 9pm, Tue-Fri 10:30 to 9pm, Sat-Sun noon to 5pm; 350 Rue Saint-Joseph Est, ☎529-0924)*, the municipal library, was named for one of French Canada's most famous writers. In her novels, this author describes the extreme poverty of people living in working-class neighbourhoods during the Depression. The library also offers special exhibition spaces to promote the work of contemporary artists.

The eastern section of Rue Saint-Joseph was once covered by a glass roof and was part of the Mail Centre-Ville, which is today limited to the eastern extremity of the street. Since the year 2000, the roof has been removed from a large part of the mall to transform it into a small-town shopping street, where cafés and shops co-exist and make strolling a charming experience. You'll notice that this wind of revival has also affected the block that stretches west of the library, where a wide array of theatres, bookstores, inns and restaurants await you.

Continue east on Rue Saint-Joseph by crossing Rue de la Couronne. You will soon see a church on your left.

Surprisingly, none of the working-class neighbourhoods have kept their old churches. Fire and the rapidly-increasing population have meant that larger and more modern buildings have replaced the old churches. The first **Église Saint-Roch** ★ *(590 Rue Saint-Joseph Est)* was erected around 1811 and was replaced by two other buildings before the present church was built between 1916 and 1923 by architects Talbot and Dionne. It is an immense neo-Romanesque structure with two steeples and a rather austere interior; however, it features interesting stained-glass windows made by the Montréal firm Hobbs (around 1920). Stuck behind the Mail Centre-Ville, Église Saint-Roch was almost forgotten in the last few years. But the revitalization of Rue Saint-Joseph gave the church and its square a prime spot in the neighbourhood.

Continue east on Rue Saint-Joseph.

Rue du Pont was named as such when the first Pont Dorchester was inaugurated in 1789 at the north end of the street. The bridge crosses Rivière Saint-Charles and links Limoilou (see below) and the northern sector of Québec City, and has been rebuilt many times. You can still find remnants of the French

Exploring

Regime settlement east of Rue du Pont. This area, which reaches as far as the columns of the Dufferin-Montmorency Highway, is where the Récollet Fathers' Saint-Roch Hermitage was situated, giving its name to the area.

In 1692, after giving up their Saint-Sauveur monastery to Monseigneur de Saint-Vallier so that it could be turned into a hospital, the Récollets settled in the east where they built a hermitage (retreat) for their priests. The hermitage consisted of a large house with an adjoining chapel; both have since disappeared. Later, a small village was created and businesses were started, thus beginning to populate the area.

Turn right on Rue du Pont to get to Boulevard Charest and go east on Boulevard Charest to return to Côte du Palais.

★
Tour G: Limoilou

(half a day)

As the winter of 1535 approached, Jacques Cartier, who was on his second exploration trip to Canada, had to find the proper spot to anchor his fleet before it was trapped by ice in the middle of the St. Lawrence River. He discovered a well-protected harbour in the bend of Rivière Saint-Charles and had a small log fort built. Towering above it, a wooden cross with the coat of arms of François I was erected. And so, Limoilou became the first French settlement in Canada. However, after Jacques Cartier left, the fort disappeared. Today, the Cartier-Brébeuf National Historic Site marks the area.

In 1625, the territory was granted to the Jesuits. They created the Seigneurie de Notre-Dame-des-Anges here and had colonists settle and cultivate the land. It was only in the middle of the 19th century that Limoilou started to urbanize, taking advantage of the prosperity of Saint-Roch's shipyards on the other side of Rivière Saint-Charles.

Large estates began to appear, each with fields, warehouses, a working-class village and, on the outskirts, the owner's residence surrounded by a landscaped garden. However, little of this period now remains. It was only at the beginning of the 20th century that the present neighbourhood took shape and acquired its name. Limoilou refers to the Manoir de Limoilou near Saint-Malo, France, where

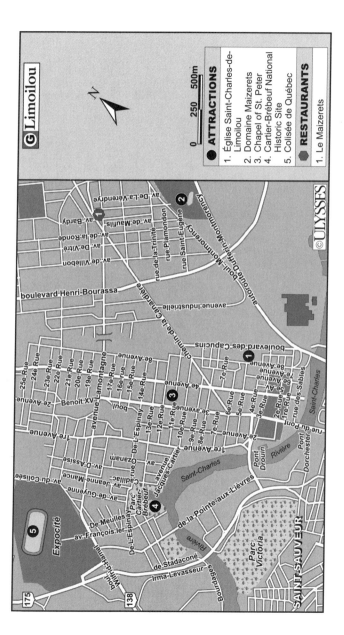

G Limoilou

0 250 500m

● **ATTRACTIONS**

1. Église Saint-Charles-de-Limoilou
2. Domaine Maizerets
3. Chapel of St. Peter
4. Cartier-Brébeuf National Historic Site
5. Colisée de Québec

◆ **RESTAURANTS**

1. Le Maizerets

©ULYSSES

Cartier retired after his numerous trips to New France.

To get to Limoilou from Vieux-Québec, take bus no. 3 from Place d'Youville. It runs along Rue du Pont and then crosses Rivière Saint-Charles. Get off at the corner of 3e Rue, which you take on the right (going east).

Aboriginal Peoples called the river *Kabir Kouba,* meaning "river with many bends," and in 1535, Cartier renamed it "Rivière Saint-Croix." The Récollets who settled on the southern banks in 1615 gave the river its present name, **Rivière Saint-Charles**, in honour of Pontoise priest Charles de Boves who had financed their establishment in New France. The river crosses the rich alluvial plane at the foot of Cap Diamant, going through the centre of Basse-Ville and isolating Limoilou from other working-class neighbourhoods. The river is made up of numerous loops that used to end in a swampy estuary, but now make up the Port de Québec and Bassin Louise.

During the Conquest in 1763 the Jesuits lost their right to teach in Canada. The last of them died in Québec City at the end of the 18th century, and the Notre-Dame-des-Anges seigneury was taken over by the King of England who redistributed the land. Around 1845, William Hedley Anderson created **Hedleyville** in his southern portion. It was the first Limoilou village to specialize in naval construction and commerce in wood. Only a few of the buildings remain from the village, which was located between 1re and 3e Rues and between 4e and 7e Avenues. Number 699 3e Rue is the former **École d'Hedleyville** *(private, no visiting)*, constructed in 1863 to give the workers' children a basic education. The school's architecture is not much different from the neighbourhood's wooden dwellings and was converted to housing quite a while ago.

Go to the end of 3e Rue, more precisely to the corner of Boulevard des Capucins, where you can admire between the pillars of the Dufferin-Montmorency Highway the view of the former **Anglo Canadian Paper Mills**, today the property of the Daishowa Company. This gigantic red-brick industrial complex looks like an impregnable stronghold and was erected in 1928 on the landfilled Rivière Saint-Charles estuary.

Return to 8e Avenue and go north (turn right if you have gone as far as Boulevard des Capucins).

Beautiful **Église Saint-Charles-de-Limoilou** ★ *(8e Avenue)* stands at the corner of 5e Rue, offering a pleasant perspective. The church and conventional buildings surrounding it were all erected on a strip of land that once belonged to Québec City's Hôtel-Dieu. Built with a typical neo-Romanesque facade (1917-1920), the nave of the Limoilou mother church has a double row of medieval-looking arches designed by architect Joseph-Pierre Ouellet. Its interior is representative of Québec City's parish churches which are generally narrower and taller than most

churches in other Québec regions. In this manner, the influence of the Notre-Dame de Québec Cathedral, a tall, long, narrow Baroque work from the mid-18th century, seems to have been felt locally right up until the Second World War.

Along 5e Rue are several of Limoilou's civic buildings such as the beautiful Beaux-Arts fire station constructed in 1910 by the city of Québec. The City had annexed the formerly autonomous Limoilou municipality the previous year, making it part of Québec City.

An option here is to explore the eastern part of Limoilou as far as Domaine Maizerets. Plan a good 30min walk to get there. Continue on 8e Avenue as far as Chemin de la Canardière and turn right. Turn right again on Avenue de la Vérendrye and go as far as Boulevard Montmorency.

On **Domaine Maizerets** ★ *(free admission; every day 9am to 9pm; 2000 Boul. Montmorency, ☎691-2385)* is the Maizerets house, one of the former summer residences of the Séminaire de Québec. The first house was built in 1697 and has been expanded three times since. It was first known as the Domaine de la Canardière because of the innumerable ducks (*canards*) that nested on the nearby sandbars. Then the house was given the name Domaine de Maizerets as a way of paying homage to Louis Ango de Maizerets, the Québec

Exploring

City seminary's superior at the time. The house, its farm and park are a rare group of rural buildings dating back to the 18th century in the Québec City region that are still intact. Its gardens, part of the Association des Jardins du Québec, are a pleasant place to relax.

To follow the main tour, go back to 8e Avenue and then turn left on 12e Rue where you will see the Chapel of St. Peter.

The **Chapel of St. Peter** *(corner of 12e Rue and 3e Avenue)* bears witness to the Anglo-Saxon Anglican presence in Limoilou during the 1920s and 1930s. Most worshippers were managerial staff or owners of the nearby factories, and the Anglican bishop had this chapel built especially for them. However, their numbers were never sufficient enough to justify transforming the chapel into a large church.

The streets around the chapel are good examples of the **architecture of Limoilou houses**; their resemblance to those in Montréal is not accidental. In fact, Limoilou saw itself as a "modern" town—later a neighbourhood—modelling itself after other North American towns at the beginning of the 20th century. Developers from Montréal as well as

the United States sold lots requiring Montréal-style constructions such as flat roofs, multi-level galleries, exterior metal staircases, parapets, alleyways and sheds. Even the shaded streets and avenues were given numbers instead of names, in all-American fashion.

Continue along 12e Rue to 1re Avenue where you turn right and then left onto 13e Rue, which runs into Rue Cadillac and Rue de l'Espinay. This is the main entrance to the Cartier-Brébeuf National Historic Site.

Cartier-Brébeuf National Historic Site ★ *(free admission to the park, open year round; exhibit: $3, early May to early Sep every day 10am to 5am, early Sep to early Oct every day 1pm to 4pm; 175 Rue de l'Espinay, ☎648-4038)* is located near the spot where Jacques Cartier and his crew spent the winter of 1535-1536. The difficult conditions of this forced winter stay resulting in the death of 25 sailors are explained at the reception and interpretation centre. A scale model of Cartier's fort is also displayed there. One must remember that Cartier's plan was not to establish a colony on Canadian soil but rather to make more lucrative discoveries, such as a passage to China or minerals as precious as the gold of the Spanish colonies.

This historic site is a pleasant green space spread out around an inlet of Rivière Saint-Charles. Bike paths cross it, leading to the Vieux-Port or to the Montmorency Falls. There was a time when this was the mouth of the Rivière Lairet, but today it has been filled in. You can see a reconstructed **Iroquois Long House** showing Aboriginal living arrangements in the St. Lawrence Valley at the time of the first explorers. But Cartier is not the only person whose memory is honoured at this historic site. Saint Jean de Brébeuf (1593-1649), a Jesuit missionary martyred by the Iroquois, arrived here in 1625 to establish the Notre-Dame-des-Anges seigneury. A monument commemorating both men was inaugurated in 1889. Cartier-Brébeuf National Historic Site has a pleasant walkway that runs along the meandering Rivère Saint-Charles to the south.

You can take Avenue Jeanne-Mance to get to Expocité. However, it is a good distance on foot and you must pass by a rather uninteresting area to get there. This excursion is particularly worthwhile if there are special events going on at the Centre de Foire (fairgrounds) during your visit. To return,

take bus no. 12 going east to the corner of 1e Rue and Avenue Lamontagne (18e Rue), then transfer to bus no. 801 for Vieux-Québec.

The **Colisée de Québec** is an indoor skating rink where the home-team favourites, the Québec Nordiques, used to play hockey. The Colisée was built in 1950 by an architect of Swiss origin, Robert Blatter, who is also responsible for several attractive international-style houses in Sillery. However, the Colisée's expansion and renovation during the 1970s was not a great success.

The Colisée is located at the centre of what is called **ExpoCité** *(250 Boulevard Wilfrid-Hamel, ☎691-7110)*. Very popular before the arrival of television, regional exhibitions were presented annually in various cities on the continent so that everyone could learn about recent discoveries and view fragments of an exotic, faraway world. These fairs also offered workers a place to relax and gave children a fun place to play. The Centre de Foire de Québec's new large functional pavilions are designed to receive the many exhibitions and fairs that are of interest to the people of Québec City and its surrounding area.

Exploring

Expocité includes the Colisée and the **Hippodrome de Québec** (*☎524-5283*) as well as some of the former pavilions that housed the annual provincial exhibitions presented here since 1892. The **Pavillon des Arts** (1913) and the **Palais Central** (1916) are two Beaux-Arts buildings that are reminiscent of the Chicago World's Fair pavilions of 1893.

Tour H: Saint-Sauveur

(half a day)

Québec writer Roger Lemelin (1919-1994) has made the neighbourhood of his childhood and romances well known through his work. His novels *Au pied de la pente douce* (1944) and *Les Plouffe* (1948) have been made into television series as well as films. He describes the harsh, ordinary day-to-day life of the Saint-Sauveur people while showing both their short-comings and kind-heartedness. At the time, this working-class quarter of Basse-Ville located west of Saint-Roch was Québec City's poorest sector and had the highest rate of un-employment.

The history of Saint-Sauveur began in 1615 when the Récollets came to the banks of Rivière Saint-Charles. These reformed Franciscans had great plans for their land. They anticipated bringing 300 families from France who would settle in a town called "Ludovica." In 1621, they built the first stone church in New France. Unfortunately, when the Kirke brothers captured Québec City in 1629, the project was brought to a halt and despite the return to French rule in 1632, the Récollets' colonisation project was never pursued any further. Only their monastery was rebuilt before being bought by the Bishop of Québec City to create the Hôpital Général (1693).

It was only after the great fire destroyed the neighbouring quarter of Saint-Roch (1845) that Saint-Sauveur became urbanized. In great confusion, hundreds of small wooden houses were built on meagre and often insalubrious land. In 1866 and again in 1889, major fires ravaged a good part of the neighbourhood, which nevertheless continued to attract a number of general workers. These days, Saint-Sauveur is known as a neighbourhood where a deep-seated spirit of Québec City can be

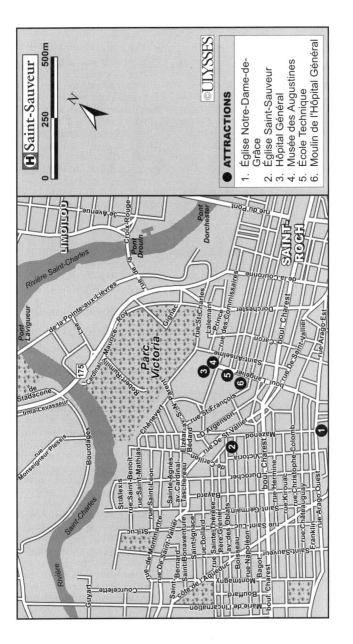

Saint-Sauveur

0 250 500m

N

© ULYSSES

● **ATTRACTIONS**

1. Église Notre-Dame-de-Grâce
2. Église Saint-Sauveur
3. Hôpital Général
4. Musée des Augustines
5. École Technique
6. Moulin de l'Hôpital Général

found in its narrow streets and doll-like houses.

Leaving Haute-Ville, take bus no. 2 from Place d'Youville. Get off at the corner of Boulevard Langelier and Boulevard Charest. Take Boulevard Langelier to the left, then turn right on Rue Arago.

Église Notre-Dame-de-Grâce
(Rue Arago at the corner of Colbert) is situated at the foot of the Haute-Ville cliff. It is an eclectic late work (1925) inspired by medieval architecture, built by Abbé Jean-Thomas Nadeau and notary Gérard Morisset. The latter also played an important role in saving Place-Royale many years later.

Turn right on charming Rue Victoria.

The small houses with mansard roofs on Rue Victoria and the surrounding streets give the neighbourhood a friendly village atmosphere. These dwellings were constructed on the tiniest plots of land marked by owners who wanted to fit a maximum number of families into a minimum space. At the beginning of the 20th century, some houses were expanded with extra storeys, along with balconies and richly-ornamented bay windows.

Église Saint-Sauveur ★ stands at the north end of Rue Victoria. It was erected in 1867, re-using the original burnt walls of the first church built in 1851. Architect Joseph-Ferdinand Peachy designed a neo-Romanesque facade with a spire to give it a Baroque look. Abundantly decorated at the end of the 19th century, the interior has a slender nave and is surrounded by high lateral galleries. Note the windows by Beaulieu and Rochon (1897).

Cross the square in front of the church to get to Avenue des Oblats, turn right and go along to Rue Saint-Vallier Ouest where you turn left.

This street is the heart of the Saint-Sauveur neighbourhood, with snack bars, Asian restaurants, secondhand dealers and workshops. There are also a few former residences of prominent personalities, which are adorned with balconies and towers. **Rue Saint-Vallier** runs through several neighbourhoods in Basse-Ville as a winding path that ends at Bassin Louise.

Take Rue de Carillon north, then turn right on Rue Elzéar-Bédard. Next, almost in front of you, take Avenue Simon-Napoléon-Parent which was named after a mayor at the end of the last century. There are several interesting Second Empire and Queen Anne-style

Victorian residences along this avenue leading to Parc Victoria.

Parc Victoria was created in 1897 to provide the neighbourhoods of Saint-Roch and Saint-Sauveur with some green space, an element that had been missing until then. Pathways and rustic log structures were built and became very popular among city dwellers. But the park lost most of its appeal when the bend in Rivière Saint-Charles was filled in, since the river had almost completely encircled the park at that time. The construction of Police Headquarters also contributed to the transformation of this green space.

Walk along Avenue Simon-Napoléon-Parent beside the park, then turn right on Avenue Saint-Anselme and right again on Avenue des Commissaires. Go around the walls of the Hôpital Général because the entrance is at the end of Boulevard Langelier.

The Récollets built the first stone church in New France in 1621 on the site of the **Hôpital Général** ★★ *(260 Boulevard Langelier)*. Their plan was to bring 300 families from France and settle on the banks of Rivière Saint-Charles in a village called "Ludovica." Although this project never came through, the institu-

tion slowly grew and took root. The present chapel was built in 1673 and in 1682, the Récollets added an arched cloister to their monastery. A few elements remain and have been integrated into the subsequent additions.

In 1693, Monseigneur Jean-Baptiste de la Croix de Chevrières de Saint-Vallier, the second Bishop of Québec City, bought the monastery from the Récollets to establish a hospital. The Augustine Hospitaller Order of the Hôtel-Dieu took charge of the institution which looked after destitute, disabled and elderly people. Today the Hôpital Général is a modern institution for long-term-care patients. However, a great deal of its past has been preserved—more, in fact, than any other institution of its kind in Québec City. There are many elements from the 17th and 18th centuries, such as the Récollets' cells, woodwork, dispensary cupboards and painted panelling. Fortunately, the hospital was never damaged by flames and only a little by the Conquest bombardments, a rarity in Québec City.

It is not possible to visit these vestiges, but you can take a tour of the **Musée du Monastère des Augustines** *(free admission; Tue-Fri by appoint-*

Exploring

Montcalm's Remains

In 1759, French general Marquis de Montcalm lost New France to the British during the Battle of the Plains of Abraham. He also lost his own life and was buried in the Ursulines monastery on Rue Donacona, in the heart of the fortified town. His remains stayed in the monastery chapel for 242 years, until, one morning in 2001 when a funeral procession carried them to their new burial site. They now rest in a mausoleum that was recently built in his honour in the Hôpital Général cemetery. This is where soldiers from both camps were buried after the hospital's Augustine nuns tried to save them, in vain. A memorial was also erected in memory of all the soldiers who died during the Seven Years' War.

ment; ☎ *529-0931)* and the small Église Notre-Dame-des-Anges. This church was redecorated in 1770 by Pierre Émond and houses the preciously guarded tabernacle made in 1722 by François-Noël Levasseur. There are some beautiful paintings such as *L'Assomption de la Vierge* by Frère Luc, painted here during the artist's visit to Canada in 1670, and several paintings by Joseph Légaré bought in 1824.

You can also visit the **Military Cemetery**, where many of the soldiers who died during the Battle of the Plains of Abraham are buried. There is also a mausoleum where the remains of the Marquis de Montcalm now rest, and nearby is the **Mémorial à la Guerre de Sept Ans**, along with a sculpture by Pascale Archambault named *Traversée sans retour.* This memorial honours the memory of the 1,058 soldiers who died between 1755 and 1760 and are buried here. In addition to French and British soldiers, French Canadians and Aboriginals who died trying to defend their land are also interred here.

Take Boulevard Langelier, leaving the hospital and museum behind you.

École Technique

(310 Boulevard Langelier), or École des Métiers, is a good example of Québec City's Beaux-Arts architecture. This is a major architectural work by René Pamphile Lemay that was built between 1909 to 1911. The long red-brick and stone building had a 22m-high central tower, but unfortunately it was demolished around 1955.

The **Moulin de l'Hôpital Général** stands in the middle of a small park at the corner of Avenue Langelier and Rue Saint-François. This old windmill is the only one of about 20 that have survived the harshness of Québec's climate. Its stone tower was erected on earlier foundations in 1730 for the nuns and patients of the Hôpital Général. It milled grain until 1862 when a fire destroyed it completely. The mill was then integrated into an industrial building and was concealed so that it disappeared from view. Only in 1976 was the tower, or what remained of it, uncovered and given a new roof.

To end this tour and return to Place D'Youville, take Rue Saint-François going east and continue for a while until you

reach Rue Dorchester. At the corner of these two streets is a bus stop where you can take Métrobus no. 800 or 801.

Tour I: Sillery to Cap-Rouge

(half a day)

This tour goes up and down along the cliff stretching from Cap Diamant to Cap-Rouge. It begins in Sillery, the affluent Québec City suburb, goes through Sainte-Foy (see p 123) and ends at the Cap-Rouge cliff. You will never be too far from the river and at times will be able to enjoy magnificent panoramas. Note that all the cities you'll cross have merged with Québec City.

Sillery

Sillery retains many traces of its colourful past, influenced by the town's dramatic topography. There are actually two sections to Sillery, one at the base and the other at the top of a steep cliff which runs from Cap Diamant to Cap-Rouge. In 1637, the Jesuits built a mission in Sillery, on the shores of the river, with the idea of converting the Algonquins and Montagnais who came to fish in the coves upriver from Québec City. They named the fortified community in honour of the mission's benefactor, Noël Brûlart de Sillery, an aristocrat who had recently been converted by Vincent de Paul.

By the following century, Sillery was already sought after for its beauty. The Jesuits converted their mission into a country house, and the bishop of Samos built Sillery's first villa (1732). Following the British Conquest, Sillery became the favoured town of administrators, military officers and British merchants, all of whom built luxurious villas on the cliff in architectural styles that were fashionable in England at the time. The splendour of these homes and their vast English gardens were in stark contrast to the simple workers houses that were clustered at the base of the cliff. The occupants of these houses worked in the shipyards where a fortune was being made building ships out of wood coming from the Outaouais region to supply the British navy during Napoleon's blockade, which began in 1806. The shipyards, set up in Sillery's sheltered coves, had all disappeared before Boulevard Champlain, now running along the river's edge, was built in 1960.

The tour begins at the entrance to Parc du Bois-de-Coulonge, on Chemin Saint-Louis, which is the extension of Grande Allee just before it branches off towards the south and becomes Boulevard Laurier.

The **Bois-de-Coulonge** ★★ *(free admission; 1215 Chemin Saint-Louis, ☎528-0773)* borders Chemin Saint-Louis to the east. This English park once surrounded the residence of the lieutenant-governor of Québec. The stately home was destroyed in a fire in 1966, though some of its buildings survived, notably the guard's house and the stables. The Saint-Denys stream flows through the eastern end of the grounds at the bottom of a ravine, and marks the spot where British troops gained access to the Plains of Abraham, where a historic battle decided the future of New France. Now Bois de Coulonge, a member of the Jardins du Québec, features magnificent gardens and an attractive arboretum.

Villa Bagatelle ★ *($3; Mar to Dec Tue-Sun 10am to 5pm; 1563 Chemin Saint-Louis, ☎688-8074)* was once home to an attaché of the British governor, who lived on the neighbouring property of Bois-de-Coulonge. Built in

Children's Favourite Attractions

Here are a few suggested sights and activities to entertain children during their visit to Québec City:

The Musée de la Civilisation always features an exhibit or two that will please children of all ages. Family workshops are often scheduled on weekends.

At the Musée du Québec, creativity abounds! On weekend afternoons, children can come and enjoy arts and crafts, such as sculpting and drawing, related to the current exhibit. A great time is guaranteed!

The Centre d'Interprétation de Place-Royale features a playroom where both young and old can dress up in period costumes and act up a storm…

After renovations are completed in 2003, the Jardin Zoologique and Aquarium will be two wonderful sites for children to see.

Several historic sites offer guided tours accompanied by characters in period costume. This type of activity is usually a hit with children who love stories.

Sound-and-light shows, such as Québec Expérience and Feux Sacrés, which light up the basilica-cathedral, are quite popular with kids.

Watch out for festivals! From the Carnaval de Québec to the Festival d'Été to the Fêtes de la Nouvelle-France, there are always activities for children. In addition, even when there are no festivals, the Vieux-Québec area (Place-Royale, Terrasse Dufferin, Place de l'Hôtel de Ville, etc.) is often animated by street performers in the summer.

And don't forget the round-trip ferry ride to Lévis!

Exploring

1848, the villa is a good example of 19th-century Gothic Revival residential architecture, as interpreted by American Alexander J. Davis. The house and its

Victorian garden were impeccably restored in 1984 and are now open to the public. There is an interesting information centre providing background information on the villas and large estates of Sillery.

On Avenue Lemoine, which runs along the south side of Bagatelle, is the **Spencer Grange Villa**, built in 1849 for Henry Atkinson *(1321 Avenue Lemoine)*. During the Second World War, it was occupied by Zita de Bourbon-Parme, the dethroned Empress of Austria.

Continue on Chemin Saint-Louis as far as the corner of **Avenue Maguire** *and Côte de l'Église. Avenue Maguire is the neighbourhood's main shopping area. Turn left on Côte de l'Église.*

A short side trip leads to the **Cimetière de Sillery**, Sillery's Catholic cemetery, where René Lévesque, founder of the Parti Québécois and Premier of Québec from 1976 to 1984, is buried. To get there, turn right on Avenue Maguire, then left on Boulevard René-Lévesque Ouest. The cemetery is just a little further.

Église Saint-Michel ★ *(at the corner of Chemin du Foulon and Côte de l'Église)* was erected in 1852 by architect George Browne. Inside are five paintings from the famous Desjardins collection. These originally hung in Parisian churches until they were sold in 1792 following the French Revolution and brought to Québec by Abbé Desjardins.

From the **Observatoire de la Pointe-à-Puiseaux**, opposite the church square, you can take a look at the vast panorama of the St. Lawrence River and south shore. On the right are the bridges that link the north and south shores. The first, to the east, is the **Pont de Québec**, a cantilever bridge that was deemed an engineering marvel when it was first built. However, its construction was marked by a tragic event: the central span collapsed when workers were attempting to put it in place for the first time in August 1907. The other bridge with great white arches is named **Pont Pierre-Laporte** in memory of the provincial government minister who was abducted and killed by members of the Front de Libération du Québec (FLQ) during the 1970 October Crisis.

At the foot of the hill, turn right on Chemin Foulon, which takes its name from a mill that was used for carding and fulling wool in the old days.

The **Maison des Jésuites de Sillery ★★** *(amission fee; Jun to Sep Tue-Sun 11am to 5pm,*

Oct to May Tue-Sun 1pm to 5pm; 2320 Chemin du Foulon, ☎654-0259) built of stone and covered with white plaster, occupies the former site of a Jesuit mission, a few ruins of which are still visible. In the 17th century, the mission included a fortified stone wall, a chapel and a priest's residence, as

storeys in front and one in back, covered with a catslide roof.

By 1824 the main building was being used as a brewery and the chapel had been torn down. The house was later converted into an office complex for various shipyards. In 1929, the Maison des Jésuites became

Pont de Québec

well as Aboriginal housing. As European illnesses such as smallpox and measles devastated the Aboriginal population, the mission was transformed into a hospice in 1702. At the same time, work began on the present house, a building with imposing chimney stacks. In 1763, the house was rented to John Brookes and his wife, writer Frances Moore Brookes, who immortalized it by making it the setting for her novel *The History of Emily Montague*, published in London in 1769. It was also during this time that the structure was lowered and the windows were made smaller, in the New England saltbox tradition. The house now has two

one of the first three buildings designated as historic by the government of Québec. Since 1948, it has housed a museum detailing the 350-year history of the property.

Continue along Chemin du Foulon then take Côte à Gignac up the embankment on the right. At the top of the hill turn right on Chemin Saint-Louis.

Domaine Cataraqui ★ *($5; Mar to mid-Dec every day 10am to 5pm, closed Mon rest of the year; 2141 Chemin Saint-Louis, ☎681-3010)* is the best-kept property of its kind still in existence in Sillery. It includes a large neoclassical residence, de-

Exploring

signed in 1851 by architect Henry Staveley, a winter garden and numerous outbuildings scattered across a beautiful, restored garden. The house was built for a wood merchant named Henry Burstall, whose business operated at the bottom of the cliff on which the house stands. In 1935, Cataraqui became the residence of painter Henry Percival Tudor-Hart and his wife Catherine Rhodes. They sold the property to the Québec government to prevent it from being divided, as many others had been. Today it is open to the public, as are its superb gardens where exhibits and concerts are regularly presented. In early fall, many concerts take place during the **Festival de Musique Ancienne de Sillery**.

Head west now on Chemin Saint-Louis.

Maison Hamel-Bruneau *(free admission; Tue-Sun 12:30pm to 5pm, Wed to 9pm; 2608 Chemin Saint-Louis, ☎654-4325)* is a beautiful example of Regency architecture, popular in British colonies at the beginning of the 19th century. This style is characterized by hip roofs with flared eaves covering low wraparound verandas. Graced with French windows, Maison Hamel-Bruneau has been carefully

restored and transformed into a cultural centre.

Turn left on Avenue du Parc to get to the Aquarium du Québec.

The **Aquarium du Québec** *(1675 Avenue des Hôtels, ☎622-0313, www.spsnq.qc.ca)* will be closed until 2003 in order to completely renovate the site and its buildings. The new installations will allow for both outdoor and indoor visits through the various ecosystems of the St. Lawrence and the polar world. Fish, mammals, invertebrates, reptiles and amphibians will live side by side in an extravaganza of shapes and colours. Watch for its reopening!

*Take Chemin Saint-Louis west towards Cap-Rouge. This way, you won't be far from **Parc de la Plage Jacques-Cartier ★** (see p 175). In Cap-Rouge, take Rue Louis-Francœur to the right before turing left down Côte de Cap-Rouge.*

Cap-Rouge

Jacques Cartier and the Sieur de Roberval tried to establish a French colony in Cap-Rouge in 1541. They called their encampments Charlesbourg-Royal and France-Roy. But the unfortunate souls who accompanied them, having no idea how cold Canada could get in January, built frail wood buildings with paper windows! Most died during the winter, victims of the cold or of scurvy, a disease caused by a lack of vitamin C. Those who survived returned to France in the spring.

A plaque has been placed at the **Site Historique de Cap-Rouge** *(at the end of Côte de Cap-Rouge)*, an historic site commemorating the first French colony in America. Cartier and Roberval had intended to make the site a base camp for expeditions heading out in search of a passage to the Orient.

Tour J: Heading North

(one day)

The area covered by this tour is in fact crossed by several highways. The tour begins in Charlesbourg, one of the first areas to be populated in New France. From there, Route 369 will take you to Wendake, a village inhabited by the Huron-Wendat community. The same road will then take you west to Sainte-Catherine-de-la-Jacques-Cartier and Lac Saint-Joseph. From Wendake, you can also choose to follow Route 371, which reaches Saint-Gabriel-de-Valcartier and Tewkesbury. Or, from Charlesbourg, Route 73 will take you to Lac Beauport, Lac Delage and Stoneham. Route 175 heads north to Parc de la Jacques-Cartier. As you may already have noticed, this entire region is a paradise for those who love the great outdoors. For more information, consult the Outdoors chapter.

Charlesbourg

In New France, seigneuries were usually shaped in long

Exploring

rectangles marked out in squares that ran up and down hills. Most of them were set up perpendicular to a significant waterway as well. Charlesbourg is the only real exception to this system, but what an exception! In 1665, when looking for different ways to populate the colony and assure its prosperity and security, the Jesuits developed an original plan to urbanize their land: the Notre-Dame-des-Anges seigneury. It is a huge square, that was divided into angled plots of land converging towards the centre where the dwellings were situated. The houses faced a square defined by a road called the Trait-Carré where there was a church, cemetery and community pasture. This concentric plan assured a better defence against the Iroquois and is still visible today in the old part of Charlesbourg. Two other initiatives of this kind, Bourg Royal to the east and Petite Auvergne to the south, did not have the same success, however, and little remains of them today.

The Notre-Dame-des-Anges seigneury was granted to the Jesuits in 1626, making it one of the first permanent settlements inhabited by Europeans in Canada. Despite this early settlement and original seigneurial design, few buildings built before the 19th century remain in Charlesbourg. The fragility of early buildings and the push to modernize are possible explanations for this. Since 1950, Charlesbourg has become one of the main suburbs of Québec City and has lost much of its original character.

It is best to park near the church and explore the Trait-Carré on foot. You can also take Métrobus no. 801 to get to Charlesbourg. This bus goes as far as the Jardin Zoologique.

Église Saint-Charles-Borromée ★★ *(135 80e Rue Ouest)* revolutionized the art of building in rural Québec. Architect Thomas Baillargé, influenced by the Palladian movement, showed particular innovation in the way he arranged the windows and doors of the facade, to which he added a large pediment. Construction of the church began in 1828 and the original design has remained intact since. The magnificent interior decor by Baillargé was done in 1833.

At the back of the choir, narrower than the nave, is the Arch de Triomphe-style retable, and in the centre is the tabernacle evoking St. Peter's Basilica in Rome. A 17th century painting by Pierre Mignard entitled *Saint Charles Borromée distribuant la communion aux pestiférés de Milan* (St. Charles Borromée giving communion to plague victims in Milan) also hangs there. Two beautiful statues by Pierre-Noël Levasseur, dating from 1742, complete the ensemble. When you step out, you can see the huge Second Empire-style 1876 presbytery, showing the village priest's privileged status in the 19th century, and the Bibliothèque Municipale (municipal library) in the former Collège Saint-Charles (1904).

Take 1re Avenue south then turn left on Rue du Trait-Carré Est, which leads to Chemin Samuel.

Maison Éphraïm-Bédard *(free admission; mid-Jun to mid-Aug Wed-Sun noon to 7pm, early Sep to end Jun Tue and Thr 1:30pm to 4pm; 7655 Chemin Samuel, ☎628-8278)* is one of the rare remaining houses in old Charlesbourg. The local historical society has been installed there since 1986 and presents an exhibition on the evolution of the Trait-Carré. Old maps and aerial photographs show the particular physical layout of Charlesbourg. Guided tours of the area are offered as well.

If you return to Rue Trait-Carré Est, you can see **Maison Magella-Paradis** *(Thu-Fri 7pm to 9pm, Sat-Sun 1pm to 5pm, ☎623-1877)* at number 7970. Built in 1833, it sometimes hosts exhibitions. A little farther along at number 7985, **Maison Pierre-Lefevbre**, built in 1846, houses **Galerie d'Art du Trait-Carré** *(free admission; Thu-Fri 7pm to 9pm, Sat-Sun 1pm to 5pm ☎623-1877)*. Works by local artists are featured here.

Turn right on 80e Rue Est. At the corner of Boulevard Henri-Bourassa is the Jesuits old mill.

The **Moulin des Jésuites** ★ *(free admission; mid-Jun to mid-Aug, every day 10pm to 7pm; mid-Aug to mid-Jun, Sat and Sun 10am to 5pm; 7960 Boulevard Henri-Bourassa, ☎624-7720)*. This pretty mill, in roughcast rubble stone, is the oldest building in Charlesbourg. It was built in 1740 by the Jesuits who were the landowners at the time. After several decades of neglect, the two-storey building was restored in 1990 and now houses the **Centre d'Interprétation du Trait-Carré** and a tourist bureau. Concerts and exhibits are also presented here.

To get to the zoo, take the Autoroute Laurentienne (Laurentian Highway) (73) north and exit at Rue de la Faune.

The **Jardin Zoologique du Québec** *(9300 Rue de la Faune,*

Exploring

☎622-0313, www.spsnq.qc.ca) will be closed until 2003 for complete renovations and general reorganization. Upon reopening its collection will specialize in birds from the world over, which will be showcased in large horticultural installations. Don't miss it once it is reopened: the birds, mammals and new installations (hothouses, gardens, aviaries) will make for an amazing visit.

Take Autoroute Laurentienne (73), this time going south to return to the vicinity of 80e Rue, which becomes Boulevard Saint-Joseph. Take Boulevard Saint-Joseph going west until it becomes Boulevard Bastien.

Wendake

Forced off their land by the Iroquois in the 17th century, 300 Huron families moved to various places around Québec before settling in 1700 in Jeune-Lorette, today known as Wendake. Visitors will be charmed by the winding roads of this village, located on the banks of the Rivière Saint-Charles. The museum and gift shop provide a lot of information on the culture of this peaceful and non-nomadic people.

The **Église Notre-Dame-de-Lorette** ★ *(140 Boulevard Bastien)*, the Huron-Wendat church completed in 1730, is reminiscent of the first churches of New France.

This humble building with a white plaster facade conceals unexpected treasures in its chancel and in the sacristy. Some of the objects on display were given to the Huron-Wendat community by the Jesuits, and come from the first chapel in Ancienne-Lorette (late 17th century). Among the works are several statues by Noël Levasseur created between 1730 and 1740, an altar-facing depicting an Aboriginal village by Huron-Wendat sculptor François Vincent (1790) and a beautiful *Vierge à l'Enfant* (Madonna and Child) sculpture by a Parisian goldsmith (1717). In addition, the church features a reliquary that was made in 1676, chasubles from the 18th century and various liturgical objects by Paul Manis (1715). However, the most interesting element remains the small, Louis XIII-style gilded tabernacle on the high altar sculpted by Levasseur in 1722. Maison Aroüanne (see below) offers guided tours.

Located near the church, **Maison Aroüanne** *(free admission; early May to late Sep every day 9am to 4pm, early*

Oct to late Apr with reserva-tions; 10 Rue Chef-Alexandre-Duchesneau, ☎845-1241) recounts Huron-Wendat culture and traditions by presenting traditional gar-ments and everyday objects. There are also temporary exhibitions and cultural events.

Onhoüa Chetek8e ★ *($6; every day 9am to 5pm; 575 Rue Stanislas-Koska, ☎842-4308)* is a replica of a Huron-Wendat village from the time of early colonization. The traditional design in-cludes wooden longhouses and fences. Visitors are given an introduction to the lifestyle and social organiza-tion of the ancient Huron-Wendat nation. Various Aboriginal dishes are also served and are worth a taste.

Parc de la Falaise et de la Chute Kabir Kouba (see p 175).

Sainte-Catherine-de-la-Jacques-Cartier

From Wendake, you can reach the **Lac Saint-Joseph region**, to the northwest. This is a popular resort area for Québec City residents who swim and practice watersports in this lake all summer long and enjoy, among other things, its beach (see p 176).

Before reaching Lac Saint-Joseph, you'll pass Sainte-Catherine-de-la-Jacques-Cartier and the **Station Écotouristique Duchesnay** ★ (see p 175), a lovely park that, come wintertime, fea-tures the famous **Ice Hotel** ★ *(guided tour $12, in French everyday, every 2hrs from 10:30am to 8:30pm, in English from 11:30am to 7:30pm; ☎875-4522 or 877-505-0423, www.icehotel-canada.com).* The Québec Ice Hotel (see p 207), a spectacular, Swedish-inspired structure, is unique in North America and definitely one of the region's "hottest" attractions. Its lifespan is obviously limited (early Jan to late Mar), but every year, build-ers return to the site to erect this stunning complex using several tonnes of ice and snow. And not only is the ice used for building, it also serves as decoration! The hotel houses an art gallery showcasing unusual snow and ice sculptures, as well as an exhibit room, a small movie theatre, a cha-pel and a bar where vodka is served in ice glasses. You'll simply be amazed!

Lac Beauport

From Charlesbourg, take Route 73, which eventually branches off towards Lac Beauport.

Exploring

Lac Beauport is a resort site that is popular throughout the year. A downhill-skiing resort, **Le Relais** (see p 185), has even been created here. Around the lake, summer visitors can enjoy lovely beaches.

Route 73 becomes Route 175 and runs along the resort towns of **Lac-Delage** and **Stoneham**, which is home to a ski resort (see p 185). A bit further, it gives access to **Parc de la Jacques-Cartier** (see p 176) and the **Réserve Faunique des Laurentides**.

To return to Québec City, head south on Route 175.

Tour K: Côte-de-Beaupré and Île d'Orléans

(one to two days)

This long, narrow strip of land nestled between the St. Lawrence and the undeveloped wilderness of the Laurentian massif, is the ancestral home of many families whose roots go back to the beginning of the colony. It illustrates how the spread of the population was limited to the riverside in many regions of Québec, and recalls the fragility of development in New France. From Beauport

to Saint-Joachim, the colony's first road, the Chemin du Roy (king's road) built under orders from Monseigneur de Laval during the 17th century, follows the Beaupré shore. Along this road, houses are built in a style characterized by a raised main floor covered in stucco, long balconies with intricately carved wood balusters and lace-curtained windows.

As for Île d'Orléans, it is a 32km-by-5km island in the middle of the St. Lawrence River downstream from Québec City. The island is close to the hearts of this region's inhabitants. You will quickly understand why when you visit the island and see the superb countryside, as well as Québec's heritage treasures that appear along Chemin Royal.

Beauport

Three types of urban development have shaped Beauport over the course of its history. Originally an agricultural settlement, in the 19th century it became an important industrial town, evolving into one of Québec City's main suburbs in the 1960s, before merging with the city in 2002. In 1634, the Beauport

Manoir Montmorency

seigneury from which the present city grew, was granted to Robert Giffard, a doctor and surgeon from the Perche region of France. During the next few years he enthusiastically set about building a manor house, a mill and a small village, establishing one of the largest seigneuries in New France. Unfortunately, wars and fires have claimed several of these buildings.

The large white house known as **Manoir Montmorency** *(2490 Avenue Royale, ☎663-3330)* was built in 1780 for British governor John Haldimand. At the end of the 18th century, the house became famous as the residence of the Duke of Kent, son of George III and father of Queen Victoria. The manor, which once housed a hotel, was severely damaged by fire in May 1993. It has been restored according to the original plans and now

features an information centre, a few shops and a restaurant (see p 248) which offers an exceptional view of the Montmorency Falls, the St. Lawrence and Île d'Orléans. The small Sainte-Marie chapel on the property and the gardens are open to the public.

The Manoir Montmorency is nestled in the **Parc de la Chute Montmorency** ★★ *(parking $7, free in winter, cablecar $7 return; accessible all year; for opening hours and parking ☎663-2877, www.chutemontmorency.qc. ca)*. Rivière Montmorency, with its source in the Laurentians, flows peacefully until it reaches a sudden 83m drop and tumbles into a void, creating one of the most impressive natural phenomena in Québec. One and a half times the height of Niagara Falls, the Montmorency Falls flow at a rate that can reach 125,000 litres-per-second

Exploring

during spring thaw. To take in this magnificent spectacle, a park has been created and a tour of the falls is offered. From the manor, follow the pretty cliff path, location of the Baronne lookout. You'll soon reach two bridges, the Pont Au-dessus de la Chute and the Pont Au-dessus de la Faille, which cross the falls and the fault respectively and offer spectacular views. Once in the park you'll find picnic tables and a playground. The bottom of the falls can be reached by the 487-step panoramic staircase or the trail. The cable car provides a relaxing and picturesque way to go back to the top. During winter, mist freezes into ice cones called "sugar-loaves" that adventurous souls can climb.

Samuel de Champlain, founder of Québec City, was impressed by the falls and named them after the viceroy of New France, Charles, Duc de Montmorency. During the 19th century, the falls became a fashionable leisure area for the well-to-do of the region who would arrive in horse-drawn carriages or sleighs.

The lower part of the park, situated opposite the falls, is accessible by a long wooden staircase or by cable car. To reach the lower part of the park by car, you must make a complicated detour: continue along Avenue Royale, turn right on Côte de l'Église, then right again on Highway 40. The parking lot is on the right. To get back to Avenue Royale, take Boulevard Sainte-Anne west, Côte Saint-Grégoire and finally Boulevard des Chutes to the right.

Take Boulevard Sainte-Anne (Highway 138) going east or take Chemin Royal, which travels through the bucolic countryside and pretty villages.

Château-Richer

Château-Richer is charming and picturesque, highlighted by the striking placement of the church on a promontory. Hundred-year-old root cellars and stone ovens are visible from the road and are still used occasionally. Throughout the village, small wooden signs have been posted in front of historical buildings, indicating any distinctive architectural features and when they were built.

The superb Petit-Pré wind-mill, which dominates the river of the same name on the edge of Chemin Royal, is where you will find (since 2001) the **Vignoble Moulin du Petit-Pré** (*free* *admission, end Jun to mid-Oct every day 10am to 5pm; 7007 Avenue Royale,* ☎*824-4411).* The windmill was rebuilt after the Conquest, modeled after the windmill that had been built by the Séminaire de Québec in 1695. Since the early 1990s, beautiful vines grow behind the windmill, and visitors can explore the vinery thanks to interpretive signs. Inside the windmill, a shop sells regional products and offers tastings of the white wine that is made on the premises.

The **Centre d'Interprétation de la Côte-de-Beaupré** ★ *($4; in summer every day 10am to 5pm, the rest of the year Mon-Fri 9am to 5pm; 7976 Avenue Royale,* ☎*824-3677),* which used to be housed in the Petit-Pré windmill, has moved for the 2002 season to a new locale in the heart of the village. Now occupying a four-storey former school, the centre features a permanent exhibit on the history and geography of Côte-de-Beaupré, as well as temporary exhibits.

For those who are curious about bees and honey, here's an interesting little museum. The **Musée de l'Abeille** *(free admission; "bee safari" $3; end Jun to mid-Oct every day 9am to 6pm, mid-Oct to end Jun 9am to 5pm; 8862 Boulevard Ste-Anne,* ☎*824-4411)* offers a brief

look into the lives of these tireless workers. Visitors can stroll through at their leisure or receive an introduction to the art of beekeeping by participating in a "bee safari." A beekeeper explains the steps involved in making honey and mead (honey wine). There is also a pastry shop and a gift shop.

To reach Sainte-Anne-de-Beaupré, you can take Boulevard Sainte-Anne (Route 138) eastbound, or Chemin Royal, which travels through the countryside and other quaint villages.

Sainte-Anne-de-Beaupré

This long, narrow village is one of the largest pilgrimage sites in North America. In 1658, the first Catholic church on the site was dedicated to Saint Anne after sailors from Brittany, who had prayed to the Virgin Mary's mother, were saved from drowning during a storm on the St. Lawrence. Soon, a great number of pilgrims began to visit the church. The second church, built in 1676, was replaced in 1872 by a huge temple, which was destroyed by fire in 1922. Finally work began on the present basilica

Exploring

which stands at the centre of a virtual compound of chapels, monasteries and facilities as varied as they are unusual. Each year, Sainte-Anne-de-Beaupré welcomes more than a million pilgrims, who stay in the hotels and visit the countless souvenir boutiques, of perhaps questionable taste, along Avenue Royale.

The **Basilique Sainte-Anne-de-Beaupré ★★★** *(information counter is loctated near the entrance, early May to mid-Sep, every day 8:30am to 5pm; 10018 Avenue Royale, ☎827-3781)*, towering over the small, metal-roofed wooden houses that line the winding road, is surprising not only for its impressive size, but also for the feverish activity it inspires all summer long. The church's granite exterior, which takes on a different colour depending on the lighting, was designed in French Romanesque Revival style by Parisian architect Maxime Roisin, who was assisted by Quebecer Louis Napoléon Audet. Its spires rise 91m high, while the nave is 129m long and the transepts over 60m wide. The wooden statue gilded with copper sitting atop the church's facade was taken from the 1872 church.

The basilica's interior is divided into five naves, supported by heavy columns with highly sculpted capitals. The vault of the main nave is adorned with sparkling mosaics designed by French artists Jean Gaudin and Auguste Labouret, recounting the life of Saint Anne. Labouret also created the magnificent stained glass, found all along the perimeter of the basilica. The left transept contains an extraordinary statue of Saint Anne cradling Mary in her right arm. Her tiara reminds visitors that she is the patron saint of Québec. In a beautiful reliquary in the background, visitors can admire the Great Relic, part of Saint Anne's forearm sent over from the San Paolo Fuori le Mura in Rome. Finally, follow the ambulatory around the choir to see the ten radiant chapels built in the 1930s, whose polychromatic architecture is inspired by the Art Deco movement. The Basilica is open all year.

Material retrieved after the demolition of the original church in 1676 was used to build the **Chapelle Commémorative ★** *(free admission; May to mid-Sep, every day 8am to 8pm; Avenue Royale, ☎827-3781)* in 1878. The steeple (1696) was designed by Claude Bailiff, an architect whose numerous other projects in 17th-century New France have all but disappeared because of war and fire. Inside, the high altar comes from the original church built during the French Regime. It is the work of Jacques Leblond-dit-Latour (1700). The chapel is adorned with paintings from the 18th century. The water from the Fontaine de Sainte-Anne, at the foot of the chapel, is said to have healing powers.

La Scala Santa ★ *(free admission; May to mid-Sep, every day 8am to 8pm; to the right of the Chapelle Commémorative)*, an unusual yellow-and-white wooden building (1891) covers a staircase which pilgrims climb on their knees while reciting prayers. It is a replica of the Scala Santa, the sacred staircase conserved in Rome at San Giovanni in Laterano that Christ climbed to get to the court of Pontius Pilate. An image of the Holy Land is inlaid in each riser.

The **Chemin de la Croix** *(behind the Chapelle du Souvenir)* is located on the side of the hill and leads to the **Monastère des Laïcs**. The Chapelle de Saint-Gérard is worth a short visit. The life-size statues were cast in bronze at Bar-le-Duc, France.

The **Cyclorama de Jérusalem** ★★ *($6; late Apr to late Oct every day 9am to 6pm, Jul and Aug every day 9am to 8pm, 8 Rue Régina, near the parking lot; ☎827-3101)*. This round building with Oriental features houses a 360° panorama of Jerusalem on the day of the crucifixion. This immense *trompe l'œil* painting, measuring 14m by 100m, was created in Chicago around 1880 by French artist Paul Philippoteaux and his assistants. A specialist in panoramas, Philippoteaux produced a work of remarkable realism. It was first exhibited in Montréal before being moved to Sainte-Anne-de-Beaupré at the very end of the 19th century. Very few panoramas and cycloramas, so popular at the turn of the century, have survived to the present day.

The **Musée de Sainte Anne** ★ *($5; late Apr to mid-Oct, every day 10am to 5pm; early Oct to late Apr, Sat-Sun 10am to 5pm; 9803 Boulevard Ste-Anne, ☎827-6873)* is dedicated to sacred art honouring the mother of the Virgin Mary. These interestingly diverse pieces were acquired over many years from the basilica but are now put on display for the public. Sculptures, paintings, mosaics, stained-glass windows and goldworks are dedicated to the cult of Saint Anne, as well as written works expressing

Exploring

prayers or thanks for favours obtained. The history of pilgrimages to Sainte-Anne-de-Beaupré is also explained. The exhibition is attractively presented and spread over two floors.

To learn more about Québec folklore, go to the **Atelier Paré** (*free admission; mid-May to mid-Oct every day 9am to 5:30pm, mid-Oct to mid-May Mon-Fri 1pm to 4pm, Sat-Sun 10am to 4pm; 9269 Avenue Royale*, ☎827-3992). All the works presented at this wood-sculpting museum are inspired by the fascinating world of local legends.

*You can follow Route 138 to the **Réserve Nationale de Faune du Cap Tourmente** ★ (see p 177), or take Route 360 Est to **Station Mont-Sainte-Anne** ★ (see p 177) and the **Grand Canyon des Chutes Sainte-Anne** (see p 177). Continuing further east on this highway, you will approach the magnificent Charlevoix region that you can visit with the Ulysses Travel Guide Québec. To continue the present tour on Île d'Orléans, take route 138 west and you will soon see signs for the bridge to the island.*

Île d'Orléans

Île d'Orléans is synonymous with old stones. In fact, of all Québec regions, it is the most evocative of life in New France. When Jacques Cartier arrived in 1535, the island was covered in wild vines which inspired its first name: Île Bacchus. However, it was soon renamed in homage to the Duc d'Orléans. With the exception of Sainte-Pétronille, the parishes on the island were established in the 17th century. The colonization of the entire island followed soon after. In 1970, the government of Québec declared Île d'Orléans a historic district. The move was made in part to slow down the development that threatened to turn the island into yet another suburb of Québec City, and also as part of a widespread movement among the Québécois to protect the roots of their French ancestry by preserving old churches and houses. Since 1936, the island has been linked to the mainland by a suspension bridge, the Pont de l'Île. Île d'Orléans is also known as the country of Félix Leclerc (1914-1988), the most famous Québec poet and *chansonnier*.

This tour around Île d'Orléans will allow you to enjoy its many charms: its old buildings dating from the French Regime, its small chapels along the road, its large fields that seem to plunge into the river, its orchards... Depending on the season, you may also be able to pick fruit (see p 181). Don't be surprised if, along the way, you see enclosed llamas or ostriches. Barely ten years ago, this island only had old-fashioned black and white cows, but today, new kinds of farming have developed, multiplying the number of discoveries you can make here!

Begin the tour of the island by taking Chemin Royal to the right on top of the hill by the bridge.

★
Sainte-Pétronille

Paradoxically, Sainte-Pétronille was the site of the first French settlement on Île d'Orléans and is also its most recent parish. In 1648, François de Chavigny de Berchereau and his wife Éléonore de Grandmaison established a farm and a Huron-Wendat mission here. However, constant Iroquois attacks forced the colonists to move further east to a spot facing Sainte-Anne-de-Beaupré. It was not until the middle of the 19th century that Sainte-Pétronille was consolidated as a village, as its beautiful

location began attracting numerous summer visitors. Anglophone merchants from Québec City built beautiful second homes here, many of which are still standing along the road. A word to music lovers: chamber music concerts are presented at the Église de Sainte-Pétronille on Sundays in the summer.

During her life, Éléonore de Grandmaison had four husbands. After the death of François de Chavigny, she married Jacques Gourdeau who gave his name to the estate, his wife's property. Overlooking the river from the top of a promontory, **Manoir Gourdeau** *(137 Chemin Royal)* has been given this name even though the house's construction date does not quite coincide with the time the couple was together. The long building was very likely built at the end of the 17th century but has been considerably expanded and changed since then.

Turn right on Rue Horatio-Walker, which leads to the river banks and a promenade.

The street is named after **Maison Horatio-Walker** ★ *(11 and 13 Rue Horatio-Walker).*

Exploring

The red-brick building and the stucco house beside it were, respectively, the workshop and residence of painter Horatio Walker from 1904 to 1938. The British-born artist liked the French culture and the meditative calm of Île d'Orléans. His workshop, designed by Harry Staveley, remains a good example of English Arts and Crafts architecture.

Return to the Chemin Royal.

The Porteous family, of English origin, settled in Québec City at the end of the 18th century. In 1900, they built the **Domaine Porteous** ★ *(253 Chemin Royal)*. This vast country house surrounded by superb gardens was christened "La Groisardière." Designed by Toronto architects Darling and Pearson, the house revived certain aspects of traditional Québec architecture. The most notable of these is the Louis XV-inspired woodwork, and the general proportions used in the design of the house, which are similar to the Manoir Mauvide-Genest in Saint-Jean. Inside, are many remounted paintings by William Brymner and Maurice Cullen depicting countryside scenes on Île d'Orléans. The building also incorporates *art nouveau* features. The property, which today belongs to the Foyer de Charité Notre-Dame-d'Orléans, a seniors' residence, was expanded between 1961 and 1964 when a new wing and a chapel were added.

The Sainte-Pétronille wharf dates back to 1855 and offers a magnificent view of Québec City. Next to it is L'Auberge La Goéliche (see p 211).

After your tour of this tip of the island, head towards Saint-Laurent by Chemin Royal. You will then cross a forest of red oaks.

Saint-Laurent

Until 1950, Saint-Laurent's main industry was the manufacturing of *chaloupes*, boats and sailboats that were popular in the United States and Europe. Though production of these boats has ceased, some traces of the industry, such as abandoned boatyards, can still be seen off the road near the banks of the river. The village was founded in 1679 and still has some of its older buildings, such as the beautiful **Maison Gendreau** built in 1720 *(2387 Chemin Royal, west of the village)* and the **Moulin Gosselin**, which was turned into a restaurant *(758 Chemin Royal, east of the village)*.

Parc Maritime de Saint-Laurent ★ *($2; mid-Jun to*

early Sep every day 10am to 5pm; 120 Chemin de la Chalouperie, ☎828-9672) has been developed on the site of the Saint-Laurent shipyard. Here you can visit the Godbout *chalouperie* workshop, a family business established around 1840. They have a collection of nearly 200 craftsmen's tools. A path behind the

Historic Québec house

building leads to the water where you can rent a small boat and go on a tour.

★★
Saint-Jean

In the mid-19th century, Saint-Jean was the preferred homebase of nautical pilots who made a living guiding ships through the difficult waters and rocks of the St-Lawrence. Some of their neoclassical or Second Empire houses can still be seen along Chemin Royal, and provide evidence of the privileged place held by these seamen who were indispensable to the success of commercial navigation.

The most impressive manor from the French Regime still

standing is in Saint-Jean. **Manoir Mauvide-Genest ★★** *($5; early May to end Oct every day 9am to 5pm; 1451 Chemin Royal, ☎829-2630)* was built in 1734 for Jean Mauvide, the royal doctor, and his wife Marie-Anne Genest. This beautiful stone building is coated with white roughcast in traditional Norman architectural style. The property officially became a seigneurial manor in the middle of the 18th century, when Mauvide, who had become rich doing business in the Caribbean, bought the southern half of the Île d'Orléans seigneury.

In 1926, Camille Pouliot, descendant of the Genest family, bought the manor house. He then restored it, adding a summer kitchen and a chapel and later transformed the house into a museum, displaying furniture and objects from traditional daily life. Pouliot was

Exploring

one of the first people to be actively interested in Québec's heritage. The manor was bought back in 1999 and its new owners have begun major works to renovate and embellish the site. Here, you can enjoy a lovely guided tour accompanied by characters in period costume and explore the three floors of the manor, which was restored in the tradition of the era to evoke the daily life of a domain under the French Regime. The tour lasts 1hr 15min.

★
Saint-François

This, the smallest village on Île d'Orléans, retains many buildings from its past. Some, however, are far from the Chemin Royal and are therefore difficult to see from the road. The surrounding countryside is charming and offers several pleasant panoramic views of the river, of Charlevoix and of the coast. The famous wild vine that gave the island its first name, Île Bacchus, can also be found in Saint-François.

As you leave the village, you will find an **observation tower ★** which provides excellent views to the north and east. Visible are the Îles Madame et Au Ruau which mark the meeting point of the fresh water of the St.

Lawrence and the salt water of the gulf. Mont Sainte-Anne's ski slopes, Charlevoix on the north shore and the Côte-du-Sud seigneuries on the south shore can also be seen in the distance.

★
Sainte-Famille

The oldest parish on Île d'Orléans was founded by Monseigneur de Laval in 1666, in order to establish a settlement across the river from Sainte-Anne-de-Beaupré for colonists who had previously settled around Sainte-Pétronille. Sainte-Famille has retained many buildings from the French Regime. Among them is the town's famous church, one of the greatest accomplishments of religious architecture in New France, and the oldest two-towered church in Québec.

The beautiful **Église Sainte-Famille ★★** (*3915 Chemin Royal*) was built between 1743 and 1747 to replace the original church built in 1669. Inspired by the Église des Jésuites in Québec City, which has since been destroyed, Father Dufrost de la Jemmerais ordered the construction of two towers with imperial roofs, which explains the single steeple sitting atop the gable. Other unusual elements such as five alcoves and the sundial

Chapel in Sainte-Famille

by the entrance (which has since been destroyed) made the building even more unique. In the 19th century, new statues were installed in the alcoves and the imperial roofs gave way to two new steeples, bringing the total number of steeples to three.

Although modified several times, the interior decor retains many interesting elements. Sainte-Famille was a wealthy parish in the 18th century, thus allowing the decoration of the church to begin as soon as the frame of the building was finished. In 1748, Gabriel Gosselin installed the first pulpit and in 1749 Pierre-Noël Levasseur completed construction of the high altar's present tabernacle. Louis-Basile David, inspired by the Quévillon school, designed the beautiful coffered vault in 1812. Many paintings adorn the church, such as *La Sainte Famille* (The Holy Family) painted by Frère Luc during his stay in Canada in 1670, the *Dévotion au Sacré Coeur de Jésus* (Devotion to the Sacred Heart of Jesus, 1766) and *Le Christ en Croix* (Christ on the Cross) by François Baillargé (1802). The church grounds offer a beautiful view of the coast.

Most of the French Regime farmhouses on Île d'Orléans were built a good distance from the road. Today these properties are much sought after and their owners jealously guard their privacy, which makes any visiting

Exploring

unlikely. Fortunately, a foundation has been set up by residents so that **Maison Drouin** ★★ *($2, end Jun to mid-Oct every day 11am to 6pm; ☎829-0330)* is open every summer to interested visitors. It is one of the oldest houses on the island and in Québec, dating from the 17th century. It stands by a bend on Chemin Royal and was build with large fieldstones and wooden beams. You will learn about its history from guides dressed in period costume acting out the daily life of its former inhabitants. The three rooms on the ground floor, as well as the upstairs, recall the environment of the first colonists. Antique furniture and tools are also displayed to help illustrate pioneer life, making it a lovely place to visit.

Saint-Pierre

The most developed parish on Île d'Orléans had already lost some of its charm before the island was declared a historic site. Saint-Pierre is particularly important to the people of Québec, since it was the home of the renowned poet and singer Félix Leclerc (1914-1988) for many years. The singer and songwriter, who penned *P'tit Bonheur* was the first musician to introduce Québécois music to Europe. He is buried in the local cemetery.

In addition, at the end of the village there is a site honouring the poet's memory that is scheduled to open in June 2002. Indeed, **Espace Félix-Leclerc** *($3; mid-Feb to mid-Dec Tue-Sun 9am to 6pm; 682 Chemin Royal, ☎828-1682)* will include a wide array of interesting features: a building housing an exhibit on the life and work of Félix Leclerc, a *boîte à chansons* (a music venue for singer-songwriters) where young and old alike can belt out Leclerc's famous tunes or come up with some new ones of their own, and hiking trails to explore the heart of the island, as Leclerc did so many times. The site covers 50ha on both sides of the road, from the sand bars to the centre of the island, knows as the *mitan*. There is also a small café and picnic tables, so plan to stay a while!

Église Saint-Pierre ★ *(1249 Chemin Royal)*, a lowly building erected in 1716, is the oldest village church still standing in Canada. The church is also a rare survivor of this kind of architecture, which was widespread in New France. It only has one portal and an oculus window on the facade. Most of these little churches with pointed roofs were destroyed in the 19th century and replaced with more elaborate structures.

Pillaged during the Conquest, the interior of Église Saint-Pierre was rebuilt at the end of the 18th century. Note in particular the altars by Pierre Émond (1795), embellished with the papal coat of arms. The paintings above the altars are by François Baillairgé.

This church was abandoned in 1955 when the larger church nearby was inaugurated. However, when it was threatened with demolition it was taken over by the Québec government.

Conserved intact, it displays furnishing no longer found in most Québec churches such as a central stove with a long iron stovepipe. The pews have doors which allowed these closed spaces to be reserved as private property and in winter, the owners kept warm with hot bricks and furs.

The tour is now over. At the traffic light, turn right, go down the hill and return to Québec City on Highway 138 Ouest.

Québec City
is certainly a choice destination for outdoor enthusiasts.

The greater Québec City region has many rich and varied natural attractions, as well as numerous beautiful parks that are scattered throughout the area as well as in the city itself.

Québec City's most beautiful gardens are grouped together by an association called **Association des Jardins du Québec** *(82 Grande Allée Ouest, ☎647-4347, www.associationdes-jardinsduquebec.com)*. These gardens are a treasure to be preserved and certainly to be explored. They are open to the public, whether they want to learn more about horticulture and botany or simply stroll around and enjoy their beauty. There are five of these gardens in Québec City, namely the Parc des Champs-de-Bataille (see p 116 or below), Jardin Roger-Van den Hende (see

p 128), Domaine Maizerets (see p 139 or below), Maison Henry-Stuart (see p 114) and Bois-de-Coulonge (see p 148).

If you feel so inclined during your stay, you will certainly get the chance to participate in several outdoor activities. To find the right equipment, you can consult our list of stores in the Shopping chapter, p 275.

Note that, just like the **Hiver Express** shuttle (see p 44), **Sherpa Plein Air** *(12 Rue Ste-Anne, ☎640-7437, www.sherpapleinair.com)* is the place to go for those who like to play outside. Sherpa Plein Air offers a shuttle service (the colourful Sherpa Bus), as well as various outdoor activities throughout the year, organized according to your needs.

Here is a general overview of the many possibilities offered to you.

Parks

Tour C: Grande Allée

The **Parc des Champs de Bataille** (see p 116), better known as the Plains of Abraham, is Québec City's undisputed park of parks. This immense green space covers about 100ha and stretches all the way to Cap Diamant, which slopes down to the river. It is a magnificent place for local residents to enjoy all sorts of outdoor activities. Strollers and picnickers abound during the summer, but there is enough space for everyone to enjoy a little peace and quiet.

Tour G: Limoilou

With its big trees and lawns, **Domaine Maizerets** *(free admission; 2000 Boulevard Montmorency, ☎691-2385)* is the perfect place for a leisurely stroll. Gardening buffs will love the arboretum *(☎660-6953)* and the landscaping; the Domaine also belongs to the Association des Jardins du Québec. In the heart of the arboretum is a butterfly aviary. Weather permitting (it is closed when it rains), visitors can walk into this world of butterflies, which features some 30 species from eastern Canada. Not only will you be amazed, but you will also learn about the different stages of their development. A number of historic buildings can also be found here, including the château (see p 139) that houses a small exhibition on the history of the estate. All sorts of outdoor activities can be enjoyed here in both summer and winter. Outdoor concerts, plays and conferences on ornithology and other subjects are held at the Domaine Maizerets all year round.

Parc Cartier-Brébeuf (see p 140) is a small park on the banks of Rivière Saint-Charles. It has recently been redesigned to make it a more pleasant spot for people to enjoy. Cement walls used to contain the river but it is now free of this yoke, at least in this area, and is adorned with aquatic plants. Flowers and decorative trees also embellish the park.

Tour I: Sillery to Cap-Rouge

On the shores of the river, at the limit of what used to be the towns of Sainte-Foy and Cap-Rouge, **Parc de la Plage-Jacques-Cartier ★** *(May to Nov; Chemin de la Plage-Jacques-Cartier, ☎654-4443)* allows residents to fully enjoy the St. Lawrence river. Indeed, there didn't use to be many places where they could leisurely stroll on the riverbanks and admire the water, the tides, the birds and boats, but today, this beach allows everyone to appreciate the majesty of this important life source.

Tour J: Heading North

Parc de la Falaise et de la Chute Kabir Kouba *(Wendake)* has several short paths running along the cliff about 40m above Rivière Saint-Charles. The Aboriginal people called this river *Kabir Kouba*, which means "the river with many twists and turns."

About 45km from Québec City, on the shore of the region's largest lake, Lac Saint-Joseph, the **Station Écotouristique Duchesnay ★** *(143 Route Duchesnay, Ste-Catherine-de-la-Jacques-Cartier, ☎529-2911 or 875-2711, www.sepaq.com/ duchesnay)* allows visitors to familiarize themselves with the Laurentian forest. Located on an area of 90km², this centre is dedicated to researching the fauna and flora of our forests and is now one of Sépaq's tourism and recreation centres. Long famous for its cross-country ski trails, it is also ideal for practicing all kinds of outdoor activities, such as hiking, on its 16km of maintained footpaths. There are also ample opportunities for watersports. The Jacques-Cartier–Portneuf bike path also traverses Duchesnay. In addition, you will find an interpretation centre that hosts educational and awareness-raising activities. The installations

Wolf

ski runs. In the summer, paths are at the disposal of hikers, mountain-bikers and horseback riders.

have been entirely renovated to offer visitors comfortable lodging and dining. In winter, the site is home to the **Ice Hotel** (see p 157).

On the shores of Lac Saint-Joseph, in the village of Fossambault-sur-le-Lac, stretches the **Plage Lac Saint-Joseph** (*$10 for the day; every day mid-Jun to mid-Sep; 7001 Route de Fossambault,* ☎*875-2242*). You're not dreaming: this is a real beach, complete with palm trees (imported from Florida annually)! In addition to swimming, you can enjoy a wide array of water activities. Note, however, that the beach attracts a large crowd on hot summer days.

The **Station Touristique Stoneham** (*Stoneham,* ☎*848-2411 or 800-463-6888*) welcomes visitors year-round. In the winter there are 30

Through out the year, hordes of visitors come to **Parc de la Jacques-Cartier** ★★★ (*$3.50; Highway 175 N., km 74,* ☎*848-3169 or 644-8844*), located in the Réserve Faunique des Laurentides, 40km north of Quebec. The area is called Vallée de la Jacques-Cartier, after the river of the same name that runs through it, winding between steep hills. As a result of the microclimate caused by the river being hemmed in on both sides, the site is suitable for a number of outdoor activities. The vegetation and wildlife are abundant and diverse. The winding and well-laid-out paths sometimes lead to interesting surprises, like a moose and its offspring foraging for food in a marsh. Before heading out to discover all the riches the site has to offer, you can get information at the nature centre's reception area. Campsites (see p 207), chalets and equipment are all available for rent.

At the park, specialists organize **Moose observation safaris** from mid-September to mid-October as well as **Nocturnal wolf-call listening sessions** (☎848-5099) from the beginning of July until mid-October, in order to familiarize people with these animals. Each of these activities lasts at least 3hrs and involves a walk through the forest.

Tour K: Côte-de-Beaupré and Île d'Orléans

Parc de la Chute-Montmorency ★★ (see p 159).

The **Cap-Tourmente National Wildlife Area** ★★★ (*$5; beg Jan to Nov; 570 Chemin du Cap-Tourmente, Saint-Joachim, ☎827-3776*) is located on pastoral, fertile land. Each spring and autumn its sandbars are visited by countless snow geese that stop to gather strength for their long migration. The reserve also has bird-watching facilities and naturalists on hand to anwser your questions about the 250 species of birds and 45 species of mammals you might encounter on the hiking and walking trails that cross the park.

Station Mont-Sainte-Anne ★★ (*2000 Boulevard Beaupre, Beaupre, ☎827-4561, www.mont-sainte-anne.com*) covers 77km² and includes the 800m-high Mont Sainte-Anne, one of the most beautiful downhill-ski sites in Québec. There are a few hotels close to the ski hill and the park. Various other activities are also offered, since the park has 200km of mountain-bike and cross-country ski trails. Sports equipment can be rented on site.

The **Grand Canyon des Chutes Sainte-Anne** (*$7; beg May to end Jun and beg Sep to end Oct, every day 9am to 5:30pm, end Jun to beg Sep 8:30am to 6:30pm; 206 Route 138, Beaupré, ☎827-4057*) is where the rushing Rivière Sainte-Anne carves a deep path through the hills near Beaupré and plunges 74m into a large pothole, 22m in diameter and formed by the resulting water current. Visitors can take in this impressive site from lookouts and a suspension bridge.

Outdoor Activities

Hiking

Tour J: Heading North

The **Station Touristique Stoneham** *(free admission; Stoneham, ☎848-2411 or 800-463-6888)* welcomes hikers with a few trails, one of which goes as far as the Parc de la Jacques-Cartier.

The trails in **Parc de la Jacques-Cartier** *($3.50; end May to mid-Oct; Hwy. 175 N., ☎848-3169)* are among the favorites for hiking in this region. Peaceful or abrupt, they will allow you to discover the hidden corners of the forest, as well as superb views on the valley and the river.

Tour K: Côte-de-Beaupré and Île d'Orléans

At **Cap Tourmente** *($5; Saint-Joachim, ☎827-3776)* you can, if your legs are willing, climb the trail that leads to a magnificent view of the river and its surroundings. You can also use the wooden sidewalks (adapted for people with disabilities) for an equally enjoyable walk.

Station Mont-Sainte-Anne *(free admission; Hwy. 360, Beaupré, ☎827-4579 or 827-4561)* has several hiking trails.

Cycling

Québec City is developing its cycling infrastructure. Today, more than 50km of cycling paths stretch out around the city. Consult the Ulysses Travle Guide *Le Québec cyclable* to obtain maps of those trails.

A bike path called **Corridor des Cheminots** *(☎649-2636)* enables cyclists and other sports enthusiasts can travel 22km through various municipalities to Val-Bélair, not far from the beginning of the Jacques-Cartier/Portneuf path (see below).

Some noteworthy bike paths have existed for a number of years, such as the one that leads to Beauport or the one that runs along the Rivière Saint-Charles. Many paths are marked out on the road or are shared routes, which makes Québec City and its neighbouring communities enjoyable places to discover by bicycle.

The Association Promo-Vélo has a great deal of information on various kinds of tours available in the region. Furthermore, this organization publishes a map of bike paths in the Québec City region.

Promo-Vélo
C.P. 700, Succ. Haute-Ville
Québec, G1R 4S9
☎*522-0087*

Bicycle Rentals

You can rent mountain bikes at Station Mont-Sainte-Anne and in Parc de la Jacques-Cartier (see above).

Cyclo Services Voyages
$20/day
Marché du Vieux-Port
84 Rue Prince-de-Galles
☎*692-4052*
Cyclo Services Voyages also organizes excursions in the city and surrounding area.

Vélo Passe-Sport Plein air
$25/day
Côte du Palais
☎*692-3643*
This organization also organizes excursions in the city and surrounding area.

Vélotek
$25/day
463 Rue Saint-Jean
☎*648-6022*

Bicycle Repairs

Bicycles Falardeau
174 Rue Richelieu
☎*522-8685*
You can also get judicious advice on bicycle touring in the area from the owner, who is a seasoned cyclist.

Mont-Vélo
1968 Avenue St-Michel, corner of Avenue Maguire, Sillery
☎*683-9979*
They specialize in the sales and repair of mountain bikes. For the keen enthusiast.

Vélotek
463 Rue Saint-Jean
☎*648-6022*
They also rent bicycles (see above)

Outdoors

Le Vélomane
957 Avenue Royale, Beauport
☎663-3930

Tour K: Côte-de-Beaupré and Île d'Orléans

A bicycle path runs from the Vieux-Port of Québec City to the Parc de la Chute Montmorency, passing through Beauport on the way. Also, roads such as Chemin du Roy, on the Côte de Beaupré and Île d'Orléans *(bike rental at the Le Vieux-Presbytère guesthouse, see p 211)*, are meant to be shared by motorists and cyclists. Caution is always in order, but these trips are definitely worth the effort.

Station Mont-Sainte-Anne *(\$6; Beaupré, ☎827-4561)* has 200km of trails to offer mountain-bike enthusiasts! Pedal your way to the top of the mountain or rush down the slopes after riding up in the cable car with your bicycle *(\$20)*. There are more than 20 trails with most evocative names such as *La Grisante* (the exhilarating one) or *La Vietnam*. This is a well-known place; World Cup Mountain Bike races are held here every year (see p 262).

Tour J: Heading North

Following the route of old railway lines, the **Piste Jacques-Cartier Portneuf** *(\$5; 100 Rue St-Jacques, C.P. 238, St-Raymond, ☎337-7525)* crosses through the Réserve Faunique Portneuf and the Station Forestière Duchesnay (where you can park your car and rent bicycles), and borders some lakes. It is 63km long, stretching from Rivière-à-Pierre to Shannon. Its magical setting and safe riding conditions have already attracted many cyclists. In winter, the path is used for snowmobiling.

In **Parc de la Jacques-Cartier** *(\$3.50; Rte. 175 Nord, ☎848-3169)* the trails are for both hikers and mountain-biking enthusiasts. Bike rental is available.

Cruises

Croisières AML *(tickets sold at Quai Chouinard, ☎692-1159 or 800-563-4643, www.croisieresaml.com)* offers cruises all summer, with a great view of Québec City and its surroundings from another angle. One of the ships owned by this company is the **M/V Louis-Jolliet** *(\$24; departures*

11:30am, 2pm, 4pm) sailing from Québec City, its port of registry. Day cruises last 1hr 30min and go as far as the Montmorency Falls. At night, you can go up to Ile d'Orleans and enjoy dinner in one of the ship's two dining rooms. These evening cruises last a few hours and feature musicians and dancing.

Croisières de la Famille Dufour *(22 Quai Saint-André, ☎827-8836, 827-8206 or 800-463-5250)* take passengers to the lovely Charlevoix region, to Pointe-au-Pic, Île-aux-Coudres and even to the heart of the breathtaking Saguenay fjord aboard a big, modern catamaran.

In-line Skating

On the **Plains of Abraham**, in front of the Musée du Québec, there is a big, paved rink for in-line skating. Scores of children and adults wearing protective helmets can be seen blading around the track on fine summer days. Equipment rentals are available at a small stand by the rink. This is the only spot on the Plains of Abraham where skating is allowed.

Jogging

Again, the place to go is the **Plains of Abraham**. The big, flat track in front of the Musée du Québec is a good place for a run, though people also go jogging on the paved streets and trails.

Fruit-Picking

Tour K: Côte-de-Beaupré and Île d'Orléans

From strawberries to raspberries, to corn, leaks and apples, the harvests follow one another all summer long continuously changing the look of the surrounding countryside. On **Île d'Orléans**, farmers open their doors to anyone, parents and children alike, who wishes to spend a day playing in an orchard or a field. Learn the secrets of picking and enjoy the fruit of your labour!

Outdoors

Bird-Watching

Tour K: Côte-de-Beaupré and Île d'Orléans

One of the best places in the region for bird-watching is definitely the **Cap Tourmente National Wildlife Area** (*$5; 570 Chemin du Cap-Tourmente, Saint-Joachim,* ☎827-3776). During spring and autumn, the thousands of migrating snow geese that overtake the area are a fascinating sight to behold. Any questions you might have after seeing these creatures up close and in such great numbers can be answered here. The reserve is also home to many other avian species. They are attracted here throughout the year by a number of bird houses and feeders.

Rafting

Tour D: Jacques-Cartier

In spring and summer the Rivière Jacques-Cartier gives adventurers a good run for their money. Two long-standing companies offer well-supervised rafting expeditions with all the necessary equipment. At **Village Vacances Valcartier** (*1860 Boulevard Valcartier, St-Gabriel-de-Valcartier,* ☎844-2200 or 888-384-5524, *www.valcartier.com*), they deliver lots of excitement during an 8km ride.

With **Excursions Jacques-Cartier** (*978 Avenue Jacques-Cartier, Tewkesbury,* ☎848-7238), you can also experience some very exciting runs.

Golf

Tour J: Heading North

The **Royal Charlesbourg** (*$32 Mon-Thu; $36 Fri-Sun; 2180 Chemin de la Grande-Ligne, Charlesbourg,* ☎841-3000) is an 18-hole golf course far from the hustle and bustle of the city.

The **Mont-Tourbillon** 18-hole golf course (*$33 Mon-Thu, $40 Fri-Sun; 55 Montée du Golf, Lac-Beauport,* ☎849-4418 or 866-949-4418, *www.monttourbillon.com*) is a great place to enjoy this sport.

Tour K: Côte-de-Beaupré and Île d'Orléans

The Station Mont-Sainte-Anne golf course, **Le Grand Vallon** (*$65 Mon-Thu, $78 Fri-Sun; 200 Boulevard Beau Pré, Beaupré, ☎827-4561, www.mont.sainte. anne.com*) was entirely redesigned in 1999. Today, it offers a par-72 course with several sand traps and four lakes, and is known as one of the most interesting courses in eastern Canada.

Ice Skating

Tour A: Vieux-Québec

Each winter, an ice rink is laid out on **Terrasse Dufferin**, enabling skaters to swirl about at the foot of the Château Frontenac with a view of the icy river. You can put on your gear at the kiosk (*free admission; mid-Dec to mid-Mar, every day 11am to 11pm, ☎692-2955*), which also rents out skates (*$2/hour*).

Tour D: Saint-Jean-Baptiste

On beautiful winter days, Place d'Youville is turned into a magical place, with skaters, snow, frost-covered Porte-Saint-Jean, the illuminated Capitole and Christmas decorations suspended from lampposts. In the centre of the square is a skating rink with music, and even if you don't feel like joining in the ice waltz, you can still enjoy the sights. The skating rink opens early in the season, around the end of October, and shuts down in late spring so that Québec City residents can skate for as long as

Outdoors

possible! There are restrooms for skaters *(free admission; Mon-Thu noon to 10pm, Fri-Sun 10am to 10pm;* ☎*691-4685).*

Tour G: Limoilou

A lovely skating rink winds beneath the trees of **Domaine Maizerets** *(free admission; 2000 Boulevard Montmorency,* ☎*691-2385).* There's a small chalet nearby where you can take off your skates and warm up next to a wood stove. Skate rentals available *($4; mid-Dec to mid-Mar Mon-Fri 1pm to 4pm, Sat and Sun 10am to 4pm, every day 6pm to 9pm).*

Once it has iced over, **Rivière Saint-Charles** is turned into a natural skating rink that, wether permitting, winds 2km between the neighbourhoods of Limoilou and Saint-Roch, in Basse-Ville. There is a heated place to rest *(free admission; Mon-Fri noon to 10pm, Sat-Sun 10am to 10pm;*

5 Rue de la Pointe-aux-Lièvres, ☎*691-5488).*

Cross-Country Skiing

Tour C: Grande Allée

The snow-covered **Plains of Abraham** provide an enchanting setting for cross-country skiing. Trails crisscross the park from one end to the other, threading their way through the trees or leading across a headland with views of the icy river. All this right in the heart of the city!

Tour G: Limoilou

Some extremely pleasant cross-country ski trails can also be found at **Domaine Maizerets** *(free admission; 2000 Boulevard Montmorency,* ☎*691-2385).* At the starting point, there is a little chalet heated with a wood-burning stove. Equipment rentals *($4; mid-Dec to mid-Mar Mon-Fri 1pm to 4pm, Sat and Sun 10am to 4pm)* are available.

Tour J: Heading North

In winter, **the Station Écotouristique Duchesnay** *($8.50; Ste-Catherine-de-la-Jacques-Cartier,* ☎*875-*

2511) is very popular among skiers in the area. In this great forest, there are 125km of well-kept trails and many little crested tits and other bird species that don't mind the cold!

Nestled in the heart of the Réserve Faunique des Laurentides, **Camp Mercier** *($9; mid-Nov to end Apr, every day 8:30am to 4pm; Rte. 175 North, Réserve Faunique des Laurentides,* ☎*848-2422 or 800-665-6527)* is criss-crossed with 192km of well-maintained trails in an extremely tranquil landscape. Given its ideal location, you can ski here from fall to spring. Long routes (up to 68km) with heated huts offer some interesting opportunities. There are also cottages for rent that can accommodate from two to 14 people.

Tour K: Côte-de-Beaupré and Île d'Orléans

Mont-Sainte-Anne *($15; Mon-Fri 9am to 4pm, Sat and Sun 8:30am to 4pm; Rte. 360, Beaupré,* ☎*827-4561, www.mont-sainte-anne.com)* has 250km of well-maintained cross-country ski trails with some heated huts set up along the way. Ski equipment can be rented.

Snowshoeing

Snowshoeing, a sport that regained its popularity when smaller, lighter models began to appear on the market, can be practiced in most of the region's cross-country skiing centres. The Station Écotouristique Duchesnay (see above), the Mont-Sainte-Anne resort (see above), as well as Parc de la Jacques-Cartier (see above) are some of the most beautiful sites.

Downhill Skiing and Snowboarding

Tour J: Heading North

Le Relais *($25/day, 1084 Boulevard du Lac,* ☎*849-1851)* has 25 downhill skiing trails, all of which are lit for night skiing.

The **Station Touristique Stoneham** *($39; Stoneham,* ☎*848-2411 or 800-463-6888, www.ski-stoneham.com)* welcomes visitors year-round. In the winter there are 30 runs, 16 of which are lighted.

Outdoors

Tour K: Côte-de-Beaupré and Île d'Orléans

Mont-Sainte-Anne *($47; Rte. 360, Beaupré, ☎827-4561, www.mont-sainte-anne.com)* is one of the biggest ski resorts in Québec. Among the 51 runs, some reach 625m in height and 14 are lit for night skiing. It's also a delight for snowboarders. Instead of buying a regular ticket, you can buy a pass worth a certain number of points, valid for two years, and each time you take the lift, points are deducted. Equipment rentals are also available.

Located 15min away from Station Mont-Sainte-Anne by Route 138, **Le Massif** *($42;* *Petite-Rivière-St-François, ☎632-5876 or 877-LEMASSIF, www.lemassif.com)* may be a bit out of the tour, but it's one of the best ski resorts in the province of Québec. First, because Le Massif features the highest vertical drop in eastern Canada (770m), and second, because every winter it receives a great deal of snow, which, aided by artificial snow, creates ideal ski conditions. And then there's the amazing natural setting! The mountain, which almost plunges into the river, offers a stunning panorama. In 2001-2002, Le Massif has been undergoing a major overhaul to modernize its infrastructure, but this in no way diminished the pleasure of skiing its slopes. There are 30 runs for all types of skiers, and a cozy

chalet now awaits you at
the summit.

Tobogganing and Waterslides

Tour A: Vieux-Québec

During winter, a hill is created on **Terrasse Dufferin**,
which you can slide down
on a toboggan. First pur-
chase your tickets at the
little stand in the middle of
the terrace *($2/ride; late Dec
to mid-Mar, every day 11am to
11pm; 692-2955)*, then grab
a toboggan and climb to the
top of the slide. Once you
get there, make sure to take
a look around: the view is
magnificent!

Tour C: Grande Allée

The hills of the **Plains of
Abraham** are wonderful for
sledding. Bundle up well
and follow the kids pulling
toboggans to find the best
spots!

Tour J: Heading North

Winter or summer, the
Village Vacances Valcartier
*(early Jun to Sep every day
10am to 7pm, early Dec to end
Mar Sun-Thu 10am to 10pm;
1860 Boulevard Valcartier, St-
Gabriel-de-Valcartier, ☎844-
2200 or 800-384-5524,
www.valcartier.com; take
Route 371 N. from Quebec
City)* is the undisputed authority when it comes to
slides. It is an outdoor-
activity centre that offers
the full range of the facilities. In the summer,
waterslides and a wave
pool draw huge crowds. In
winter, ice slides will help
you forget the cold for a
little while. There are also
snow rafting and skating on
a 2.5km-long ice rink that
snakes through the woods.
There is also a restaurant
and bar.

Accommodations

Québec City has all kinds of accommodations to offer: two youth hostels, plenty of bed and breakfasts, inns and luxury hotels.

You will certainly find a suitable place to stay, whether it is for one night or one week.

Although comfort may be a little rudimentary in the smaller inns, most hotels offer very comfortable conditions, and include many services. There are quite a few bed and breakfasts in Québec City. They are reasonably priced and offer the advantage of a home-style atmosphere. In Québec, bed and breakfasts are known as *gîtes du passant*. These establishments are members of the Fédération des Agricotours du Québec and must conform to their regulations and standards to ensure a high level of quality. The *Ulysses Gîtes du Passant au Québec* travel guide is available and lists the various accommodations and ser-

vices for each Québec region.

Hospitalité Canada Tours is a free telephone service operated by the Maison du Tourisme de Québec *(12 Rue Ste-Anne; ☎800-665-1528 or from Montreal ☎514 252-3117, www.hospitality-*

canada.com). Depending on what kind of accommodations you're looking for, the staff will suggest various places belonging to the network and even make reservations for you.

Rates

Rates may vary from one season to another. Rooms are more expensive during the summer or high season, and the weeks of the Festival d'Été (Summer Festival) in July and Carnaval in February are the busiest of the year. We recommend that you reserve well in advance if you plan to visit Québec City during these periods.

The prices mentioned here are for a standard room for two people in high season, unless otherwise indicated.

$	less than $50
$$	$50 to $100
$$$	$100 to $150
$$$$	$150 to $200
$$$$$	more than $200

However, room prices may vary within the same hotel. Also, many hotels and inns offer considerable discounts to employees of corporations or members of automobile clubs (CAA, AAA). Be sure to ask about corporate and other discounts, as they are often very easy to obtain.

The following accommodations are classified according to price starting with the least expensive. Remember to add the 7% federal tax and the 7.5% Québec sales tax to the given rate when making your calculations. The federal tax is refundable to non-residents (see p 56). A non-refundable tax called "Taxe Spécifique sur l'Hébergement" (accommodation tax) is also applied to accommodation costs. The amount is $2 per night regardless of the total bill or the type of accommodation.

Symbols in this Guide

The various services offered by each establishment are indicated with a small symbol, which is explained in the legend in the opening pages of this guidebook. By no means is this an exhaustive list of what the establishment offers, but rather the services we consider to be the most important.

Please note that the presence of a symbol does not mean that all the rooms have this service; you sometimes have to pay extra to get, for example, a whirlpool tub. And likewise, if the symbol is not attached to an establishment, it means that the establishment cannot offer you this service. Please note that unless otherwise indicated, all hotels in this guide offer private bathrooms.

The Ulysses Boat

The Ulysses boat pictogram is awarded to our favourite accommodations and restaurants. While every establishment recommended in this guide was included because of its high quality and/or uniqueness, as well as its value for the money, every once in a while we come across an establishment that absolutely wows us. These, our favourite establishments, are awarded a Ulysses boat. You'll find boats in all price categories: next to exclusive, high-priced establishments, as well as budget ones. Regardless of the price, each of these establishments offers the most for your money. Look for them first!

Ulysses's Favourites

For history buffs:
Château Frontenac (p 197), Hôtel Clarendon (p 196),

Le Vieux-Presbytère
(p 211),
Auberge Baker (p 208).

For the view:
Château Frontenac (p 197), Hôtel Loews Le Concorde (p 202), Hôtel Dominion 1912 (p 199), Château Bellevue (p 196), Château de Pierre (p 196), La Goéliche (p 211).

For the décor:
Auberge Saint-Antoine (p 199), Hôtel du Capitole (p 203), Hôtel Dominion 1912 (p 199), Auberge Saint-Pierre (p 199), Hôtel Germain-des-Prés (p 204).

For the warm welcome:
Auberge du Quartier (p 200), Auberge du Petit Pré (p 208).

For peace and quiet:
Château Bonne-Entente (p 204), Auberge Canard Huppé (p 211), Chaumière Juchereau-Duchesnay (p 207).

For the friendly atmosphere:
Auberge de la Paix (p 192), Le Krieghoff B&B (p 200), L'Autre Jardin (p 205), Hôtel Belley (p 197).

For business people:
Hilton Québec (p 202), Hôtel Loews Le Concorde (p 202), Radisson Hôtel Gouverneur (p 202), Hôtel Royal William (p 205).

Tour A: Vieux-Québec

Centre International de Séjour (Hostelling International)
$
19 Rue Ste-Ursule, G1R 4E1
☎694-0755 or 800-461-8585
from Montréal
☎(514) 252-3117
The Centre International de Séjour is a youth hostel with 240 beds for young people. The rooms can accommodate from three to six people, the dormitories from eight to 10, and there are also private double rooms.

Auberge de la Paix
$ bkfst incl.
plus $2 for bedding
if you don't have your own
sb, K
31 Rue Couillard, G1R 3T4
☎694-0735
Behind its lovely white facade in Vieux-Québec, Auberge de la Paix has a youth-hostel atmosphere. It has 60 beds in rooms able to accommodate from two to eight people, as well as a kitchenette and a living room. This inn lives up to its name by providing a friendly and fun place to relax. In the summer, a lovely garden is filled with flowers. Children are welcome!

Maison Sainte-Ursule
$-$$
pb/sb
40 Rue Ste-Ursule, G1R 4E2
☎694-9794
⇌694-0875
Maison Sainte-Ursule is a small, charming house with green shutters.
Unfortunately, its rooms are oddly shaped and dark. In low season, though, prices are quite affordable.

Auberge de la Chouette
$$
≡, ℜ
71 Rue D'Auteuil, G1R 4C3
☎694-0232
Occupying two floors above the Apsara restaurant (see p 221), Auberge de la Chouette's 10 rooms are simply decorated and furnished with antiques. The bathrooms were recently renovated. The Vietnamese family that manages the restaurant and the inn will welcome you with a smile.

Manoir LaSalle
$$
pb/sb, K
18 Rue Sainte-Ursule, G1R 4C9
☎692-9953
Manoir LaSalle is a small hotel with 11 rooms, one of which has a private bathroom. This red-brick building is exemplary of the architectural style of some of the first homes built in the city.

A Vieux-Québec

ACCOMMODATIONS

1. Au Jardin du Gouverneur
2. Auberge de la Chouette
3. Auberge de la Paix
4. Auberge du Trésor
5. Auberge Saint-Louis
6. Cap-Diamant
7. Centre International de Séjour
8. Château Bellevue
9. Château de Léry
10. Château de Pierre
11. Château Frontenac
12. Clarendon
13. Clos Saint-Louis
14. Hôtel du Vieux-Québec
15. Maison Acadienne
16. Maison du Fort
17. Maison Sainte-Ursule
18. Manoir LaSalle
19. Manoir Victoria
20. Marquise de Bassano

Auberge Saint-Louis
$$ bkfst incl.
pb/sb, ℜ, ≡
48 Rue Saint-Louis, G1R 3Z3
☎**692-2424** or **888-692-4105**
⇌**692-3797**

Located on busy Rue Saint-Louis, Auberge Saint-Louis is a small, pleasant hotel. Room prices vary according to amenities offered. Less expensive rooms do not have private bathrooms. The hotel is well maintained.

Au Jardin du Gouverneur
$$ bkfst incl.

≡
16 Rue Mont-Carmel, G1R 4A3
☎**692-1704**
⇌**692-1713**

Au Jardin du Gouverneur is a charming little hotel a in small blue and white house opposite Parc des Gouverneurs. Rooms are a good size but there is nothing special about the decor. No smoking.

Marquise de Bassano
$$ bkfst incl.
sb
15 Rue des Grisons, G1R 4M6
☎**692-0316**
www.total.net/~bassano

Vieux-Québec has been home to some colourful characters throughout its history. At the corner of the Rue des Grisons and Avenue Sainte-Geneviève is a small Victorian house which, it is said, was built for one such character. The dark panelling that decorates the inside surely guards some secrets of the Marquise de Bassano. The house has been transformed into a welcoming bed and breakfast, with charming rooms and a cheerful sitting room with a piano and a fireplace. During breakfast, which sometimes lasts into the afternoon, the young hosts take pleasure in animating the discussions!

Maison du Fort
$$ bkfst incl.
≡, *K*
21 Avenue Ste-Geneviève, G1R 4B1
☎**692-4375**
⇌**692-5257**

Maison du Fort is tucked away in a quiet neighbourhood around Parc des Gouverneurs. This small residence offers adequate rooms, and the service is quite welcoming.

Maison Acadienne
$$-$$$
pb/sb, ⊛, ≡, ℝ
43 Rue Ste-Ursule, G1R 4E4
☎**694-0280**

A number of old houses on Rue Sainte-Ursule have been made into hotels. Among these, Maison Acadienne stands out with its large, white facade. The rooms are rather lacklustre, although some have been renovated.

Château de Léry
$$-$$$
≡, ⊛, *K*
8 Rue Laporte, G1R 4M9
☎*692-2692 or 800-363-0036*
⇄*692-5231*
Located next to Parc des Gouverneurs and overlooking the river, the Château de Léry has comfortable rooms. Rooms facing the street offer a good view. This hotel is in a quiet neighbourhood in the old part of the city, but is just a few minutes' walk from the bustle of downtown.

Le Clos Saint-Louis
$$-$$$ bkfst incl.
sb/pb, ⊛, ≡, ℜ
71 Rue St-Louis, G1R 3Z2
☎*694-1311 or 800-461-1311*
⇄*694-9411*
Le Clos Saint-Louis comprises in two imposing Victorian houses dating from 1844 on Rue St-Louis. Located close to Vieux-Québec and its attractions, this hotel has 25 rooms spread out on four floors. The rooms have all been arranged to make their historic aspect especially welcoming: some have four-poster beds with canopies, others old-fashioned bookcases or fireplaces. The rooms on the second floor are particularly attractive with their stone walls and exposed wooden beams. Even if some of the bathrooms must be shared,

they are all modern and well equipped. In the morning, coffee and croissants are served in the basement.

Auberge du Trésor
$$-$$$
ℜ, ≡
20 Rue Sainte-Anne, G1R 3X2
☎*694-1876 or 800-566-1876*
Auberge du Trésor was built in 1676. Renovated many times since then, it maintains an impressive appearance. Rooms are modern and comfortable. All rooms have private bathrooms and colour televisions.

Manoir Victoria
$$$
≡, ≈, ☉, △, ℜ, *K*, ⊛
44 Côte du Palais, G1R 4H8
☎*692-1030 or 800-463-6283*
⇄*692-3822*
www.manoir-victoria.com
Manoir Victoria is a 145-room hotel nestled on Côte du Palais. Decorated in true Victorian style, it succeeds in being both chic and very comfortable. The lobby, at the top of a long flight of stairs, is inviting and contains both a bar and a dining room. Manoir Victoria offers well-equipped suites and a number of cultural and sports packages.

Cap-Diamant
$$$
≡, ℝ, ℑ
39 Avenue Ste-Geneviève, G1R 4B3
☎*694-0313*
www.hcapdiamant.qc.ca
The Cap-Diamant hotel is located in an old house in Vieux-Québec. This is the kind of house where even the walls have secrets… and many stories to tell. It is the perfect place to immerse yourself in the family life of bygone days. The long staircase, the creaking floors, and even the wallpaper contribute to its charm and quaint appearance. In the summer you can enjoy the porch or wander in the flower-filled garden and sit by the stream.

Hotel Clarendon
$$$
≡, ℜ, ⊛
57 Rue Ste-Anne, G1R 3X4
☎*692-4652 or 888-554-6001*
⇋*692-4652*
www.hotelclarendon.com
Built in 1870, the Hotel Clarendon is one of the oldest hotels in the city (see p 75). The hotel has an unpretentious exterior while the elegant interior is decorated in Art Deco style. The entrance hall is very attractive. The rooms in this hotel have been renovated many times over the years and are spacious and comfortable. This a very good place to stay in Vieux-Québec. Its restaurant, Le Charles-Baillargé (see p 225), serves elegant meals, and there is also a lively bar, L'Emprise (see p 252), which plays jazz music.

Château Bellevue
$$$
≡
16 Rue Laporte, G1R 4M9
☎*692-2473 or 800-463-2617*
⇋*692-4876*
The Château Bellevue has an impressive view of the river. The rooms are reasonable but equipped with rather sterile modern furniture.

Château de Pierre
$$$
≡
17 Avenue Ste-Geneviève, G1R 4A8
☎*694-0429 or 888-694-0429*
⇋*694-0153*
The Château de Pierre is housed in an old colonial-style house. The ostentatious entrance of this hotel is quite striking and somewhat flashy. The rooms are comfortable.

Hôtel du Vieux-Québec
$$$
≡, K, ⊛
1190 Rue St-Jean
☎*692-1850 or 800-361-7787*
⇋*692-5637*
Hôtel du Vieux-Québec is a modern establishment that exudes a kind of cool ambiance often associated with modernism. Although the decor is not extravagant, it is quite

comfortable and friendly. The rooms are spacious and several of them have kitchenettes. There also is a terrace.

⛵ Château Frontenac
$$$$$
ℜ, ≡, ♿, ⊛, ≈, ☺
1 Rue des Carrières, G1R 4P5
☎692-3861 or 800-268-9420
⇄692-1751
www.fairmont.com

The Château Frontenac is by far the most prestigious hotel in Québec City (see p 69). Enter its elegant lobby with its wood panelling and warm colours and let yourself be transported back in time. The Château Frontenac was built in 1893 and over the years has been the setting of several historic events. The decor exudes a classic, refined richness that is truly worthy of a castle. Its restaurant also offers a taste of luxury (see Le Champlain, p 227). The sumptuous rooms provide the most comfortable environment possible, and although the size and benefits of the hotel's 618 rooms vary greatly, all are quite pleasant. The rooms overlooking the river have beautiful bay windows and, of course, the view is magnificent.

Tour B: Petit-Champlain to Vieux-Port

See map page 91.

⛵ Hôtel Belley
$$
K
249 Rue St-Paul, G1K 3W5
☎692-1694 or 888-692-1694
⇄692-1696

The pleasant Hôtel Belley stands opposite the market at the Vieux-Port. A hotel since 1877, this handsome building will leave you with fond memories for years to come. It has eight simply decorated, cozy rooms, some with exposed brick walls, others with wooden beams and skylights. The ground floor is home to a bar called Taverne Belley (see p 254), whose breakfasts and lunches, served in two lovely rooms, are very popular with locals. A number of extremely comfortable and attractively decorated lodgings, some with terraces, are also available in another house across the street. These may be rented by the night, by the week or by the month.

Accommodations

Hayden's Wexford House
$$ bkfst incl.
sb, ≡
450 Rue Champlain, G1K 4J3
☎*524-0524*
≈*648-8995*

Located on a magnificent street between Cap Diamant and the river, Hayden's Wexford House has proudly displayed its facade since 1832. Its name, in fact, is inscribed in the brickwork. This house has managed to maintain all of its former charm. The four small rooms nestled on the top floor have lovely views from the dormer windows and are tastefully decorated with wood trim and floral patterns. The bathrooms have been recently renovated and are modern. To add to the guests' comfort, quality mattresses have been made to measure. Breakfast is served in a stone-walled dining room which is every bit as charming as the rest of the house. No smoking.

Appartements du Cap-Blanc
$$$
ℑ, K
444 Rue Champlain, G1K 4J3
☎*524-6137*
≈*648-8995*

Do you want to spend a few days in Québec City in a well-situated *pied-à-terre* with all the necessary conveniences? Appartements du Cap-Blanc will surely please you since they are right next door to the owner's bed and breakfast (see Hayden's Wexford House). Each apartment occupies one floor of a renovated old house. Two of them have fireplaces so you can spend pleasant moments in front of the hearth in this cozy stone and wood setting. Each apartment has a living room, well-equipped kitchenette, dining room, bathroom and closed bedroom, all attractively decorated. You'll never want to leave! There is a minimum stay of two nights and no smoking.

Le Priori
$$$ bkfst incl.
⊛, ℜ, ℑ, *K*, ≡
15 Rue du Saul-au-Matelot, G1K 3Y7
☎*522-8108 or 800-351-3992*
≈*692-0883*

Le Priori is located on a quiet street in the Basse-Ville. The building is very old but has been renovated in a very modern style. The decor successfully contrasts the old stone walls of the building with up-to-date furnishings. Its appearance is striking and even the elevator is distinctive. Le Priori is highly recommended.

Auberge Saint-Pierre
$$$$ bkfst incl.

K, ⊛, ≡
79 Rue St-Pierre, G1K 4A3
☎ ***694-7981 or 888-268-1017***
⇰ ***694-0406***
www.auberge.qc.ca

A lovely inn has recently opened in a building that had housed Canada's first insurance company since the end of the 19th century. The historic charm of the Auberge Saint-Pierre was conserved when the building was renovated. The rooms are similar to the neighbouring apartments, with their various landings and narrow hallways. Each room has beautiful, dark hardwood floors and sumptuously coloured walls. Those on the lower floors have lovely high ceilings, while those higher up provide a wonderful view.

Hôtel Dominion 1912
$$$$ bkfst incl.

≡, ⊛
126 Rue St-Pierre, G1K 4A8
☎ ***692-2224 or 888-833-5253***
⇰ ***692-4403***
www.hoteldominion.com

Dating from 1912 as its name implies, this beautiful buildings on Rue Saint-Pierre has been newly renovated into a hotel that charms its chic clientele. The luxurious Hôtel Dominion 1912 has a modern aspect with materials such as glass and wrought iron, but still maintains its original character. Elements of interior decoration such as cream-and-sand-coloured draperies and cushions, and luxuriously soft sofas and bedspreads add an extremely comfortable touch. Black-and-white photographs of the neighbourhood hang in each room, inviting you to go out and visit it. The upper floors have magnificent views of the river on one side and of the city on the other.

Auberge Saint-Antoine
$$$$$ bkfst incl.

⊛, ≡, K, ℑ
10 Rue St-Antoine, G1K 4C9
☎ ***692-2211 or 888-692-2211***
⇰ ***692-1177***
www.saint-antoine.com

Auberge Sainte-Antoine is located near the Musée de la Civilisation. This lovely hotel is divided into two buildings. Guests enter through a tastefully renovated old stone building. The entrance hall is distinguished by exposed wooden beams, stone walls and a beautiful fireplace. Each room is wonderfully decorated according to a different theme and has its own unique charm.

Tour C: Grande Allée and Avenue Cartier

See map page 107.

La Maison d'Elizabeth et Emma
$$ bkfst incl.
sb, K
10 Grande Allée Ouest, G1R 2G6
☎647-0880

Over the last few years, residents of Grande Allée have established several places for visitors to stay. You will easily recognize the warm colours of Maison d'Elizabeth et Emma. Located at the corner of Rue De Salaberry, the house's entire second floor is given over to guests. There are four rooms, including a large one in front that may be a little noisy, and a small former maid's room at the back. However, they are all adorned with period furniture and beautiful dark woodwork. Large windows provide plenty of light and there is a small reading area and kitchen. When the weather is warm, breakfast is served on the balcony.

Le Krieghoff B&B
$$ bkfst incl.
ℜ, ℝ, ≡
1091 Avenue Cartier, G1R 2A6
☎522-3711
⇄647-1429
www.cafekrieghoff.com

Café Krieghoff offers travellers a bed and breakfast combination. The novelty, however, is that breakfast is served in the café itself (see p 236) which guarantees both good food and pleasant surroundings! The friendly staff makes sure that guests feel right at home in the family-like atmosphere. The five rooms nestled above the restaurant are modest and clean. Each one has access to a private bathroom (even if it is not connected to the room), and they all share a small sitting room and balcony with a view of lively Avenue Cartier.

Auberge du Quartier
$$-$$$ bkfst incl.
≡
170 Grande Allée Ouest., G1R 2G9
☎525-9726 or 800-782-9441
⇄521-4891

Looking for a charming little neighbourhood inn? Situated opposite the imposing Église Saint-Dominique, just 5min from the Plaines d'Abraham and the Musée du Québec, Auberge du Quartier should please you. This large white house has a dozen clean, well-lit, attractive and modern rooms. They are spread out on three floors, with a suite in the attic. Reception by the owner and staff is very friendly.

Relais Charles-Alexandre
$$$ bkfst incl.
pb/sb
91 Grande Allée Est, G1R 2H5
☎ *523-1220*
⇄ *523-9556*

Relais Charles-Alexandre offers some 20 comfortable rooms on three floors where everything is brand new. Breakfast is served in a former art gallery, a well-lit room decorated with several reproductions. Friendly reception.

Auberge Louis-Hébert
$$$
ℜ
668 Grande Allée Est, G1R 2K5
☎ *525-7812*
⇄ *525-6294*
www.louishebert.com

Directly located on lively Grande Allée, Auberge Louis-Hébert is a warm and charming 17th-century home. It is also very peaceful. Rooms here have been tastefully decorated and offer several amenities. The service is quite good.

Manoir Lafayette
$$$
≡, ℜ
661 Grande Allée Est, G1R 2K4
☎ *522-2652 or 800-363-8203*
⇄ *522-4400*

Manoir Lafayette is attractive and elegant. The hotel was recently renovated and some rooms are equipped with comfortable antique furniture. The Lafayette has an excellent location.

Hôtel Château Laurier
$$$
≡, ℜ, ⊛, ℑ
1220 Place George-V Ouest, G1R 5B8
☎ *522-8108 or 800-463-4453*
⇄ *524-8768*

For several years, Château Laurier has been situated in an old house with a beautiful stone facade on the corner of Grande Allée. The hotel recently adopted a new image. The small guestrooms have been renovated, retaining their original character, while a large modern wing with classical decor has been added at the back. The rooms, however, are fairly cramped and some have a view of the parking lot. They will suit people looking for fresh new accommodations as well as business people, since some of the rooms offer Internet access.

Château Grande Allée
$$$
≡
601 Grande Allée Est, G1R 2K4
☎ *647-4433 or 800-263-1471*
⇄ *646-7553*

The Château Grande Allée is a recent addition to busy Grande Allée. The well-kept rooms are so large that they look under-furnished. Making up for this slight shortcoming are various features, including large bathrooms.

🏨 Hôtel Loews Le Concorde
$$$-$$$$
&, ≡, ≈, ☉, △, ℜ, ⊛
1225 Place Montcalm, G1R 4W6
☎*647-2222 or 800-463-5256*
⇄*647-4710*

Just outside Vieux-Québec is the Hôtel Loews Le Concorde. It is part of the Loews hotel chain and has spacious, comfortable rooms with spectacular views of Québec City and the surrounding area. There is a revolving restaurant on top of the hotel (see L'Astral p 239).

Tour D:
Saint-Jean-Baptiste

See map page 119.

Chez Pierre
$$ bkfst incl.
pb/sb, ℜ
636 Rue d'Aiguillon, G1R 1M5
☎*522-2173*

Chez Pierre is a bed and breakfast with three rooms. Two of them are situated in the renovated basement, but the third room is upstairs and has all the charm of a faubourg Saint-Jean-Baptiste apartment. However, the bathroom of the latter room is also situated in the basement. Pierre, your host, is a painter and his large

coloured canvases brighten up the house. He serves a generous breakfast in the morning.

Hilton Québec
$$$
≡, ≈, ☉, △, ℜ, &
1100 Boulevard René-Lévesque Est
G1J 1H3
☎*647-2411 or 800-447-2411*
⇄*647-6488*

Located just outside Vieux-Québec, the Québec Hilton offers rooms with the kind of comfort one expects of an international hotel chain. The Place Québec shopping mall is located in the lobby, which is connected to the new Centre des Congrès.

Radisson Hôtel Québec Centre
$$$
≈, ≡, ☉, &, △, ℜ
690 Boulevard Rene-Lévesque Est
G1R 5A8
☎*647-1717 or 888-884-7777*
⇄*647-2146*

The Radisson Hôtel Québec Centre is linked to the Centre des Congrès. This hotel has over 375 rooms, all nicely decorated. Standard rooms are furnished with slightly rustic but elegant pine furniture. The hotel's heated outdoor pool is open all year.

Palace Royal
$$$
≈, ℜ, ≡, ☺, △, ⊛, ᏸ
775 Avenue Dufferin, G1R 6A5
☎*694-2000 or 800-567-5276*
≠*380-2552*
www.jaro.qc.ca
Newly built on Place
D'Youville, this hotel may
not be top of the line, but
its 230 rooms provide a
most comfortable lair. The
rooms surround an indoor,
skylight-topped courtyard
that features a small
swimming pool, a whirlpool
bath, a few fountains and
plants that create a lovely
effect. Some of the suites
boast a balcony overlooking
the courtyard. The rooms'
decor is classical in style,
with friezes, patterned
lamps and draped curtains.

Hôtel du Théâtre Capitole
$$$$
ℜ, ≡, ⊛
972 Rue St-Jean, G1R 1R5
☎*694-9930 or 800-363-4040*
≠*647-2146*
www.lecapitol.com
Adjoining the renovated
theatre (see p 120), the
Hôtel du Théâtre Capitole is
not luxurious, but the
rooms are amusing, with a
decor that resembles a stage
set. At the entrance is the Il
Teatro restaurant (see
p 243).

**Tour E:
Chemin Sainte-Foy**

Sainte-Foy

Université Laval
$
sb
Université Laval, Pavillon Parent
Office 1604, G1K 7P4
☎*656-2801*
It is possible to rent a room
on the university campus
from the beginning of May
to mid-August. The Service
des Résidences on campus
is responsible for renting
these rooms, which offer
the basic comfort of a single
bed and a bureau. The
bathrooms are shared by all
residents on the floor. This
is an inexpensive place to
stay and is worth
considering. A weekly rate
is also available. It is better
to reserve in advance.
Public transportation serves
this area well; it takes about
10min to get downtown.

YWCA
$
sb, ≈
855 Avenue Holland, G1S 3S5
☎*683-2155*
≠*683-5526*
The YWCA residence is
located on the border of
Sillery and Québec City. For
a modest sum you can rent,
for either a long or short
stay, one of the small
rudimentary rooms. There is

Accommodations

a cafeteria, laundry room, swimming pool and parking.

Château Bonne-Entente
$$$$

ℜ, ≡, K, ⊛, ≈, ✪, ℑ
3400 Chemin Sainte-Foy, G1X 1S6
☎*653-5221 or 800-463-4390*
653-3098
www.chateaubonneentente.com

This magnificent old-English-style property is spread out over 4.5ha and is covered with greenery and flowers. Rooms have been decorated with taste and refinement, and the entire inn has plenty of comfort and charm. You can also participate in a number of indoor and outdoor activities here, or simply enjoy watching the ducks splash about in the nearby pond. Château Bonne-Entente offers all the advantages and benefits of a country resort right in the city. Its restaurant, Le Pailleur (see p 243), serves gourmet Québécois cuisine. There are also several conference rooms.

Hôtel Gouverneur Sainte-Foy
$$$$

ℜ, ≡, ⊛, ≈
3030 Boulevard Laurier, G1V 2M5
☎*651-3030 or 888-910-1111*
651-6797

Hôtel Gouverneur is a topnotch establishment with warm-coloured rooms that provide maximum comfort. It is judiciously located near the bridges, a few minutes away from the shopping centres and right next to the expressways that lead to the region's various sports centres. It's dining room, restaurant La Verrière, will delight your taste buds as well as your eyes. A large area in the back has been landscaped with lush greenery and a lovely swimming pool.

Hôtel Germain-des-Prés
$$$$

ℜ, ≡
1200 Avenue Germain-des-Prés, G1V 3M7
☎*658-1224 or 800-463-5253*
658-8846
www.germaindespres.com

Hôtel Germain-des-Prés is a classic in the Québec City region. Established a few years ago, it was the first of what is now a chain of four extremely well-reputed boutique hotels. Its rooms, decorated with utmost care, are very welcoming and offer all the amenities you need for total relaxation: bathrobes, comfy armchairs, duvets and feather pillows... not to mention those little extras that are typical of this type of establishment, which provides personalized service despite its 126 rooms. The rooms will please business travellers, with its work desks and Internet access, as well as leisure travellers. There are also meeting rooms.

Near the Airport

The area around the airport is not particularly pleasant and travellers usually spend only one night here.

Château Repotel
$$ bkfst incl.

≡, ⊛, ㋐
6555 Boul. Wilfrid-Hamel, G2E 5W3
☎872-1111 or 800-463-5255
⇌872-5989

Château Repotel is well-equipped to make your stay pleasant. The rooms are not luxurious but they are peaceful and have large bathrooms.

Motel Confortel
$$ bkfst incl

≡, ⊛, ㋐
6500 Boul. Wilfrid-Hamel, G2E 2J1
☎877-4777 or 800-363-7440
⇌877-0013

As its name indicates, Confortel Québec is a hotel concerned with comfort. Furnished in bland colours and modern furniture, the rooms seem a bit austere but they are spacious.

Confort Inn L'Ancienne-Lorette
$$-$$$

≡, ㋐
1255 Autoroute Duplessis, G2G 2B4
☎872-5900
⇌872-9550

Confort Inn L'Ancienne-Lorette is on the road leading to the airport. The rooms are attractive even though they are furnished with laminated furniture.

Tour F: Saint-Roch

See map page 131.

🏨 L'Autre Jardin
$$ bkfst incl.

≡
365 Boulevard Charest Est, G1K 3H3
☎523-1790 or 877-747-0447
⇌523-9735
www.autrejardin.com

L'Autre Jardin is an inn unlike any other, created thanks to Carrefour Tiers-Monde, a non-governmental organization working in the field of international development. All profits from the inn are therefore reinvested towards international solidarity projects. Now there's a great way to spend your hard-earned dollars: pampering yourself in a cozy inn while simultaneously supporting projects that aim to improve social conditions both in Québec and in developing countries. The inn's decor on each of its three floors is simple yet warm, with a few original touches here and there, and the staff is friendly and welcoming.

Hôtel Royal William
$$$$

ℜ, ≡, ⊛
360 Boulevard Charest Est, G1K 3H4
☎521-4488 or 888-541-0405
www.royalwilliam.com

The Saint-Roch neighbourhood is in a

period of restoration. The opening of the Hôtel Royal William was in keeping with this spirit of revival. This large hotel, located on Boulevard Charest has helped to liven up the surrounding area. Business people are particularly pleased with the practical aspect of the 40-odd rooms. In fact, the rooms are equipped with work tables, telephone outlets and Internet access. The decor is modern and comfortable, like most hotels in this category.

Tour J: Heading North

Lac-Delage

Manoir du Lac Delage
$$$$
≡, ≈, ☺, ℜ, ℑ, ◠, ✪
40 Avenue du Lac, G0A 4P0
☎*848-2551 or 800-463-2841*
≈*848-6945*
www.lacdelage.com
Manoir du Lac Delage offers a wide array of installations that will charm sports-lovers in both winter and summer. The centre features a skating rink and is located near cross-country ski trails and slides. In summer, the lakeshore is ideal for practicing several watersports. The rooms and their wood furnishings are comfortable.

Lac-Beauport

Château du Lac-Beauport
$$
≈, ℜ, ⊛, K
154 Chemin Tour-du-Lac, G0A 2C0
☎*849-1811 or 800-463-2692*
≈*849-2895*
Resembling a large ski chalet, Château du Lac-Beauport is quite comfortable, providing several sports facilities. Facing Lac Beauport, it features a lovely beach that allows visitors to enjoy activities such as surfing, kayaking, canoeing and sailing. In winter, a skating rink is created on the frozen lake. This site is fabulous for those who love spending time outdoors.

Sainte-Catherine-de-la-Jacques-Cartier

Station Écotouristique Duchesnay
$$
pb/sb, ℜ, K
143 Route Duchesnay, G0A 3M0
☎*875-2112 or 877-511-5885*
≈*875-2868*
www.sepaq.com/duchesnay
In the heart of a 90km² forest, on the shore of Lac Saint-Joseph (see p 175), several cottages and log cabins were recently renovated to welcome visitors. A number of packages are available, all including nature and

comfort. Whether you wish to rent a cabin for the entire family and enjoy the lake and footpaths, or rent a romantic room for two and take advantage of the many cross-country ski trails, you will undoubtedly be seduced by this place.

Chaumière Juchereau-Duchesnay
$$
ℜ, ≈
5050 Route Fossambault, G0A 3M0
☎*875-2751 or 800-501-2122*
⇌*875-2752*
Not far from Station Forestière de Duchesnay, where you can take part in a variety of outdoor activities, Chaumière Juchereau-Duchesnay offers room and board. Its nine pastel-coloured rooms are all similarly decorated. They are very comfortable despite the fact that they do not have the same antique elegance as the dining room. This inn, with its trees, swimming pool and terrace, will allow you to relax in peace and quiet.

Ice Hotel
$$$$$ ½b
sb, ℜ
143 Route Duchesnay,
Pavillon L'Aigle, G0A 3M0
☎*875-4522 or 877-505-0423*
⇌*875-2833*
www.icehotel-canada.com
It's hard to believe that a hotel could actually be made of ice…but it really is (see p 157)! This

(see p 157)!

magnificent structure is built from thousands of tonnes of ice and snow. Adventurous travellers come from all over the continent to spend the night in this chilly castle. Note, however, that because the ice provides natural insulation, the temperature always remains between -2°C and -6°C within the hotel walls. So you can snooze quite comfortably in one of its 31 rooms, all wrapped up in a thick sleeping bag laid atop deer pelts. And if you're new to winter camping, don't worry: the hotel staff is available day and night. Furthermore, the shared bathrooms are heated, and breakfast and dinner are served in a warm chalet. On site, guests can enjoy a multitude of outdoor activities. An unforgettable experience is guaranteed!

Parc de la Jacques-Cartier

Parc de la Jacques-Cartier
$
Centre d'Accueil et d'Interpretation, Stoneham, G0A 4P0
☎*848-7272*
In Parc de la Jacques-Cartier you can camp in magnificent surroundings. Along the river, there are numerous campsites, some rustic, others with some facilities. And of course there's no lack of things to do!

Accommodations

| Tour K: |
| Côte-de-Beaupré |
| and Île d'Orléans |

Beauport

Journey's End
$$

®, ≡

240 Boulevard Sainte-Anne, G1E 3L7

☎*666-1226 or 800-465-6116*

⇄*666-5088*

This member of the
Journey's End hotel chain
lives up to company
standards. It offers travellers
comfortable rooms where
they can relax. Journey's
End is better known for its
low prices than for its
variety of services.

Ramada Hôtel Ambassadeur
$$$$

⊘, △, ℜ, ®

321 Boul. Ste-Anne, G1E 3L4

☎*666-2828 or 800-363-4619*

⇄*666-2775*

www.ramadaquebec.com

This hotel was built on the
outskirts of town in an area
where travellers usually
only stop for one night. The
rooms are large and
attractive, and there is a
good Chinese restaurant on
the ground floor.

Château-Richer

Auberge du Petit Pré
$$ bkfst incl.
sb
7126 Avenue Royale, G0A 1N0

☎*824-3852*

⇄*824-3098*

At the Auberge du Petit Pré,
situated in an 18th-century
house, you will be warmly
received and well treated.
Their four bedrooms are
cosy and tastefully
decorated. There's a large
picture window which is
open on warm sunny days,
two lounges—one with a
T.V. and the other with a
fireplace, as well as two
bathrooms with clawfoot
tubs. Breakfasts are generous and finely prepared.
Also, if requested in
advance, the owner will
prepare one of his delicious
dinners for you. The
splendid aroma of the
home-cooking fills the
house and adds to its
overall warmth.

Auberge Baker
$$ bkfst incl.
pb/sb, ℜ, K
8790 Avenue Royale, G0A 1N0

☎*666-5509*

⇄*824-4412*

www.auberge-baker.qc.ca

For over 50 years, the
Auberge Baker has been
established in this hundred-
year-old Côte-de-Beaupré
house. Its stone walls, low
ceilings, wood floors and
wide-frame windows never

fail to enchant visitors. The five bedrooms are on the dimly-lit upper floor but there is also a kitchenette, a bathroom and an adjoining terrace on the same floor. The rooms are meticulously decorated in authentic period-fashion and furnished with antiques. The inn's restaurant serves delicious meals (see p 248).

Sainte-Anne-de-Beaupré

Auberge La Bécassine
$$
ℜ, ≡
9341 Boulevard Sainte-Anne, G0A 3C0
☎*827-4988 or 877-727-4988*
La Bécassine is located less than 10min from Mont Sainte-Anne. It is actually a motel since most of the rooms are next to the main building. The rooms are simply but quite pleasantly decorated. There is also a large dining room, and the kitchen's specialty is game.

Beaupré (Mont Sainte-Anne)

Camping Mont Ste-Anne
$
☎*827-4561, 826-2323 or 800-463-1568*
Camping Mont Ste-Anne located at Station Mont-Sainte-Anne (see p 177), has 166 campsites in a wooded area traversed by

the Rivière Jean-Larose. Essential services are offered, and, the campground is superbly located close to all the park's outdoor activities.

Village Touristique Mont-Sainte-Anne
$$$$
≡, K, ⊛, ℑ, ≈, ⊘
2000 Boulevard Beaupré, G0A 1E0
☎*827-2002 or 800-463-7775*
Situated at the foot of the mountain, Villégiature Mont-Sainte-Anne is the dream spot for those who prefer to stay put rather than travel from one place to another. There are several apartments of varying sizes that can accommodate from two to eight people. Some rooms have whirlpool baths and a mezzanine. All accommodations are equipped with modern kitchens and functional fireplaces and are very comfortable. Several apartments have views overlooking the trails.

Hôtel Val des Neiges
$$-$$$
≈, ⊘, △, ℜ, ⊛, ℑ
201 Val des Neiges, G0A 1E0
☎*827-5711 or 888-554-6005*
≠*827-5997*
Many chalets have recently been built in newly developed areas around the base of Mont Sainte-Anne. Among these is the Hôtel Val des Neiges The decor is rustic and the rooms are

comfortable. The complex also includes small, well-equipped condos. They also offer cruise packages.

⚓ La Camarine
$$$

≡, ℜ, ℑ, ⊛
10947 Sainte-Anne, G0A 1E0
☎*827-5703 or 800-567-3939*
⇄*827-5430*
www.camarine.com

La Camarine faces the Saint Lawrence River. This charming high-quality inn has thirty rooms. The decor successfully combines the rustic feel of the house with the more modern wooden furniture. This is a delightful spot and its restaurant has a very good reputation (see p 249).

Île d'Orléans

On île d'Orléans, there are about 50 bed and breakfasts! A list can be obtained from the tourist office. There are also a few guesthouses with solid reputations, a hostel and a campground. There are plenty of options therefore for getting the most out of your stay on this enchanting island.

Camping Orléans
$

≈
357 Chemin Royal, St-François, G0A 3S0
☎*829-2953*
⇄*829-2563*

Camping Orléans has close to 80 campsites, most of which are shaded and offer a view of the river. Many services are offered. There is access to the river bank where you can go for a pleasant walk.

Auberge Le P'tit Bonheur
$ dormitory
$$ private room
sb
183 and 186 Côte Lafleur, St-Jean, G0A 3W0
☎*829-2588*
⇄*829-0900*

Auberge Le P'tit Bonheur, situated on Île d'Orléans, is named after a song by Félix Leclerc, who fell in love with this island in the middle of the St. Lawrence River. This youth hostel offers an affordable alternative to those who wish to discover this part of the region. Both the 300-year-old main house and the site offer a most friendly atmosphere. Several outdoor activities are available in winter and summer.

Le Vieux-Presbytère
$$ bkfst incl.
pb/sb, ℜ
1247 Avenue Monseigneur-d'Esgly St-Pierre, G0A 4E0
☎828-9723 or 888-282-9723
⇆828-2189
www.presbytere.com
The guesthouse Le Vieux-Presbytère is in fact located in an old presbytery just behind the village church. The structure is predominantly made out of wood and stone. Low ceilings with wide beams, wide-frame windows and antiques such as woven bed-covers and braided rugs take you back to the era of New France. The dining room and the lounge are inviting. It is a tranquil spot with rustic charm.

Auberge Canard Huppée
$$$ bkfst incl.
ℜ, ⊛, ℑ
2198 Chemin Royal, St-Laurent, G0A 3Z0
☎828-2292 or 800-838-2292
⇆828-0966
www.canard-huppe.qc.ca
Le Canard Huppée has enjoyed a very good reputation over the last few years. Their clean, comfortable, country-style rooms are situated in two old houses each with decorative wooden ducks scattered throughout. The restaurant is also just as renowned and appealing (see p 250). The service is conscientious, and the surroundings, beautiful.

Auberge Chaumonot
$$$
≈, ℜ
425 Chemin Royal
Saint-François, G0A 3S0
☎829-2735
☎800-520-2735
This small inn only has eight rooms and is open exclusively in the summer. Located on the south shore of the island, Auberge Chaumonot was built near the banks of the river and is surrounded by charming countryside, far from the village and the road. The country-style rooms are comfortable.

La Goéliche
$$$
ℜ, ≈, ≡, K, ⊛
22 Chemin du Quai,
Ste-Pétronille, G0A 4C0
☎828-2248 or 888-511-2248
⇆828-2745
La Goéliche has reopened in a new building, after the former inn burned to the ground in 1996. The new establishment is slightly smaller, and does not have the antique charm that made the original such a hit. Nevertheless, the modern setup still has a certain country-style appeal. The 18 rooms are comfortable and offer a lovely view of Québec City. There is a small living room with a fireplace and games. The restaurant (see p 250) is worth the trip.

Restaurants

Fine dining
is without question one of Québec City's best attractions.

Whether you wish to enjoy a gourmet meal, a light healthy snack or simply an espresso, your only difficulty will be choosing among the great selection of romantic restaurants and charming cafés.

As a general rule, restaurants offer, from Monday to Friday, specials that include a full menu at a reasonable price. Served at lunch only, theses *menus du jour* often feature a choice of appetizers and main courses with coffee and dessert. In the evening, the *table d'hôte* (same formula at a slightly higher cost) is often quite interesting as well.

Prices in this guide apply to **dinner** for one person **excluding** taxes, tip (see p 56) and drinks. The restaurants are listed according to their corresponding

tours, starting with the least expensive. The price scale is as follows:

$	less than $10
$$	$10 to $20
$$$	$20 to $30
$$$$	more than $30

It is always preferable to make reservations, especially for groups. This also allows you to make sure the restaurant you have chosen is open that evening. Some restaurants are closed at the beginning of the week in the winter; however, most of them are open every day in high season (summer).

If you are travelling by car to Vieux-Québec, check with the restaurant to see if they offer valet service when you make reservations. This will save you a lot of trouble. If they do not provide this service, you should try to find an indoor parking garage. They are usually easy to locate.

Bring Your Own Wine

There are in fact many restaurants here where you can bring your own bottle of wine, a practice that often seems unusual to Europeans. This tradition stems from the fact that in order to serve alcohol, an establishment must purchase a rather expensive liquor license.
Consequently, restaurant owners who wish to offer their clientele a more economical solution prefer a license which allows customers to bring their own wine. In such cases, there is usually a sign in the window.

Here's another unusual tradition: there exists, in addition to the liquor license, a bar license. In other words, restaurants who solely display a liquor license can only sell you beer, wine or other drinks when you order a meal. Some restaurants, however, have both permits and can sell you alcohol without you having to order a meal.

Cafés

Many Québécois are fans of espresso, which is why cafés and small, friendly restaurants are highly popular. These types of establishments have often been part of their neighbourhoods for many years. The gleaming coffee machine is usually the most popular attraction, but you can also find lovely light dishes such as soups, salads and *croque-monsieur* (an open-faced sandwich of ham and cheese broiled and served hot), as well as croissants and desserts, of course!

On weekends, breakfast is usually served until early

afternoon. To find the list of cafés we recommend, look under "Restaurants by Type of Cuisine."

This chapter recommends the best places to eat. The selection was made with all budgets and tastes in mind. There are two indexes: the first is by type of cuisine (see below) and the second, in alphabetical order, is under "Restaurants" in the index at the end of the guide. We have also compiled a list of Ulysses's Favourites (see below), which are also indicated with a boat logo next to each establishment (see also p 191). These pointers should help you make a wise choice. *Bon appétit!*

Ulysses's Favourites

The finest establishments in Québec City and surroundings:
Laurie Raphaël (p 233), La Grande Table de Serge Bruyère (p 227), La Closerie (p 239) Le Champlain (p 227), La Camarine (p 249), La Fenouillère (p 244), Initiale (p 232) and Michelangelo (p 247).

For the romantic atmosphere:
Le Saint-Amour (p 226), Le Graffiti (p 239), La Crémaillère (p 226), Michelangelo (p 247), Le Sainte-Victoire (p 245) and Poisson d'Avril (p 232).

For the terrace:
Il Teatro (p 243), À la Bastille Chez Bahüaud (p 224), Café-Resto du Musée (p 237), Buffet du Passant (p 246) and Moulin Saint-Laurent (p 249).

For traditional Québec cuisine:
Aux Anciens Canadiens (p 225) and Auberge Baker (p 248).

For the view:
L'Astral (p 239), Manoir Montmorency (p 248), La Goéliche (p 250), Café de la Terrasse (p 227) and Café-Resto du Musée (p 237).

For elegant decor:
Voo Doo Grill (p 238), Le Marie Clarisse (p 232), Café du Monde (p 231), Aviatic Club (p 231), Cosmos Café (p 234) and Le Montego (p 247).

For originality:
Café du Clocher Penché (p 245), Le Bonnet d'Âne (p 240) and Dazibo Café (p 240).

Restaurants by Type of Cuisine

Belgian

Restaurants

Tour A:
Vieux-Québec

Brûlerie Tatum
$
1084 Rue St-Jean
☎692-3900
Brûlerie Tatum is located in
a lovely narrow building

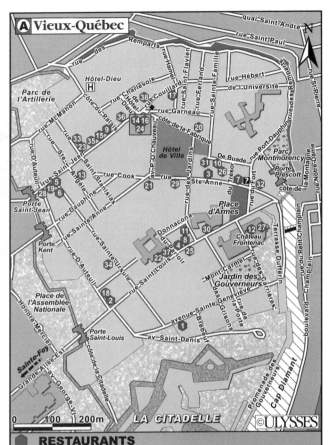

A Vieux-Québec

RESTAURANTS

1. À la Bastille Chez Bahüaud
2. Apsara
3. Au Café Suisse
4. Au Parmesan
5. Au Petit Coin Breton
6. Au Petit Coin Latin
7. Auberge du Trésor
8. Aux Anciens Canadiens
9. Brûlerie Tatum
10. Café Buade
11. Café de la Paix
12. Café de la Terrasse
13. Café d'Europe
14. Café Serge Bruyère
15. Casse-Crêpe Breton
16. Chez Livernois
17. Chez Temporel
18. Élysée-Mandarin
19. Entrecôte Saint-Jean
20. Fleur de Lotus
21. Guido Le Gourmet
22. La Caravelle
23. La Crémaillère
24. La Grande Table
25. La Petite Italie
26. La Ripaille
27. Le Champlain
28. Le Chantauteuil
29. Le Charles Baillairgé
30. Le Continental
31. Le D'Orsay
32. Le Gambrinus
33. Le Patriarche
34. Le Saint-Amour
35. Le Saint-James
36. Les Frères de la Côte
37. L'Omelette
38. Portofino

with a mezzanine and is decorated in reddish hues. This café roasts its own beans in a gleaming coffee machine installed at the entrance. They serve mouth-watering light meals such as *croque-monsieur* and sandwiches, as well as a great selection of coffee and hot chocolate.

Casse-Crêpe Breton
$
1136 Rue St-Jean
☎692-0438
Little Casse-Crêpe Breton is a popular spot that draws big crowds. Though it has been expanded, patrons still have to line up for a taste of its delicious crepes. Prepared right before your eyes, these delights are filled with your favourite ingredients by waitresses who manage to keep smiling in the midst of the hubbub. High-backed, upholstered seats help lend the place a warm atmosphere.

Chez Temporel
$
25 Rue Couillard
At Chez Temporel, the food is prepared right on the premises. Whether you opt for a rich butter croissant, a *croque-monsieur*, a salad or the special of the day, you can be sure it will be fresh and tasty. To top it all off, this establishment serves the best espresso in town! Tucked away on little Rue Couillard, the two-storey Temporel has been welcoming people of all ages and all stripes for over 20 years now. Open early in the morning to late at night.

Le Petit Coin Latin
$
8½ Rue Sainte-Ursule
☎692-2022
Petit Coin Latin serves homestyle cooking in an ambiance reminiscent of a Parisian café. The decor is dominated by parlour chairs and mirrors, creating a relaxed, convivial atmosphere. The menu includes *croûtons au fromage*, quiche and salads. You can also snack on *raclette* (a swiss meal) served at the table on small burners with potatoes and cold cuts. Delicious! During summer, a lovely outdoor seating area enclosed by stone walls is open out back; to get there from the street, use the carriage entrance.

Le Chantauteuil
$-$$
1001 Rue St-Jean
☎692-2030
The Chantauteuil is a quaint resto-bar. The pretty decor is reminiscent of Paris with its lace curtains and attractive paintings hanging on the stone walls. This café has lots of character, service is friendly and communication is easily

established between staff and customers. Lunch time always features a delicious *menu du jour*. Light meals such as *croque-monsieur* and sandwiches are served all day.

L'Entrecôte Saint-Jean
$$
1011 Rue Saint-Jean
☎*694-0234*
The Entrecôte Saint-Jean serves steaks prepared in a variety of ways accompanied by matchstick potatoes. Try the salad with nuts and the chocolate profiteroles, which make a perfect ending to your meal. Great value for your money.

Apsara
$$
71 Rue d'Auteuil
☎*694-0232*
The Apsara is located near Porte Saint-Louis and features Southeast Asian cuisine. Complete meals are served at both lunch and dinner time and prices are reasonable.

Café Buade
$$
31 Rue de Buade
☎*692-3909*
Near Rue du Trésor and Terrasse Dufferin, Café Buade has a large dining room with an attractive but modest decor. It is a pleasant establishment with a family atmosphere where you can enjoy a good meal

without having to spend a fortune. The house specialty is roast beef.

Le D'Orsay
$$
65 Rue de Buade
☎*694-1582*
Le D'Orsay is a *brasserie* where people congregate to eat and drink. It has a pub atmosphere and a slightly preppy clientele. During the summer, a *chansonnier* usually entertains the crowd on the large back terrace.

Fleur de Lotus
$$
38 Côte de la Fabrique
☎*692-4286*
Popular for its Asian music, peaceful atmosphere and courteous service, Fleur de Lotus is also appreciated for its delectably different cuisine, which will transport you to the heart of Asia.

L'Omelette
$$
64 Rue St-Louis
☎*694-9626*
L'Omelette is a very friendly place that serves copious breakfasts early in the morning. Later in the day, choose from a large variety of omelettes, pasta, pizza, hamburgers and submarines. Quality food at a reasonable price.

Restaurants

Au Petit Coin Breton
$$
1029 Rue St-Jean
☎**694-0758**

The atmosphere, decor and traditional costumes worn by the staff at Au Petit Coin Breton will surprise you. And the crepes, filled with your very own choice of ingredients, are quite satisfying. The dessert crepes are especially yummy.

La Petite Italie
$$
49 ½ Rue St-Louis
☎**694-0044**

La Petite Italie serves Italian specialties at affordable prices. The menu features pizza and pasta and the decor is pleasant to the eye. This restaurant is right in the heart of a lively tourist area.

Le Saint-James
$$
1110 Rue St-Jean
☎**692-1030**

The Saint-James bistro is part of Manoir Victoria (see p 195) even though it has its own entrance on Rue St-Jean. The decor is elegant, similar to that of the Manoir. An innovative formula lets you create your own meal combination from a large choice of pasta and sauces. There are also steaks, sandwiches and an interesting *table d'hôte*.

Café Serge Bruyère
$$-$$$
1200 Rue St-Jean
☎**694-0618**

An institution in Vieux-Québec, Maison Serge-Bruyère is located in Maison Livernois, a large bourgeois residence built in the 19th century. The premises actually comprises three restaurants, which increase in refinement as you climb the stairs. The top floor is occupied by La Grande Table (see p 227). On the ground floor, the Café offers a typical menu of salads, sandwiches and pastries to accompany a beer or an espresso. In the cellar is an Irish pub, Pub St-Patrick, which serves all kinds of beer and occasionally presents Celtic music.

Chez Livernois
$$-$$$
1200 Rue St-Jean
☎**694-0618**

Chez Livernois is a bistro located inside Maison Livernois now called Maison Serge-Bruyère. It is named after photographer Jules Livernois, who set up his studio in this imposing 19th-century house in 1889. The excellent cuisine consists mainly of pasta and dishes from the grill, and the atmosphere is a bit more relaxed than at La Grande Table (see p 227).

Les Frères de la Côte
$$-$$$
1190 Rue St-Jean
☎692-5445

Les Frères de la Côte serves delicious bistro fare, including pasta, grilled items, and thin-crust pizzas baked in a wood-burning oven and topped with delicious fresh ingredients. Unlimited mussels and fries are also available on certain evenings. The atmosphere is lively yet relaxed and the place is often packed, in keeping with the bustling activity on Rue St-Jean. Guests can take in the action through the restaurant's large windows.

Portofino Bistro Italiano
$$-$$$
54 Rue Couillard
☎692-8888

Portofino was designed to resemble a typical Italian trattoria. A long bar, blue glasses, mirrors on the wall and soccer banners on the ceiling help create a warm, lively atmosphere. Don't be surprised if the owner greets you with a kiss! To top it all off, the mouth-watering Italian aromas will whet your appetite for the upcoming delights. During tourist season, the place is always full. Valet parking.

Au Café Suisse
$$$
32 Rue Sainte-Anne
☎694-1320

All kinds of fondues (Swiss, Chinese, Bourguignonne and even seafood) are on the menu at Café Suisse, along with *raclette*, grilled dishes and light meals. The terrace, which opens onto the pedestrian-only, Rue Sainte-Anne, will make your summertime dinner even more pleasant. You can watch painters and caricaturists at work and occasionally listen to street musicians.

Au Parmesan
$$$
38 Rue St-Louis
☎692-0341

Upon entering Au Parmesan, one is struck by the extensive collection of pots and bottles exhibited on the cornices along the walls. If you are looking for a quiet spot to have a private conversation, this is not the place. A *chansonnier* playing the accordion contributes to the animated atmosphere, and in the summer, it is *la dolce vita* every evening of the week! The clientele is mostly made up of tourists. The specialties are French and Italian; pasta, seafood platters and smoked salmon are among the favourites.

Restaurants

🌴 Café de la Paix
$$$
44 Rue des Jardins
☎**692-1430**

Café de la Paix occupies a narrow space a few steps from the sidewalk on little Rue des Jardins. It has been around for years and enjoys a solid reputation among Québec City residents. The menu features traditional French cuisine such as frog's legs, beef Wellington, rabbit with mustard and grilled salmon.

🌴 L'Élysée-Mandarin
$$$
65 Rue d'Auteuil
☎**692-0909**

L'Élysée-Mandarin, which also boasts prime locations in Montréal and Paris, serves excellent Szechuan, Cantonese and Mandarin cuisine in a decor that features a small indoor garden and Chinese sculptures and vases. The food is always succulent and the service extremely courteous. If you are with a group, try the sampler menu: it would be a shame not to sample as many dishes as possible!

Le Patriarche
$$$
17 Rue St-Stanislas
☎**692-5488**

Le Patriarche's decor is charming and unpretentious. The dining room has beautiful stone walls creating quite a relaxed, pleasant atmosphere. The reception is warm and the service very friendly. The inviting menu of French cuisine includes wild game and seafood.

La Ripaille
$$$
9 Rue de Buade
☎**692-2450**

Right near the Château Frontenac and quaint Rue du Trésor, La Ripaille always offers lovely surprises, whether it is the French or the seafood dishes. The atmosphere is warm and inviting.

🌴 À la Bastille Chez Bahüaud
$$$
47 Avenue Ste-Geneviève
☎**692-2544**

À la Bastille Chez Bahüaud is located near the Plains of Abraham and is surrounded by trees. The wonderfully quiet terrace makes this the ideal spot for an intimate moonlit dinner. Inside, the decor is both elegant and comfortable and includes a billiard table. There is also a charming downstairs bar with a more intimate atmosphere. Fine French cuisine awaits you.

Auberge du Trésor
$$$-$$$$
20 Rue Sainte-Anne
☎**694-1876**

Established in a house built in 1679 during the French

winter, pure white snow, Christmas decorations and sparkling lights
bathe the city in magic and romance. - *T. Philiptchenko*

Cap Diamant affords a lovely view of the multicoloured roofs in the Basse-Ville sector of Vieux Québec.
- *S. Schanz*

February is Carnaval de Québec time, when many activities are held all over the city and its surroundings. Here, a canoe race through the icy river.
- *Y. Tessier*

Regime, the Auberge du Trésor's clientele is mostly made up of tourists. French cuisine is served here in an ambiance that recalls an Old French manor house. During the summer, the terrace is an ideal spot to enjoy a drink and admire the magnificent view of Château Frontenac and the various activities taking place in Parc de la Place d'Armes. Musicians perform here in the evening. Note however that a simple coffee on the terrace may cost more than you expect.

La Caravelle
$$$-$$$$
68 ½ Rue St-Louis
☎694-9022
Located on Rue St-Louis, a popular street for tourists, La Caravelle is busy at all hours of the day and night. A mixed clientele frequents this attractive, luxuriously decorated restaurant. The stone walls, wood panelling, lighting and plants give it a pleasant, inviting atmosphere. The staff here caters to your every need, attentively making every effort to serve you. In the evening, a *chansonnier* entertains the appreciative audience. Exquisite French cuisine is served here, with a few Spanish additions to the menu.

Le Charles-Baillargé
$$$-$$$$
57 Rue Sainte-Anne
☎692-2480
The Charles-Baillargé restaurant is located on the main floor of the beautiful Hôtel Clarendon (see p 196). Discriminating diners come here for excellent, traditional French cuisine served in comfortable surroundings.

Le Continental
$$$-$$$$
26 Rue St-Louis
☎694-9995
Le Continental, just steps away from the Château Frontenac, is one of the oldest restaurants in Québec City. The continental cuisine includes seafood, lamb and duck, among other dishes. Service is *au guéridon* (pedestal table) in a large, comfortable dining room.

Aux Anciens Canadiens
$$$-$$$$
34 Rue St-Louis
☎692-1627
Located in one of the oldest houses in Québec City (see Maison Jacquet p 72), the restaurant Aux Anciens Canadiens serves upscale versions of traditional Québecois specialties. Dishes include ham with maple syrup, pork and beans, and blueberry pie.

Restaurants

Café d'Europe
$$$-$$$$
27 Rue Sainte-Angèle
☎*692-3835*

Café d'Europe has a sober, slightly outdated decor. There is limited amount of space, and when the place is busy, the noise level gets pretty high. The service is courteous with a personal touch. Sophisticated French and Italian cuisine is presented in a traditional manner and served in generous portions. The flambée dishes are expertly prepared, and the smooth, flavourful sauces make this an unforgettable culinary experience.

La Crémaillère
$$$-$$$$
21 Rue St-Stanislas at the corner of Rue St-Jean
☎*692-2216*

Friendly service and exquisite cooking with a European flavour await you at La Crémaillère. A great deal of attention is given here to make your meal memorable. The attractive decor adds to the charm of this inviting restaurant.

Le Gambrinus
$$$-$$$$
15 Rue du Fort
☎*692-5144*

Le Gambrinus is a beautiful restaurant that has a good reputation with the people of Québec City. The welcoming dining room is adorned with lace curtains reaching midway to the small paned windows. The entire room is decorated with ivy, and elegant ornamental plates hang on the walls. The atmosphere could not be more enjoyable in this warm and appealing room. On summer evenings guests are entertained by a singer, who makes the ambiance even more inviting. The terrace overlooks Château Frontenac. The French cuisine features a large selection of fish and seafood.

Guido Le Gourmet
$$$-$$$$
73 Rue Sainte-Anne
☎*692-3856*

Guido Le Gourmet will transport you to the world of fine dining. The menu, made up of French and Italian cuisine, includes quail, veal, salmon and other delicacies from both land and sea. The elegant decor and the large, lovely plates on the table provide a good indication of the pleasures that await you. Brunch is served on weekends.

Le Saint-Amour
$$$-$$$$
48 Rue Sainte-Ursule
☎*694-0667*

Chef and co-owner Jean-Luc Boulay creates succulent, innovative cuisine that is a feast for both the eyes and the palate. The desserts concocted in the *chocolaterie*, on the second floor, are absolutely divine. A truly gastronomic experience! To top it all off, the setting is beautiful and comfortable with a wonderful warm atmosphere. The solarium, open year-round and decorated with all sorts of flowers and plants, brightens up the decor. Valet parking.

🏮 Café de la Terrasse
$$$$
1 Rue des Carrières
☎692-3861

The Café de la Terrasse, in the Château Frontenac, has picture windows looking out onto Terrasse Dufferin. Attractive decor and delicious French cuisine.

🏮 Le Champlain
$$$$
1 Rue des Carrières
☎692-3861

Le Champlain is the Château Frontenac's own restaurant. Needless to say, its decor is extremely luxurious in keeping with the opulence of the rest of the hotel. The outstanding French cuisine also does justice to the Château's reputation. Chef Jean Soular, whose recipes have been published, adds a unique touch to the classic dishes. Impeccable service.

🏮 La Grande Table de Serge Bruyère
$$$$
1200 Rue St-Jean
☎694-0618

La Grande Table in Maison Serge-Bruyère has a solid reputation that extends far beyond the walls of the old city. First established by the late Serge Bruyère, an excellent cook who gave the place its name, this restaurant's reputation has been maintained from year to year thanks to the skills of various well-known chefs. Since the beginning of the year 2000, Serge Bruyère's former student, Martin Côté, has carried on the tradition after travelling all over the world perfecting his art. He creates magnificent French gastronomic dishes with the most exquisite, creamy sauces you will ever taste. La Grande Table is on the top floor of an historic house situated between Rue Garneau and Rue Couillard. The decor is attractive and paintings by Québec artists hang on the walls. Valet parking.

Restaurants

Tour B: Petit-Champlain to Vieux-Port

Buffet de l'Antiquaire
$
95 Rue St-Paul
☎*692-2661*
Buffet de l'Antiquaire is a pleasant snack bar that serves homestyle cooking. As indicated by its name, it is located in the heart of the antique dealers' quarter and is a good place to take a little break while treasure-hunting. It is also one of the first restaurants to open in the morning (6am).

La Crêperie de Sophie
$$
48 Rue St-Paul
☎*694-9595*
The charms of Brittany are recaptured in the food as well as the decor of this establishment, where peasant scenes of rural France grace the walls. The crepes here are innovatively prepared, and taste comes second to presentation, which is exemplary.

Asia
$$
89 Rue Sault-au-Matelot
☎*692-3799*
Asia serves excellent cuisine from Thailand and Vietnam. Vegetarians will also be delighted with the selection of dishes available. Their trademark dishes are prepared on the grill or in a wok, resulting in light, healthy meals.

Le Cochon Dingue
$$
46 Boulevard Champlain
☎*692-2013*
Cochon Dingue is a charming café-bistro located between Boulevard Champlain and Rue du Petit-Champlain. Mirrors and a checkerboard floor create a fun, attractive decor. The menu features bistro-style dishes such as *steak-frites* and *moules-frites* combos (steak and fries or mussels with fries). The desserts are heavenly!

Pizza Mag
$$
363 Rue St-Paul
☎*692-1910*
For a delicious thick-crusted all-dressed pizza, stop at one of the Pizza Mag counters. The toppings are quite unusual, with choices such as La Biquette (with goat cheese), La Crème et Poireaux (cream and leeks), La Parmentière (potatoes dusted with parmesan cheese), La Louloutte Escargots (snails) or La Kamouraska with smoked sturgeon. Although mainly a take-out place, there are also a few tables where you can sit and relax while you eat. Free delivery.

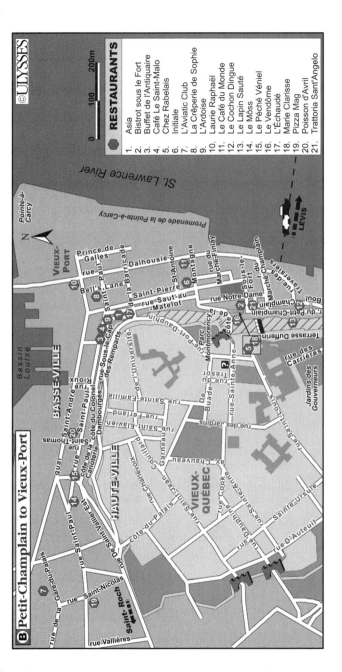

B Petit-Champlain to Vieux-Port

St. Lawrence River

0   100   200m

©ULYSSES

Le Péché Véniel
$$-$$$
233 Rue St-Paul
☎*692-5642*
Once inside Péché Véniel
you will find a most
enjoyable atmosphere.
Whether for breakfast,
lunch or dinner, the meals
are always excellent. To
name just a few specialties,
we suggest the smoked
meat sandwich on a
baguette, *moules poulettes*
(mussels), steak and fries
and the popular Lac Saint-
Jean *tourtière* (meat pie). A
more elaborate *table d'hôte*
is also available and just as
tasty.

Café Le Saint-Malo
$$-$$$
75 Rue St-Paul
☎*692-2004*
Café Le Saint-Malo is a
small restaurant that has
been on Rue St-Paul for
almost 20 years. It is
decorated with many
assorted objects that create
a friendly atmosphere, as
do the low ceilings, booths
and fireplace. French
cuisine specialties can be
enjoyed here. The *cassoulet*
(bean casserole) and *boudin
aux pommes* (blood sausage
with apples) are particularly
good.

Bistro Sous-le-Fort
$$-$$$
48 Rue Sous-le-Fort
☎*694-0852*
Bistro Sous le Fort has a
somewhat stark decor and

is frequented mainly by
tourists. The restaurant
serves delicious, reasonably
priced Québécois cuisine.

Trattoria Sant'Angelo
$$-$$$
10 Rue Cul-de-Sac
☎*692-4862*
Discover Italy at Trattoria
Sant-Angelo, in the heart of
the Petit-Champlain
neighbourhood. The decor
is a little austere but the
wood fire in the centre of
the restaurant provides a
cheerful touch. And on a
starlit summer evening,
your dining experience will
be enhanced if you eat out
on the terrace. During high
season the clientele is
mostly made up of tourists,
and is mixed the rest of the
year. As the advertising
states, "Pasta-Pizza-Amore,"
the menu has a great
variety of pasta and pizza
cooked with love in a
wood-burning oven.

Le Lapin Sauté
$$-$$$
52 Rue du Petit-Champlain
☎*692-5325*
Located in a 200-year-old
house in the Petit-
Champlain neighbour-
hood, Lapin Sauté is
furnished in a
simple manner. The rough
walls are white with a few
spots of colour. The terrace
is next to the Maison de la
Chanson, at the foot of Cap
Diamant. You may have
guessed that they serve

lapin (rabbit) prepared in many different ways.

Café du Monde
$$-$$$
57 Rue Dalhousie
☎692-4455

Café du Monde is a large Parisian-style brasserie that serves dishes one would expect from such a place, including *magret de canard* (duck filet), *tartare* (raw minced steak with herbs, etc.), *bavette* (beef steak) and of course, *moules-frites* (mussels and french fries). The lunch menu is interesting with its delicious *profiteroles* (cream puffs) served for dessert. On the weekend there are great brunches as well. The bright decor is condusive to relaxation and discussion: there are black-and-white tiles on the floor, leather seats, large windows overlooking the port and a long bar adorned with an imposing copper coffee machine. There is also a singles bar at the entrance. The waiters, dressed in long aprons, are quite helpful.

Le Môss
$$$
255 Rue St-Paul
☎692-0265

Le Môss is a Belgian bistro with a somewhat cold decor that includes black tables, brick walls, a stainless-steel counter and halogen lights. However, its *moules-frites* combo, dishes

from the grill and desserts made with Belgian chocolate are delicious.

L'Aviatic Club
$$$
450 de la Gare-du-Palais
☎522-3555

There are two restaurants in the magnificent Gare du Palais: a brand-new one with the evocative name of Charbon, which serves, as you might have guessed, food from the grill, and a second, which has been there for a number of years. The Aviatic Club takes you back in time with its mid-19th-century English-style decor featuring rattan armchairs, burgundy curtains, palm trees and a cosmopolitan menu.

L'Ardoise
$$$
71 Rue St-Paul
☎694-0213

On a street lined with antique shops and art galleries, the chic little bistro L'Ardoise is an ideal spot to take a break from touring the town. Although the service tends to be pretentious at times, this is a place where you will feel quite at ease. The mahogany panelling combines harmoniously with the stone walls. Among the dishes prepared are *boudin grillé aux pommes* (grilled blood sausage with apples) *foie de veau à l'anglaise* (English-style

Restaurants

liver), *entrecôte* (rib steak) and a selection of fish. Breakfast is also served.

Le Vendôme
$$$
36 Côte de la Montagne
☎692-0557

Le Vendôme is located halfway up Côte de la Montagne, and is one of the oldest restaurants in Québec City. It serves classic French dishes like Chateaubriand, *coq au vin* and *duck à l'orange* in an intimate setting.

Poisson d'Avril
$$$
115 Rue St-André
☎692-1010

Poisson d'Avril is in an old house with stone walls and wooden beams that lend a great deal of charm. The decor is enhanced by clever lighting and also by the shell-patterned fabric on the chairs. The menu includes well-prepared pasta, grilled dishes and seafood. Try the mussels!

Two good restaurants are perched on picturesque Escalier Casse-Cou, which leads to Rue du Petit-Champlain. On the top floor, **Chez Rabelais** (*$$$-$$$$; 2 Rue du Petit-Champlain*, ☎694-9460) serves French cuisine with an emphasis on seafood. A little lower down is **Marie-Clarisse** (*$$$$; 12 Rue du Petit-Champlain*, ☎692-0857),

where everything, except for the stone walls, is as blue as the sea—and with good reason: seafood is the house specialty. These divine dishes are served in a lovely dining room that has been very ornately decorated. When the cold weather sets in, a crackling fire warms you up.

🐟 L'Échaudé
$$$-$$$$
73 Rue Sault-au-Matelot
☎692-1299

L'Échaudé is an appealing restaurant with an Art Deco decor featuring a checkerboard floor and a mirrored wall. Relaxed atmosphere. Sophisticated cuisine prepared daily with fresh market ingredients.

Initiale
$$$$
54 Rue St-Pierre
☎694-1818

Initiale is situated on Rue St-Pierre in an old bank building with a high ceiling and decorative mouldings. Formerly located in Sillery, the restaurant's devoted clientele has followed it here in appreciation of the fine food prepared by chef Yvan Lebrun. His exquisite creations feature lamb, salmon, *filet mignon*, and kidneys served alongside *foie gras poêlé* (foie gras cooked in a pan) and, for the adventurous, pigeon! In a classical decor with a semicircular bar and light streaming in through high windows, you will be won over by these delicious dishes. The atmosphere is welcoming, although slightly stiff.

Laurie Raphäel
$$$$
17 Rue Dalhousie
☎692-4555
Chef and co-owner Daniel Vézina is well known and one of the best chefs in Québec. When creating his mouth-watering dishes, Vézina draws inspiration from culinary traditions from all over the world, preparing giblets, sea food, meat, and other dishes. in innovative ways. It goes without saying, that the food at Laurie Raphäel is delicious! The restaurant is located in spacious quarters with a semi-circular exterior glass wall. The elegant decor includes creamy white curtains, sand and earth tones and a few decorative, wrought-iron objects.

Tour C: Grande Allée and Avenue Cartier

Bügel
$
164 Rue Crémazie Ouest
☎523-7666
Craving a bagel? You'll find all different kinds at Bügel, a bagel bakery on pretty

little Rue Crémazie. In a warm atmosphere enhanced by the aroma of a wood fire, you can snack on bagels with salami, cream cheese or veggie pâté and stock up on goodies to take back home.

Les Finesses de Charlot
$
1125 Avenue Cartier
☎524-5636
Les Finesses de Charlot has excellent made-to-order submarines of all kinds. For a picnic, tuck one or two into a basket and head for the Plains of Abraham (only a 10min walk away!) If it is raining you can always eat inside the restaurant. In the summer, it is also an ice cream parlour.

Sushi Taxi
$-$$
813 Avenue Cartier
☎529-0068
Maki, sashimi, temaki... got a craving for raw fish? Then stop by the Sushi Taxi counter or, as its name hints, have this delicious Japanese treat delivered to your door. You can also savour the dishes, prepared before your eyes, in the restaurant itself, a tiny room with a Zen-style decor. Sushi Taxi also has an outlet in Sainte-Foy.

Restaurants

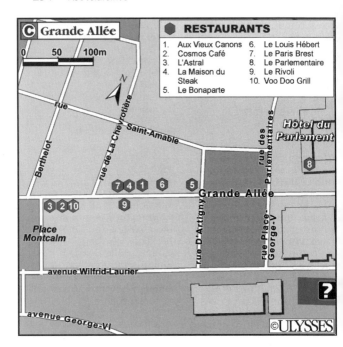

C Grande Allée

0   50   100m

N

Rue

Berthelot

rue de La Chevrotière

Saint-Amable

rue des Parlementaires

Hôtel du Parlement

RESTAURANTS

1. Aux Vieux Canons
2. Cosmos Café
3. L'Astral
4. La Maison du Steak
5. Le Bonaparte
6. Le Louis Hébert
7. Le Paris Brest
8. Le Parlementaire
9. Le Rivoli
10. Voo Doo Grill

7 4 1   6   5   Grande Allée

8

3 2 10   9

rue D'Artigny

rue Place-George-V

Place Montcalm

avenue Wilfrid-Laurier

avenue George-VI

?

©ULYSSES

Le Parlementaire
$-$$
Tue-Fri
at the corner of Ave. Honoré-Mercier and Grande Allée
☎**643-6640**
Visitors who might want to rub shoulders with members of Québec's National Assembly should have breakfast at Le Parlementaire. The menu features European and Québécois dishes. The restaurant is often packed, particularly at lunch, but the food is good. Open only for breakfast and lunch.

Cosmos Café
$$
575 Grande Allée Est
☎**640-0606**
The Cosmos Café promises a good time in a hip atmosphere, serving burgers, sandwiches and salads with a cosmopolitan flavour. Breakfasts here are quite good. A new Cosmos has opened in Sainte-Foy.

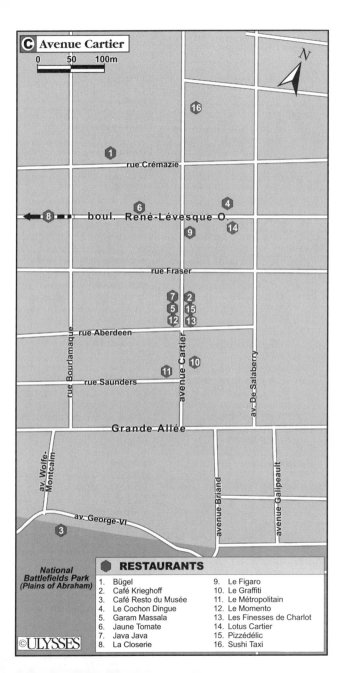

C **Avenue Cartier**

0   50   100m

N

rue Crémazie

boul. René-Lévesque O.

rue Fraser

rue Bourlamaque

rue Aberdeen

avenue Cartier

rue Saunders

av. De-Salaberry

Grande Allée

av. Wolfe-Montcalm

avenue Briand

avenue Galipeault

av. George-VI

National Battlefields Park (Plains of Abraham)

RESTAURANTS

1. Bügel	9.	Le Figaro
2. Café Krieghoff	10.	Le Graffiti
3. Café Resto du Musée	11.	Le Métropolitain
4. Le Cochon Dingue	12.	Le Momento
5. Garam Massala	13.	Les Finesses de Charlot
6. Jaune Tomate	14.	Lotus Cartier
7. Java Java	15.	Pizzédélic
8. La Closerie	16.	Sushi Taxi

©ULYSSES

Café Krieghoff
$$
1809 Avenue Cartier
☎521-3711
Named after the Dutch-born artist whose former home is located at the end of Avenue Cartier, Café Krieghoff occupies an old house on the same street. It serves tasty light meals (quiche, salads, etc.) and also has a good daily menu. The casual, convivial atmosphere is reminiscent of a Northern European café. During summer, its two outdoor seating areas are often packed.

Java Java
$$
1112 Avenue Cartier
☎522-5282
The subtle and original decor at Java Java creates a fun atmosphere. This is an excellent place to savour a light meal when you need a bite, or to merely wish to watch the world go by.

Lotus Cartier
$$
29 Boulevard René-Lévesque Ouest
☎649-9991
Here at Le Lotus Cartier, flavourful cuisine from Southeast Asia is served in a calm, pleasant atmosphere. The soups are particularly delicious.

La Piazzetta
$$
1191 Avenue Cartier
☎649-8896
(see p 241).

Pizzédélic
$$
1145 Avenue Cartier
☎525-5981
This is a pizza place with a colourful setting and a welcoming staff. At Pizzédélic you can taste the latest trend in pizza, as they prepare it in hundreds of different ways. You can even choose your own combination of ingredients. The clientele here is young and lively.

Le Cochon Dingue
$$
46 Boulevard René-Lévesque Ouest
☎523-2013
A pretty terrace in the back of this Boulevard René-Lévesque establishment is heated when the temperature is cool.

Le Figaro
$$-$$$
1019 Avenue Cartier
☎525-3535
A pleasant bistro located in a lovely spot on Avenue Cartier, Le Figaro offers delicious bistro-style cuisine. The decor is beautiful and the service courteous. In summer, people sit on the terrace to watch others and to be seen. Brunch is served on the weekends.

Jaune Tomate
$$-$$$
120 Boulevard René-Lévesque Ouest
☎ **523-8777**

This is a pretty yellow and red restaurant on Boulevard René-Lévesque near Avenue Cartier. It serves good Italian cuisine in a country-style decor. Come here on Saturday and Sunday mornings to sample the delicious and inventive brunches. The eggs benedictine with hollandaise sauce flavoured with a zest of orange or teriyaki will make your weekend mornings a delight.

Aux Vieux Canons
$$-$$$
650 Grande Allée Est
☎ **529-9461**

The terrace at Aux Vieux Canons is very lively during the summer season. Try the delicious wine-flavoured French cooking or the succulent, expertly flambéed dishes. The atmosphere is festive thanks to singers, dancers and musicians performing gypsy music.

Café-Restaurant du Musée
$$-$$$
same hours as the museum
1 Avenue Wolfe-Montcalm
☎ **644-6780**

Inside the Musée du Québec, you'll find the lovely Café-Restaurant du Musée. Run by a nearby hotel-management school,

the restaurant's top priority is offering well-prepared food and outstanding service. Guests can gaze out at the Plains of Abraham and the river through large windows; in summer, the same view can be enjoyed from the patio.

Le Momento
$$-$$$
1144 Avenue Cartier
☎ **647-1313**

Momento is decorated in modern fashion with warm colours and adorned with a fresco taken from a Boticelli painting. As you may have guessed, they serve refined, original Italian cuisine that is sure to offer some pleasant surprises. Prepared with basil, oregano, dried tomatoes, capers and olives, the sauces are rich, but not excessively, and they are quite savoury. The marinated salmon is perfectly prepared and will melt in your mouth.

Le Rivoli
$$$
601 Grande Allée Est
☎ **529-3071**

The Rivoli is an Italian trattoria with lots of charm. Its decor features stone walls and pink woodwork. You can enjoy the sun on the terrace during the summer months as you sample the pizza, which is served in hundreds of different ways, along with veal and pasta.

Restaurants

Le Bonaparte
$$$
680 Grande Allée Est
☎647-4747

Le Bonaparte is an excellent restaurant when it comes to French gourmet cooking. To add to the experience, why not participate in one of the "Murder Mystery" evenings where intrigue and suspense are part of the fun? The terrace overlooks Grande Allée, which is popular among the young fashionable crowd.

Garam Massala
$$$
1114 Avenue Cartier
☎522-4979

At Garam Massala you can savour curry, tandoori and other spicy dishes from the Indian menu. Though the restaurant has the disadvantage of being located in a basement, its decor is nonetheless attractive. Pleasant Indian music adds to the ambiance.

Le Louis-Hébert
$$$
668 Grande Allée Est
☎525-7812

An elegant restaurant with a plush decor, Le Louis-Hébert serves French cuisine and delectable seafood. There is a plant-filled solarium at the back. Courteous, attentive service.

Voo Doo Grill
$$$
575 Grande Allée Est
☎647-2000

This old house was once the social club of the Union Nationale, the political party of the unforgettable Maurice Duplessis. Thus the name of the nightclub, Maurice, occupying the building's two upper floors (see p 255) where you can end the evening after a copious meal. Located on the second floor, the restaurant has kept some of the building's original architectural features and displays a most ingenious decor. A collection of African art work featuring masks, sculptures and dolls among other things, creates an entrancing effect. Unfortunately the music is not African, but *djumbé* players occasionally perform in the evening, adding a bit of rhythm to the already lively atmosphere. The VooDoo Grill menu has grilled food, of course—meat, fish and fowl as well as dishes cooked in a wok and served on spicy rice or satay with choice of sauce. All are tasty, creatively prepared and beautifully presented. The kitchen is open late.

Le Métropolitain
$$$-$$$$
1188 Avenue Cartier
☎649-1096

Le Métropolitain is *the* place for sushi in Québec City. These delicious Japanese morsels are a real feast, prepared before your very eyes by expert hands behind the glass counter. Other Oriental specialties, including fish and seafood dishes, are available here as well. The restaurant used to be located in the basement of another building and had a big sign at the entrance similar to those adorning certain métro stops in Paris. Its new, two-storey quarters are brighter.

Le Paris-Brest
$$$-$$$$
590 Grande Allée Est, corner De La Chevrotière
☎529-2243

At the Paris Brest, French cuisine is the specialty. Prepared with care, the food here will satisfy the most demanding gourmets. In summer, the restaurant opens its small terrace which looks onto Grande Allée.

L'Astral
$$$-$$$$
Hotel Loews Le Concorde
1225 Place Montcalm
☎647-2222

A rotating restaurant located atop one of the city's largest hotels, L'Astral serves excellent French food and provides a stunning view of the river, the Plains of Abraham, the Laurentian mountains and the city. It takes about one hour for the restaurant to make a complete rotation. This is a particularly good place for Sunday brunch.

Le Graffiti
$$$-$$$$
1191 Rue Cartier
☎529-4949

Le Graffiti's old-fashioned decor, is distinguished by exposed beams and brick walls, creating a warm ambience, where you can savour excellent French cuisine.

La Maison du Steak
$$$-$$$$
641 Grande Allée Est
☎529-3020

La Maison du Steak is the most popular steakhouse in town. High quality food is served in a very cheerful atmosphere. In addition to the house specialty, French cuisine is also offered. There is a terrace.

La Closerie
$$$$
966 Boulevard René-Lévesque Ouest
☎687-9975

La Closerie serves fine French cuisine. The chef, who has a well-established reputation, creates meals from fresh, prime quality ingredients. The exterior of this townhouse, located at a distance from tourist

Restaurants

attractions, is no indication of what's inside—a gorgeous, intimate decor that guarantees pleasurable moments.

Tour D: Saint-Jean-Baptiste

See map page 119.

Dazibo Café
$-$$
Tue-Sat
526 Rue St-Jean
☎525-2405

Dazibo Café is very small but quite pleasant. It is painted in warm colours and offers Irish specialties in a friendly family atmosphere. The most popular item on the menu is *briks*, small rolls of crusty pastry garnished to order.

Chez Victor
$$
145 Rue St-Jean
☎529-7702

Located in a basement with a retro decor, Chez Victor serves salads and burgers—and not just any old burgers! The menu offers several different kinds (including a delicious veggie burger), all big, juicy and served with fresh toppings. The homemade fries are sublime! Cordial service.

Thang Long
$$
869 Côte d'Abraham
☎524-0572

Thang Long, located on Côte d'Abraham, is tiny, but its menu will transport you to Vietnam, Thailand, China and even Japan! The decor of this neighbourhood restaurant is simple and unpretentious; the cuisine is truly up to the mark, and the service, very attentive. Try one of the meal-size soups– comfort food at bargain prices!

Le Bonnet d'Âne
$$
298 Rue St-Jean
☎647-3031

The theme here is elementary school and the menu is as varied as the subjects after which the dishes are named. Hamburgers, pizza and light meals are served on big beautiful plates that will delight both young and old. The theme extends to the decor, which includes blackboards, school desks and old toys, as well as lovely wood trim. There is a pretty terrace in the summer.

Le Commensal
$$
860 Rue St-Jean
☎647-3733

The buffet style of Le Commensal has earned the public's affection over the years. Vegetarian dishes are the specialty here and are sold by weight. Strangely enough though, the plants are all artificial. However, this open space features a modern and tidy decor, which helps make it an enjoyable setting for a meal.

Le Hobbit
$$
700 Rue St-Jean
☎*647-2677*

Le Hobbit has occupied an old house in the Saint-Jean-Baptiste neighbourhood for years, and its stone walls, checkerboard floor and big windows overlooking bustling Rue St-Jean have not lost their appeal. There are two sections: the first is a café-style room where you can linger over an espresso and have a light meal; the second, a dining room with a delicious menu that changes daily and is never disappointing. Works by local artists are displayed here regularly.

La Piazzetta
$$
707 Rue St-Jean
☎*529-7489*

The layout of modern-looking Piazzetta is not really suitable for intimate dining. The restaurant is generally crowded but lively. An infinite variety of European-style pizzas is served. There are many franchises of this restaurant all over Québec; this one is the original,

located in a house on Rue St-Jean.

La Pointe des Amériques
$$
964 Rue St-Jean
☎*694-1199*

La Pointe des Amériques is located in the heart of lively Place d'Youville. This large restaurant is charming and attractively decorated, featuring gourmet pizza as its specialty. Let yourself be tempted by the many toppings inspired by cooking from around the world. If you are a small party, you can each choose a different kind of pizza and ask that they give a slice to everyone. You will certainly have a hard time deciding which is your favourite!
The ambiance is delightful.

La Campagne
$$-$$$
bring your own wine
555 Rue St-Jean
☎*525-5247*

La Campagne is located on the second floor of a house on Rue St-Jean, behind a large window filled with green plants. This establishment is well-known for its tasty, well-prepared Vietnamese dishes.

Restaurants

Les Épices du Széchouan
$$-$$$
215 Rue St-Jean
☎648-6440

For exotic cuisine with succulent flavours and enticing aromas, try Les Épices du Széchouan, which occupies an old house in the Saint-Jean-Baptiste quarter. Its pretty decor is enhanced by a thousand and one Chinese trinkets. One table with a banquette is nestled beneath a corbelled wall. The house is a little ways from the street, so be careful not to miss it!

Carthage
$$-$$$
399 Rue St-Jean
☎529-0576

Le Carthage is a superb restaurant decorated in typical North African style. The ceiling is finely-crafted and adorned with gilt. Mahogany-coloured woodwork is found everywhere, as well as a good number of Tunisian decorative objects. Here, a wonderful gastronomic experience awaits you. Seated on a cushion on the floor, a stool or simply at a table, you will be delighted by the Tunisian specialties. For example, couscous with vegetables and merguez (spicy sausages) or chicken are among the mouth-watering choices. Belly dancers are also occasionally on hand to liven up the celebrations.

La Grolla
$$-$$$
Tue-Sun
815 Côte d'Abraham
☎529-8107

La Grolla welcomes you with the cozy atmosphere of a Swiss chalet. Wood beams, dried flowers and even the traditional Swiss cuckoo clock are all part of the decor. Next to a lovely wood fire, enjoy the delicious *raclette*, fondue, *röstis* or buckwheat crepes served by waitresses who are experts in the art of putting you at ease. The apple cider is light and delicious, and although this is not specified on the menu, it is non-alcoholic.

La Playa
$$$
780 Rue St-Jean
☎522-3989

La Playa, a small restaurant with a beautiful, cozy decor, offers Californian cuisine and dishes from other sunny spots. Top billing on the menu goes to pasta, which is served with flavourful sauces. The restaurant also has a *table d'hôte* featuring delicious meat and fish dishes. During summer, guests can dine on a charming little patio.

Il Teatro
$$$
972 Rue St-Jean
☎*694-9996*

Il Theatro, located inside
the magnificent Théâtre
Capitole, serves excellent
Italian cuisine in a lovely
dining room with a long bar
and big, sparkling windows
all around. The courteous
service is on a par with the
delicious food. During
summer, guests can dine in
a small outdoor seating area
sheltered from the hustle
and bustle of Place
d'Youville.

Ciccio Café
$$$-$$$$
875 Rue Claire-Fontaine
☎*525-6161*

Ciccio Café is located on a
quiet street near the Grand
Théâtre de Québec. The
atmosphere is relaxed and
beautiful stone walls
enhance the decor.
Progressive French cuisine,
gourmet pizza and excellent
pasta are featured on the
menu.

Tour E: Chemin Sainte-Foy

Sainte-Foy

Mille-Feuilles
$$
1405 Chemin Ste-Foy
☎*681-4520*

Mille-Feuilles is a vegetarian
restaurant. They offer dishes
that are both healthy and
delicious, as well as
carefully prepared. Located
on a section of Chemin Ste-
Foy that has a few shops
and restaurants, its decor is
a bit cold, but the ambiance
is relaxed. They also have a
little bookstore that sells
health-related books.

Cosmos Café
2813 Boulevard Laurier
☎*692-2001*
See p 234.

Le Pailleur
$$$
3400 Chemin Sainte-Foy
☎*653-5221*

As Château Bonne-Entente's
dining room (see p 204),
Le Pailleur has just been
renovated to offer its
guests a higher level of
comfort. The decor is
attractive and beautiful
streams of light seep in
through large windows,
which overlook the
grounds and the swimming
pool. Well-prepared
gourmet Québec cuisine,

Restaurants

such as of rabbit, duck, deer and salmon is served here. On weekends there is also a large buffet brunch.

Le Bistango
$$$
1200 Avenue Germain-des-Prés
☎658-8780

Located in the Hôtel Germain-des-Prés complex (see p 204), Le Bistango combines *savoir-faire* and a casual ambiance. The good-sized dining room is decorated with taste and originality, and is very busy, both at lunch and dinner. Comfortably seated in a chair or booth, you can savour fine dishes prepared and served with care. The menu features such delicacies as fish filet, chicken breast, duck confit, a salad of Japanese-style shrimp and tuna, and the simple but delicious sirloin. This is a great spot if you find yourself in Sainte-Foy. On certain evenings, musicians liven up the atmosphere.

La Tanière
$$$$
2115 Rang St-Ange
☎872-4386

La Tanière specializes in wild game, as you might have guessed (*tanière* is a den or lair). Although located in Sainte-Foy, this restaurant is slightly off the tour, near the airport. Paradoxically housed in a bungalow, the restaurant

features a hunting-style decor, complete with stuffed trophies. Here you can experience tasty and delicious specialties from the forests of Québec.

La Fenouillère
$$$$
3100 Chemin St-Louis
☎653-3886

At La Fenouillère, the menu of refined and creative French cuisine promises a succulent dining experience. This restaurant also claim lays of one of the best wine cellars in Québec. The decor is simple and comfortable.

Tour F: Saint-Roch

See map page 131.

Humani'terre
$
Tue-Sat
281 Rue de la Couronne
☎529-3447

This small café, which is actively engaged in humanitarian causes, serves vegetarian dishes in a simple decor of wood furnishings and colourful tablecloths. But there is much more than meets the eye here: the place hosts conferences, workshops, concerts, and other events. It is the meeting place of neighbourhood social activists.

Tam Tam Café
$
Mon-Fri
421 Boulevard Langelier
☎*523-4810*

The Tam Tam Café is an interesting spot, adjoined to a youth community centre and serving as training grounds for those who wish to learn about the restaurant business. Here, you can enjoy tasty family-style dishes while supporting staff-in-training! The decor is quaint, occasionally featuring the works of young artists. The community centre provides various types of training to the young, as well as Internet access.

Café du Clocher Penché
$-$$
203 Rue St-Joseph Est
☎*640-0597*

In an old bank building in the Saint-Roch neighbourhood, across from the church with the leaning steeple, Café du Clocher Penché serves great little dishes prepared with a touch of originality. If you go for breakfast on the weekend, try the "Voleur de bicyclette" ("bicycle thief"—from the title of a movie)! Located on a street corner, it has several windows that make up for the austere high ceilings.

Les Salons d'Edgar
$-$$
Wed-Sun
263 Rue St-Vallier Est
☎*523-7811*

In the attractive Salons d'Edgar, which is also a bar (see p 257), the food is simple and hearty. European hot-dogs and beef bourguignon, among others, are flavourful and presented with a creative touch, such as a green salad topped with blueberries. The muffled atmosphere creates a slightly dramatic setting just right for relaxing and chatting.

La Part du Diable
$$
275 De St-Vallier Est
☎*522-3666*

Contrary to what its name might indicate (*diable* means "devil"), this place is not hot as hell, even though, come wintertime, a nice fire heats up diners, or rather, the atmosphere! You'll be tempted by their menu of pizza, sandwiches, beef and chicken dishes, and appetizers.

Le Sainte-Victoire
$$$-$$$$
380 Boulevard Charest Est
☎*525-5656*

A grand piano occupies centre stage at Le Sainte-Victoire, where a pianist plays jazz tunes on Friday and Saturday evenings. The bistro is decorated in red and gold and features

Restaurants

banquettes, woodwork and large windows. In the kitchen, is a young talented chef, Jean-François Girard. It seems he particularly enjoys concocting fish dishes, but his menu proves that he can do much more, as guinea fowl, lamb, duck, and horse create a lovely symphony of flavours.

Tour G: Limoilou

Le Maizerets
$$
2006 Chemin de la Canardière
☎661-3764

It is said that Le Maizerets serves "the best pizza west of Rome." Well, this is true! For a really delicious pizza with a thin spicy crust cooked in a wood oven, make sure to drop by here. There is also a terrace.

Tour I: Sillery to Cap-Rouge

Sillery

Buffet du Passant
$
Apr-Oct
1698 Côte de l'Église
☎681-6583

In Sillery, stop in at Buffet du Passant, located halfway down the steep Côte de l'Église. You may ask yourself why, since it appears to be just a

traditional snack bar serving hamburgers and french fries. But a little-known treasure lies hidden away at the back: from Rue des Voiliers, there is a superb view of the River and both its shores. A few picnic tables have been set up there so that you can eat lunch and enjoy the view.

Le Cochon Dingue
$$
1365 Avenue Maguire
☎683-8111
see p 228.

Brynd
$
1360 Rue Maguire
☎527-3844

Brynd is the place to go for smoked meat. There are also items on the menu for those who don't wish to try the house specialty. (Quite a shame!) The meat is smoked and sliced right in front of your eyes, in the authentic delicatessen tradition.

La Fougasse
$$
1648 Chemin St-Louis
☎682-6585

This small Italian restaurant is established in a house on Chemin St-Louis in Sillery and is worth the detour. In fact, La Fougasse offers an appealing menu of classical Italian cuisine at very reasonable prices. The decor is fashionable with long velvet drapes, and a clientele of regulars faithfully shows up for lunch, dinner and brunch on the weekend.

Pizza Mag
$$
465 Avenue Maguire, Sillery
☎**683-1561**
Like its sister establishment on Rue Saint-Paul (see p 228), this restaurant serves great pizza. Its facade is decorated with a bright, Mediterranean-inspired mural.

Le Montego
$$$
1460 Avenue Maguire
☎**688-7991**
The Montego restaurant-club promises a "sunny experience." The warmly decorated interior, large colourful plates and food presentation are indeed a pleasure. And the cooking will delight your tastebuds with sweet, hot and spicy flavours inspired by the cuisine of California and other sunny places.

Paparazzi
$$$
1363 Avenue Maguire
☎**683-8111**
Paparazzi serves Italian dishes. The salad with warm goat-cheese, spinach and caramelized walnuts is a true delight, as are other ménu items. The decor is modern and pleasant with pretty tables

covered in ceramic tiles set up on various levels.

Sainte-Foy

Le Galopin
$$$-$$$$
3135 Chemin St-Louis
☎**652-0991**
The Galopin dining room is in a Sainte-Foy hotel, near the bridges. It is very large and comfortable, and the quality gourmet cuisine is served in a pleasant manner.

Michelangelo
$$$-$$$$
3111 Chemin St-Louis
☎**651-6262**
Michelangelo serves fine Italian cuisine that both smells and tastes wonderful. The classically decorated dining room, although busy, remains warm and intimate. The courteous and attentive service adds to the pleasure.

Restaurants

| **Tour J: Heading North** | **Tour K: Côte-de-Beaupré and Île d'Orléans** |

Wendake

 Nek8arre
$$-$$$
9am-5pm
575 Rue Stanislas-Kosca
☎ *842-4308*
⇒ *842-3473*

In Onhoüa Chetek8e, the Huron-Wendat village (see p 157), a pleasant restaurant whose name means "the meal is ready to be served" will introduce you to traditional Huron-Wendat cooking. Wonderful dishes such as clay trout, caribou or venison *brochettes* with mushrooms accompanied by wild rice and corn, are some of the items on the menu. The wood tables are engraved with texts explaining the eating habits of Aboriginal cultures. Numerous objects scattered here and there will arouse your curiosity, and luckily, the waitresses act as part-time "ethnologists" and can answer your questions. All this can be enjoyed in a pleasant atmosphere. The entry fee to the village will be waived if you're only going to the restaurant.

Beauport

Manoir Montmorency
$$$
closed Jan
2490 Avenue Royale
☎ *663-3330*

Manoir Montmorency (see p 159) benefits from a superb location above the Montmorency Falls. From the dining room surrounded by bay windows, there's an absolutely magnificent view of the falls, the river and Île d'Orléans. Fine French cuisine, prepared with the best products in the region, is served in pleasant surroundings. A wonderful experience for both the view and the food! The entrance fee to the Parc de la Chute Montmorency (where the restaurant is located) and the parking fees are waived upon presentation of your receipt or by mentioning your reservation.

Château-Richer

Auberge Baker
$$$
8790 Avenue Royale
☎ *824-4852 or 824-4478*

The Auberge Baker (see p 208) has two dining

rooms. One has stone walls and a fireplace, while the other features a more somber decor. Both serve fine traditional Québecois cuisine: game, meat and fowl are well-prepared and presented with care.

Beaupré
(Mont Sainte-Anne)

La Camarine
$$$$
10947 Boulevard Sainte-Anne
☎*872-1858*
La Camarine (see p 210) has an excellent restaurant that serves Québec nouvelle cuisine. The dining room is peaceful with a simple decor. The innovative dishes are a feast for the senses. In the basement of the inn is another small restaurant, the Bistro, which offers the same menu and prices as upstairs, but is only open in the winter. Equipped with a fireplace, it is a cozy spot for *après-ski*. It is open in the evening for drinks.

Île d'Orléans

Café de mon Village
$$
May to mid-Oct
3963 Chemin Royal, Sainte-Famille
☎*829-3656*
Café de Mon Village offers a good *menu du jour* as well as bagels, croissants and

salads. The decor is simple and the staff friendly. In the summer, the terrace has a magnificent view of the river.

Le Vieux-Presbytère
$$$
1247 Avenue Mgr-d'Esgly, St-Pierre
☎*828-9723*
The Vieux-Presbytère (see p 211) specializes in unusual meat such as bison, wapiti and ostrich. This is because the next-door neighbour raises them! You may even be able to see the animals on the farm. The restaurant prepares these and other dishes in a most delectable manner. The attractive dining room of this historic building also offers a superb view of the river.

Le Moulin de Saint-Laurent
$$$-$$$$
May to mid-Oct
754 Chemin Royal, Saint-Laurent
☎*829-3888*
The Moulin de Saint-Laurent serves Québécois cuisine and is charmingly decorated with antiques. In the large dining room, which regularly receives groups, the chairs, wooden beams, stone walls and copper utensils hung here and there harmoniously complement this old building. The food is well presented and varied. On sunny days you can sit on the terrace which has a

Restaurants

view of the waterfalls beside the mill.

Auberge Canard Huppé
$$$-$$$$
2198 Chemin Royal, St-Laurent
☎828-2292

The dining room of the Auberge Canard Huppé (see p 211) serves fine regional cuisine. Prepared with fresh ingredients so abundant to the area, such as duck, trout and maple products, these little dishes will delight the most demanding palate. Although the room is somewhat dark (forest green being the predominant colour) the country decor is, on the whole, quite pleasant.

La Goéliche
$$$-$$$$
22 Chemin du Quai, Ste-Pétronille
☎828-2248

The dining room at La Goéliche has unfortunately lost its old-time splendour (see p 211), though it is still a pleasant spot offering one of the most beautiful views of Québec City. This restaurant serves fine French cuisine: stuffed quail, nuggets of lamb and saddle of hare.

Ententertainment

A s well as possessing undeniable charm, Québec City is a highly entertaining town.

Whether you are in the mood for cultural activities, festivals or simply bars and nightclubs, this unique place will not disappoint you.

In many Québec City shops, restaurants and bars, you will find three newspapers containing information on current cultural activities. **Québec Scope**, published every two weeks, is a small bilingual magazine that gives a brief overview of Québec City's main cultural events. The weekly **Voir** provides a few articles on current events as well as a listing of the main cultural activities. **Le Clap** is a magazine published by the movie theatre of the same name (see p 260). It features films reviews and articles on the movie industry. All three publications are free. Ask for them!

Bars and Nightclubs

All year long, the city's bars and nightclubs are filled with people from all walks of life. Whether it be the nightclubs on the young and dynamic Grande Allée, the coolest spots on Avenue Cartier or the few "underground" bars in the Saint-Jean-Baptiste and Vieux-Québec areas, there are countless places to choose from. Why not discover them all?

There is no cover charge at most bars and nightclubs in Québec City, except when they are hosting a special event or a show. During winter, most places require customers to check their coats, which costs a dollar or two.

Tour A: Vieux-Québec

L'Arlequin
1070 Rue Saint-Jean
☎654-9464
For the best in underground sounds, live or mixed by a DJ, visit L'Arlequin. Located upstairs in a house on Rue Saint-Jean, its fantastic decor and party atmosphere are sure to get your feet moving.

Le Chantauteuil
1001 Rue Saint-Jean
Le Chanteuteuil is a pleasant bistro at the foot of the hill on Rue d'Auteuil. People spend hours here chatting away, seated on benches around tables strewn with bottles of wine or beer.

Chez Son Père
24 Rue Saint-Stanislas, corner Saint-Jean
☎692-5308
This bar is one of the rare spots where you can listen to Québécois music. An air of nationalism prevails in this place… The decor is nothing special: a large hall with a small stage. *Chansonniers* regularly perform hit songs by Québécois singers such as Paul Piché, Beau Dommage, Michel Rivard and Robert Charlebois. The atmosphere is often festive and audience members show their enthusiasm by clapping their hands and tapping their feet.

L'Ostradamus
29 Rue Couillard
For a laid-back atmosphere, go to L'Ostradamus, a gathering place for non-conformists of all sorts. It is this peculiar ambiance that makes the place interesting. Unusual-sounding music also invites you to just have a good time!

L'Emprise
57 Rue Sainte-Anne
☎692-2480
The oldest hotel in the city (see Hôtel Clarendon p 196) houses L'Emprise. This elegant bar is recommended to jazz fans. There is a long *L*-shaped bar and, in the centre of the room, a magnificent black grand piano. While relaxing

comfortably in an armchair, you can listen to one of the informal shows that are frequently presented here. There is no cover charge.

Le Kashmir
1018 Rue Saint-Jean
☎694-1648

Upstairs in a Rue Saint-Jean building is Le Kashmir, a rock and roll bar which often features live entertainment. The dance floor and the shows generally draw a large crowd.

Frankie's
48-C Côte de la Fabrique

At Frankie's nightclub, musicians of various musical persuassions are regularly invited to play. Neither of its two floors, which are decorated in lovely tones of red and black, features an actual dance floor, but patrons can "get down and boogie" pretty much wherever they want.

Le Saint-Alexandre
1087 Rue Saint-Jean
☎694-0015

Le Saint-Alexandre is a typical English pub. The Scottish-green colour and stone walls blend perfectly with the mahogany wood panelling and furniture. At the back of the room is a beautiful black grand piano: unfortunately, it is seldom used. Here, great care is given to detail and authenticity. The impressive line-up of imported beers behind the bar is eye-catching and will give you a taste of the exotic. In fact, 200 varieties of beer are served, including about 20 on tap, their handles decorating the long bar. Good light meals are also served.

Le Sainte-Angèle
26 Rue Sainte-Angèle
☎692-2171

Tucked away in the basement of a building on Rue Saint-Angèle, the Sainte-Angèle looks like an English pub. It's decor is a bit worn, but the place is still comfortable. Though space is cramped, that does not stop local residents of all ages from packing in here. Regulars sit at the bar and chat with the bartender. Good selection of reasonably priced scotches and cocktails.

Les Yeux Bleus
1117 1/2 Rue Saint-Jean
☎694-9118

The *chansonniers* of Les Yeux Bleus take turns performing and give the bar a festive air. This place is not chic or exceptional, but it's fun nevertheless. This is the kind of place where friends meet for a drink or two, or perhaps three... The clientele, aged 25 to 35, is very lively. There is also a terrace.

Entertainment

Tour B:
Petit-Champlain to
Vieux-Port

L'Inox
37 Rue Saint-André
☎692-2877

A bistro-style brewery and the last bastion of the brewing tradition, L'Inox also has an economuseum (see p 101). The decor is original and the stainless steel central bar quite eye-catching. The clientele is young and varied. As well as serving beer, they have hot-dogs to satisfy growling stomachs. There are many different activities throughout the year so you should inquire; for example, it might be fun to attend a session of *peinture en direct* where artists paint and then auction the pictures, or take part in a CD launching.

Le Pape-Georges
8 Rue Cul-de-Sac
☎692-1320

Le Pape George is a pleasant wine bar. Beneath the vaults of an old house in Petit Champlain, guests can sample a wide variety of wines while nibbling on snacks like cheese and *charcuteries*. The atmosphere is warm, especially when there's a *chansonnier* to liven things up.

Taverne Belley
249 Rue Saint-Paul
☎692-4595

The Taverne Belley in front of the Marché du Vieux-Port, has a few typical tavern features such as a pool table and small, round, metal tables. The decor of its two rooms is both warm and fun with colourful paintings hanging on exposed brick walls. A tiny fireplace warms the air nicely in winter.

Pub Thomas Dunn
369 Rue Saint-Paul
☎692-4693

Pub Thomas Dunn is named after the Honourable Thomas Dunn, a provincial civil servant and politician for many years. At this typical English pub situated opposite the Gare du Palais you will find one of the best selections of beer in Québec City. The neat and tidy decor of mahogany and Scottish-green complement each other perfectly. The clientele is very mixed—from university graduates to workers of all kinds. The atmosphere is friendly and relaxed.

Le Troubadour
29 Rue Saint-Paul
☎694-9176

Located near Place Royale, Le Troubadour is nestled beneath a vaulted ceiling. This place is made entirely of stone, which, in addition to the long white candles placed in bottles on the wooden tables, makes you feel as if you've stepped back in time to the Middle Ages. During winter, a crackling fire helps banish the cold.

Tour C: Grande Allée

Le Dagobert
600 Grande Allée Est
☎522-0393
Better known as the Dag, Le Dagobert is one of the largest clubs in town. According to the regulars, it is the best nightclub for flirting… Taking up three floors of an old house, the Dag is actually very chic-looking, as is its clientele. The dance floor is quite large and a horseshoe-shaped mezzanine is ideal for those who prefer to watch rather than join the dancing crowd. Hanging above the crowd, a giant screen shows the latest rock videos. In the summer, the terrace is always packed. There are also shows upstairs.

Maurice
575 Grande Allée Est
☎640-0711
The Maurice nightclub resembles no other in town. The decor is so original that it is difficult to describe. There is red all over the place, and the avant-garde furniture is amazing. The large dance floor in the centre is lined with small bars. Here the doormen cleverly handpick the customers, who are always hip, beautiful and aged between 20 and 35. The atmosphere is quite unique. On the top floor, a cigar room called **Charlotte** features a similar style decor. This is a room with sofas that serves its purpose well, later on you can get up and jive on a dance floor where live shows are sometimes presented. Sunday is Latino day. Cover charge.

Jules et Jim
1060 Avenue Cartier
☎524-9570
Little Jules et Jim has graced Avenue Cartier for several years now. It has a smooth atmosphere with banquettes and low tables reminiscent of Paris in the 1920s.

Le Turf
1175 Avenue Cartier
On the lively Avenue Cartier, Le Turf (formerly known as the Merlin) is the place to be for the "beautiful" crowd (30 and over). In the basement, an English pub serves imported beer to the same type of clientele.

Pub Sherlock Holmes
1170 Rue d'Artigny
☎529-8271
Aside from its name, there is very little evidence that Pub Sherlock Holmes is an

Entertainment

English pub. The decor is unassuming and the music rather commercial without being dance music. The student customers take their minds off their studies by playing pool and darts. The atmosphere here is quite relaxed and easygoing.

Vogue
1170 Rue d'Artigny
☎529-9973

The Vogue is very popular, as its name indicates, with the 20 to 35 crowd. Attractively decorated and spread out on two floors, this club attracts the beautiful people. Following the beat of the infectious dance music, the frenzied crowd lets loose on the small dance floor. A modest terrace overlooks the Parc de la Francophonie and Grande Allée.

Tour D: Saint-Jean-Baptiste

L'Étrange
275 Rue Saint-Jean
☎522-6504

L'Étrange has been located upstairs in a house in the Saint-Jean-Baptiste neighbourhood for many years. Its specials and giant screen continue to attract the young and not-so-young. L'Étrange recently added another feather to its cap by providing Internet access to its customers.

Fou Bar
519 Rue Saint-Jean

The Fou Bar is an appealing place with a regular clientele who come here to drink, chat with friends or check out the current works of art on display.

Le Sacrilège
447 Rue Saint-Jean
☎649-1985

Sacrilège is a bar in the Saint-Jean-Baptiste neighbourhood with a lovely back terrace where you can just relax and get away from the hustle and bustle of the city.

Le Temps Partiel
698 Rue d'Aiguillon

For over a decade, the Fourmi Atomik club in Vieux-Québec was the haunt of a colourful, underground crowd. Forced to shut down in the summer of 2001, it more or less reopened under this new name in the Saint-Jean-Baptiste district. The co-op team that manages the bar is the same that used to run the Fourmi. The clientele has also been transplanted from the former nightclub, as has the music, which includes *black beat, punk rock,* alternative and 1980s techno, as well as the latest tunes.

Autumn's lovely colours surround Maison Chevalier,
which displays the same warm hues. - *Y. Tessier*

Québecers love bistros. In spring, when the warm weather returns, the terraces are irresistible. - *Y. Tessier*

Tour E: Chemin Sainte-Foy

Sainte-Foy

Le Cactus
814 Rue Myrand
☎527-9111
A little bit of Mexico in Québec City? Yes, it's possible! Located near the university, Le Cactus welcomes students who come for a drink and the spicy specialtes. There is a terrace.

Mundial
965 Route de l'Église
☎652-1170
Mundial has adopted a formula that's sure to please everyone. The ground floor has a small bar, ideal for quiet chats or for enjoying one of the shows that are regularly presented here. The upstairs is reserved for those who want to put on their dancing shoes. There is a lively ambiance on the dance floor where the latest hits can be heard. The clientele is rather young.

La Grimace
2376 Rue Galvani
☎527-3359
Located in Sainte-Foy, away from the tourist circuit, La Grimance attracts a clientele of regulars who enjoy evenings spent with a *chansonnier* who sings well-known Québecois tunes.

Tour F: Saint-Roch

Les Folies de Paris
Le Cabaret de Québec
252 Rue St-Joseph Est
☎523-4777 or 888-775-9977
This is a nightclub that offers dinner-shows to those seeking an impressive evening of entertainment. The kitchen is on the way to creating an enviable reputation for itself in this city.

La Barberie
310 Rue St-Roch
☎522-4373
www.labarberie.com
Set up in a slightly deserted neighbourhood, La Barberie was initially supposed to be just a brewery,. Now open to the public, it has been revamped and painted with warm colours for the occasion. The different beers offered at the counter, which are also available in various bars around the capital and surrounding area, are, for the most part, delicious. Their ales are fermented in oak barrels.

Les Salons d'Edgar
263 Rue Saint-Vallier Est
☎523-7811
Can't decide whether to eat something, have a drink with friends or play pool? Then go to Salons d'Edgar where all of these possibilities are offered. The beautiful decor, complete with screens and large

Entertainment

white draperies, will give you the slight feeling of being on stage. In a long narrow room at the back you'll find high ceilings, armchairs, pool tables, table hockey and, as in any self-respecting lounge, a fireplace. The music is well chosen and live entertainment is often featured.

Le Scanner
291 Rue Saint-Vallier Est
☎523-1916

Are you overcome by a desire to surf? No need to panic, Québec City has its fair share of Internet bars and cafés. Evocatively named, Le Scanner has two computers to help you out and a bar on two floors. Aside from the computers, there are table games such as pool and soccer as well as parlour games. And when Le Scanner presents a musical evening, it would be hard to imagine staying glued to the computer screen.

Le Bar à Vin
Tue-Sun
624 Rue Saint-Joseph

Located on the rejuvenated Rue Saint-Joseph, this friendly wine bar is simply ideal for savouring the nectar of the gods, either by the glass or the bottle. You can accompany your beverage with appetizers such as sandwiches and cheese plates.

Tour G: Limoilou

Bal du Lézard
1049 3e Avenue
☎529-3829

The Bal du Lézard is a small bar in the Limoilou neighbourhood with underground music and decor. In the summer, the Bal opens out onto a terrace with wooden floors overlooking the street. Shows are regularly presented here.

Gay and Lesbian Clubs

L'Amour Sorcier
789 Côte Sainte-Geneviève
☎523-3395

L'Amour Sorcier is a small bar in the Saint-Jean-Baptiste quarter. The atmosphere really heats up here sometimes. During summer, it features a pretty patio.

Zazou
811 Saint-Jean
☎524-4982

Zazou replaced the Ballon Rouge, an institution in the Saint-Jean-Baptiste district for many years. Zazou brings a breath of fresh air to the gay and lesbian scene, offering a warm ambiance and lively shows.

Le Drague
804 Rue St-Joachim
☎*649-7212*
This large gay nightclub has been completely renovated and today displays one of the most beautiful decors in Québec City. There is a spacious dance floor in the basement, and on Sunday evenings, drag queen shows are presented that create a wild atmosphere.

Cultural Events

The intensity of Québec City's cultural life varies from season to season but reaches its peak during the summer. However, you can enjoy discovering different facets of Québec culture all year long through the many shows, concerts and exhibitions that are presented. There are films from all over the world, concerts from here and abroad, exhibitions of all kinds and festivals for the public at large. To choose from the many possibilities, consult the region's daily newspapers, the magazines mentioned at the beginning of this chapter or the **Télégraphe de Québec Web site** *(www.telegraph.com)*.

Ticket prices vary from one place to another. Many venues also offer student discounts.

Outdoor Activities

In the summer many shows are presented in the city parks, whether it be the gardens of the Hôtel-de-Ville, the Parc de la Francophonie (behind the Parlement, see p 111) or Place d'Youville. They are all very lively, especially during the Festival d'Été International de Québec (Québec City International Summer Festival, see p 262). **L'Agora du Vieux-Port** *(84 Rue Dalhousie, ☎692-4672)* near the river and the **Pavillon de Musique Edwin-Bélanger** *(☎648-4071),* set up in the centre of the Plains of Abraham, also add to the excitement.

Music

The **Orchestre Symphonique de Québec**, the oldest in Canada, often performs at the Grand Théâtre de Québec *(269 Blvd. René-Lévesque E., ☎643-8131).*

Theatres

Le Périscope
2 Rue Crémazie Est
☎*529-2183*
This theatre presents experimental plays.

Entertainment

Théâtre de la Bordée
315 Rue Saint-Joseph Est
☎**694-9631**

Théâtre du Trident
Grand Théâtre de Québec
269, Boul. René-Lévesque Ouest
☎**643-8131**

Le Petit Théâtre de Québec
190 Rue Dorchester
☎**522-0321**

Concert Halls

Auditorium Joseph-Laverge
Bibliothèque Gabrielle-Roy
350 Rue Saint-Joseph Est
☎**529-0924**
All kinds of shows are
presented in this small
theatre.

Grand Théâtre de Québec
269 Boul. René-Lévesque Est
☎**643-8131**
See p 112.

Maison de la Chanson
68-78 Rue Du Petit-Champlain
☎**692-4744**
Excellent concerts are held
in this intimate hall.

Palais Montcalm
995 Place d'Youville
☎**691-2399**, *tickets* ☎**670-9011**
Concerts as well as thematic
exhibitions are presented
here.

Salle de l'Institut
42 Rue Saint-Stanislas
☎**691-6981**, *tickets* ☎**691-7411**

Capitole de Québec
Cabaret du Capitole
972 Rue Saint-Jean
☎**694-4444**
First inaugurated in 1903,
this theatre was restored in
1992. It is now one of the
most beautiful theatres in
Québec City.

Salle Albert-Rousseau
Cégep de Ste-Foy
2410 Ch. Ste-Foy, Ste-Foy
☎**659-6710**
Various shows are featured
here.

L'Autre Caserne
325 5ᵉ Rue
☎**691-7709**

Movie Theatres

Le Clap
Centre Innovation
2360 Chemin Sainte-Foy, Sainte-Foy
☎**650-2527**
Le Clap shows first-run and
repertory films. A program
is available (see p 251).

Cinéma Imax
5401 Boul. des Galeries, Galeries de la
Capitale
☎**627-8222**

Cinéma des Galeries de la
Capitale
5401 Boul. des Galeries
☎**628-2455**

Place Charest
500 Rue du Pont
☎**529-9745**

Spectator Sports

The Montréal Canadien's farm team, the **Citadelles**, shares the Colisée de Québec *(250 Boulevard Wilfrid-Hamel, ☎691-7211)* with the **Remparts** of the Major Junior League which always attracts hockey fans.

Right next door is the **Hippodrome du Québec** *(ExpoCité, 250 Boulevard Wilfrid-Hamel, ☎524-5283)* where fans can watch horse races.

The municipal stadium in Parc Victoria is the home of the **Capitales** baseball team.

Festivals

February

Carnaval de Québec *(☎626-3716 or 888-737-3789)*, Québec City's winter carnival, takes place annually during the first two weeks of February. It is an opportunity for visitors and residents of Québec City to celebrate the beauty of winter. It is also a good way to add a little life to a cold winter that often seems to never end. Various activities are organized. Some of the most popular include night-time parades, canoe races over the partially frozen St. Lawrence River as well as the international ice and snow sculpture contests on the Plains of Abraham and in front of the carved ice castle at Place du Parlement. This can be a bitterly cold period of the year, so dressing very warmly is essential.

During Carnaval (see above), the city hosts a number of sporting events, including the **Tournoi International de Hockey Pee-wee de Québec** *(☎524-3311)*.

June

The **Concours Hippique de Québec** *(☎647-2727)* (equestrian show-jumping) at the end of June is the preliminary for this sport's Coupe du Monde (World Cup). It takes place in the magnificent Parc des Champs-de-Bataille.

Entertainment

July and August

At the end of June, the **Coupe du Monde de Vélo de Montagne** (World Cup Mountain Bike Race) (☎827-1122) is held at Mont-Saint-Anne. Here you can watch top men and women professional racers compete.

Estival Juniart (☎691-6284) is the time to discover up-and-coming youths performing at shows and concerts in Vieux-Québec. This event takes place at the end of July.

The **Festival d'Été de Québec** (mid-Jul; ☎1-888-992-5200) is generally held for 10 days in early July when music, songs, dancing and other kinds of entertainment from all over the world liven up Québec City. The festival has everything it takes to be the city's most important cultural event. The outdoor shows are particularly popular. For most theatres' indoor shows, you must buy tickets. However, those presented outdoors are free.

In early August, Québec City celebrates the beginnings of the colonization period with the **Fêtes de la Nouvelle-France** (☎694-3311). People dress in period costume, a marketplace is recreated on Place Royale and many festive activities mark the occasion which lasts a few days.

Wednesday and Saturday evenings at the end of July and beginning of August, the Parc de la Chute-Montmorency comes to life with the **Grand Feux Loto-Québec** (☎523-3389 or 800-923-3389). The fireworks sparkle above the falls in a spectacular show, while on the river, passengers aboard a multitude of boats admire the display of colours.

Place du Parlement houses the **Plein Art** (late Jul or early Aug; every day 10am to 11pm; ☎694-0260) exhibit. All kinds of arts and crafts are displayed and sold.

People from the Québec City region have been enjoying themselves at **Expo-Québec** (Parc d'ExpoCité, ☎691-7110) every August for 50 years now. This huge fair, complete with an amuseument park, is held in front of the coliseum for about 10 days at the end of the month.

September

For movie buffs, the start of fall (end of August, early September) marks the beginning of the **Festival International du Film de Québec** (☎681-5720). This festival presents the best films from here and abroad.

October

In October, Québec City bars and theatres host musical entertainment and evenings of tales and legends during the **Festival International des Art Traditionnels** (☎647-1598).

Some institutions such as the Musée de la Civilisation and the Bibliothèque Gabrielle-Roy also present traditional crafts as part of the festival.

The **Festival de l'Oie des Neiges de Saint-Joachim** (*Cap Tourmente*, ☎827-3776) is the perfect opportunity to observe an impressive congregation of thousands of snow geese. They stop in the marshes and fields of Cap Tourmente (see p 177) before setting off on their long voyage south.

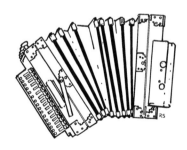

Shopping

Whether you are looking for Québec-made or imported goods, you will find everything your heart desires in Québec City's shops.

There are many shopping centres in the Québec City region. Here are a few: **Galeries de la Capitale** on Boulevard des Galeries; **Place Québec** on Avenue Dufferin (Tour D); **Promenades Sainte-Anne** at 10909 Boulevard Sainte-Anne (Tour K) that includes a few factory outlets. There are also three shopping centres on Boulevard Laurier in Sainte-Foy, namely **Place Laurier**, **Place Ste-Foy** and **Place de la Cité**.

Avenue Maguire is Sillery's most pleasant shopping street. You can make some interesting discoveries here.

In Sainte-Foy, the Laudance area has been set up to resemble a small European town. Brick dwellings with stores on the ground floor, an urban park and a finely designed marketplace are grouped together along **Rue Campanile**. Adorned with a clock tower, the covered market is a long and narrow passageway with stalls on both sides.

Here are a few shops where some wonderful treasures await you.

Antiques

If you are an antique lover, you should not miss attractive **Rue Saint-Paul**. In fact, the street is known for its many antique and second-hand shops that offer great discoveries.

Then, there is **Machins Chouettes** *(835 Rue Turnbull,* ☎*525-9898)* whose wonderful name (thingamabobs) is a perfect description.

Art Galleries

As a city admired by artists, Québec City offers numerous art galleries exhibiting works from many periods and schools. There are also half a dozen galleries scattered around Île d'Orléans and several in the village of Saint-Jean. Here are some Québec City addresses:

Beauchamp & Beauchamp
10 Rue Sault-au-Matelot
☎*694-2244*

Galerie Estampe Plus
49 Rue Saint-Pierre
☎*694-1303*

Galerie d'Art Linda Verge
1049 Avenue des Érables
☎*525-8393*

Galerie d'Art Madeleine Lacerte
1 Côte Dinan
☎*692-1566*

Galerie d'Art Royale
53 Rue Saint-Pierre
☎*692-2244*

Le Chien D'Or
8 Rue du Fort
☎*694-9949*

Engramme
501 Rue De Saint-Vallier Est
☎*529-0972*

Bookstores

Québec City has many bookstores to offer, but the ones listed here sell English books or books on specific topics such as art. The Saint-Jean-Baptiste neighbourhood abounds in used bookshops, although the books are mainly in French. At the following addresses you will also receive good tips.

Librairie du Musée du Québec
Parc des Champs-de-Bataille
☎*643-0529*
Beautiful books on art.

La Maison Anglaise
Place de la Cité, Sainte-Foy
☎*654-9523*
The best selection of English books in Québec City.

CDs and Cassettes

Here are two good places to buy discs and tapes. They both sell all kinds of music and will advise you on the latest releases.

Sillons Le Disquaire
1149 Avenue Cartier
☎ *524-8352*

Archambault Musique
1095 Rue Saint-Jean, Vieux-Québec
☎ *694-2088*

Clothing

Ladieswear

Atelier La Pomme, **Les Vêteries**, see "Crafts Shops and Artisans' Studios."

La Cache
1150 Rue Saint-Jean
☎ *692-0398*
La Cache is a Canadian chain of quality clothing. The clothes are made from beautiful rich-coloured fabrics with unusual designs inspired by the nature and culture of India where they are handmade. There are also attractive objects for the house as well as bed coverings made of the same attractive fabrics.

Chez Boomer
970 Avenue Cartier
☎ *523-7047*

Chez Boomer is filled with comfortable and well-made clothes for men, women and children, as well as accessories.

L'Exile
714 Rue Saint-Jean
☎ *524-4752*
L'Exile is a charming shop selling carefully selected quality clothing, and fine jewellery.

O'Clan
52 Boulevard Champlain
☎ *692-1214*
If you enter O'Clan by Boulevard Champlain, you will find well-made clothes in the latest fashions. The men's department is upstairs and can be accessed via Rue Petit-Champlain (see "Men's Clothing," see below).

Simons
20 Côte de la Fabrique
☎ *692-3630*
Place Sainte-Foy
Galeries de la Capitale
Simons stores have existed since 1840 and are a part of Québec City tradition. In Québec City homes during the holidays, the Christmas trees are often piled high with Simons' characteristic green boxes. All three stores provide everything to dress men, women and children from head to toe and in several different styles. Clothing accessories and bed linens are also sold.

Shopping

Paris Cartier
1180 Avenue Cartier
☎529-6083
This shop offers lovely
women's clothing.

In a small area of Boulevard
René-Lévesque, between
Rue Turnbull and Rue
Salaberry, there are several
Québec designer boutiques
selling exclusive creations
for women.

In the old town, along Rue
Saint-Jean, you will find the
large popular chains selling
fashionable clothing such as
Bedo, Gap, Jacob, Le
Château, Roots and San
Francisco.

Men's Clothing

Chez Boomer, see above.

Louis Laflamme
1192 Rue Saint-Jean
☎692-3774
Louis Laflamme features
two floors of chic clothing
for men.

O'Clan
67 1/2 Rue du Petit-Champlain
☎692-1214
If you enter O'Clan by the
Rue Petit-Champlain
entrance, you will find
great-looking, well-made
clothes for men. Women's
clothes are downstairs.

Simons, see above.

In the old town, the large
popular chain stores selling
fashionable clothing such as
America, Bedo, Gap, Le
Château and Roots are
located on Rue Saint-Jean.

Furriers

Laliberté JB
595 Charest Est
☎525-4841
In the Mail Centre-Ville, the
Laliberté JB department
store sells a variety of fur
coats as well as coats for
every season.

Shoes and Hats

In the old town, large
Canadian shoe-store chains
such as Aldo, Pegabo and
Nero Bianco are found
along Rue Saint-Jean.

For all kinds of hats visit
Bibi et Compagnie *(40 Rue
Garneau,* ☎*694-0045).*

Jewellery

Lazuli, see "Crafts Shops and
Artisans' Studios."

Origines
54 Côte de la Fabrique
☎694-9257
The small shop Origines
mainly sells jewellery. The
pieces may be simple or
elaborate, but they are all
very original and elegant.

For original creations by experienced jewellers: **Louis Perrier** *(48 Rue du Petit-Champlain, ☎692-4633)* or **Pierre Vives** *(23 1/2 Rue du Petit-Champlain, ☎692-5566)*.

Craft Shops and Artisans' Studios

Abaca
38 Rue Garneau
☎*694-9761*
Hidden away on little Rue Garneau, Abaca abounds with beautiful objects from Africa and Asia.

Aux Multiples Collections
69 Rue Sainte-Anne
☎*692-4298*
43 Rue de Buade
Aux Multiples Collections specializes in Inuit art. Handsome serpentine sculptures depicting daily life in the Far North, as well as other handmade objects fill these two attractive shops.

Inuit carving

Atelier La Pomme
47 Rue Sous-le-Fort
☎*692-2875*
Atelier La Pomme makes leather goods and clothes, and is one of Petit-Champlain's oldest workshops. The various

different kinds and colours of leather accentuate the originality and quality of the clothing. Some of the items you will find here include: coats, skirts, hats and even mittens.

Boutique du Musée de la Civilisation
85 Rue Dalhousie
☎*643-2158*
This small shop within the Musée de la Civilisation sells beautiful handcrafted objects from around the world. There are truly great finds to be made here in all price ranges.

Boutique du Musée du Québec
Parc des Champs-de-Bataille
☎*644-1036*
The Musée du Québec gift shop also features a lovely collection of objects and reproductions.

Cinq Nations
20 Rue Cul-de-Sac
25 1/2 Rue du Petit-Champlain
At Cinq Nations, an Aboriginal art gallery, you can admire and purchase crafts made by First Nations peoples. There is also some superb jewellery.

Corporation des Artisans de l'Isle d'Orléans
1249 Chemin Royal
☎828-9824
On Île d'Orléans you will find a few crafts and antique shops, as well as woodworking studios. Behind Église de Saint-Pierre, you can also find the Corporation des Artisans de l'île.

Still in Saint-Pierre, the **Boutique Hang'Art** *(751 Chemin Royal,* ☎*828-2519)* is also an *Économusée* of rugs presenting an assortment of woven coverings. In Saint-Jean, in the old presbytery in front of the church facing the river, **Les Échoueries** *(2001 Chemin Royal)* displays a great many objects made by skilled craftspeople.

Forge à Pique-Assaut
2200 Chemin Royal, Saint-Laurent
☎828-9300
On Île d'Orléans, the Forge à Pique-Assaut is a tiny economuseum that introduces visitors to the blacksmith's art and presents various wrought iron objects such as chandeliers, furniture and curios. There are also other kinds of handicrafts.

Galerie-Boutique Métiers d'Art
29 Rue Notre-Dame
☎694-0267
Galerie-Boutique Métiers d'Art brings together a whole range of articles made by Québec craftspeople. Located in a beautiful building on Place Royale, the gallery overflows with a variety of wonderful items that include clothing, ceramics and jewellery.

La Corriveau
24 Côte de la Fabrique
☎694-0062
La Corriveau is a large crafts shop. With three floors to peruse, you will find anything and everything you might want as a souvenir of Québec City.

Lazuli
774 Rue Saint-Jean
☎525-6528
Lazuli, an attractive shop, sells crafts from around the world. Silver, wood and ceramic objects of exceptional quality are finely made for those who can appreciate them.

Les Trois Colombes
46 Rue Saint-Louis
☎694-1114
Les Trois Colombes on Rue Saint-Louis sells crafts as well as quality clothing. Among the items are beautiful handmade wool coats.

L'Oiseau du Paradis
80 Rue du Petit-Champlain
☎692-2679
A pretty Petit-Champlain shop, L'Oiseau du Paradis sells all kinds of paper goods as well as handmade

paper from Québec
workshops.

Pot-en-ciel
27 Rue du Petit-Champlain
☎*692-1743*
Behind its large windows,
Pot-en-ciel exhibits all sorts
of curios that come in a
rainbow of colours,
especially the ceramics.

Le Sachem
17 Rue Desjardins
☎*692-3056*
Sachem is situated in the
Antoine-Vanfelson historic
house (see p 75). Its two
rooms are filled with
Aboriginal art objects and
crafts. They also sell
greeting cards, postcards
and attractive T-shirts.

La Soierie Huo
91 Rue du Petit-Champlain
☎*692-5920*
At La Soierie Huo you can
purchase lovely silk scarves
with designs that are as
varied as they are colourful.
You may also get the
chance to see Dominique
Huot as she creates them,
paintbrush in hand.

Transparence
193 Rue St-Jean
☎*692-3477*
Transparence is a small,
aptly named store that sells
glass objects, mostly made
by craftspeople. Stop by
and admire these beautiful
objects which reflect the
coloured light of the various
tints of glass.

Verrerie La Mailloche
58 Rue Sous-le-Fort
☎*694-0445*
Verrerie La Mailloche (see
p 90) sells blown-glass
objects made in the
workshop such as bottles,
vases and dishes of all
shapes and colours.

Les Vêteries
31 1/2 Rue Du Petit-Champlain
☎*694-1215*
At Vêteries you will find
hand-woven clothing from
a regional weaving studio.
The clothes are classical in
their colours and cut, but
are nonetheless quite
original.

Decorative Objects

La Cache, see above under
Women's Clothing.

La Dentellière
56 Boulevard Champlain
☎*692-2807*
La Dentellière sells lace,
lace and more lace! For
romantics only.

Simons, see above listed
under "Ladieswear."

Zone
999 Avenue Cartier
☎*522-7373*
Behind its large windows,
Zone, much like its
Montréal shops, overflows
with objects for the house.
You will find all sorts of
items like funny lemon
squeezers, casserole dishes

Shopping

or picnic baskets that will make your life easier or simply more pleasant.

Food

Chez Nourcy
131 Avenue Cartier
☎523-4772
Chez Nourcy is a gourmet food store that has been around for a long time, with two locations—one in Sillery and another in Québec City. The bread, cakes, cheese, sorbets and so on are positively mouth-watering. There are also Lebanese dishes and a selection of salads.

Le CRAC and **La Carotte Joyeuse** *(690 Rue Saint-Jean, ☎647-6881)* are two adjoining shops where you will find a whole range of health food including organically grown fruit and vegetables.

Délicatesse Tonkinoise
732 Rue Saint-Jean
☎523-6211
The small Délicatesse Tonkinoise sells Asian products to use when preparing exotic dishes, as well as delicious food for take-out.

Épicerie Européenne
560 Rue Saint-Jean
☎529-4847
Épicerie Européenne sells European gourmet products, particularly from

Italy where the shopowners came from. In French or Italian, they will kindly offer you judicious advice. If you like blue cheese, you must taste their Stilton with port.

Épicerie Méditerranéenne
64 Boulevard René-Lévesque
☎529-9235
Épicerie Méditerranéenne is a chic specialty grocery store adorned with granite, a tiled floor and glass counters. All sorts of tempting dishes are offered from different Mediterranean countries. Products in this store can also be found in a large store in the Saint-Roch neighbourhood *(85 Rue Saint-Vallier Est)* where bread is baked daily on the premises.

Épicerie J.-A.-Moisan
699 Rue Saint-Jean
☎522-8368
What a pleasure it is to shop at J.-A.-Moisan (see p 122). This old grocery store carries all kinds of fresh products such as fruit, vegetables, seafood, spices, bread and delicious cheeses. This gourmet shop also has a few tables where you can enjoy a snack and a counter where delicious sushi is prepared before your eyes.

For fresh fruit and vegetables in the summer, go to the **Marché du Vieux-Port** (see p 103) or **Marché**

de la Place in Sainte-Foy *(Rue de la Place, near Route de l'Église and Boulevard Hochelage)*. Every day farmers from the region bring their flavourful fresh products here for sale. On Sunday in Sainte-Foy, the market also houses a flea market that's sure to please anyone looking for a bargain.

Pâtes à Tout
42 Boulevard René-Lévesque
☎ *529-8999*
For fresh pasta and tasty sauces, Pâtes à Tout is the one to go to. They also sell take-out meals and homemade bread.

Poissonnerie Jean-Pierre
951 Avenue Cartier
☎ *525-5067*
Poissonnerie Jean-Pierre used to belong to a seasoned connoisseur from Îles-de-la-Madeleine. Today it still carries all kinds of fresh fish and seafood.

Take advantage of your visit to Île d'Orléans to sample its many goodies. There are market gardeners who sell their produce at road-side stands in the summer, sugar shacks in the spring, as well as small, diverse shops scattered around the island. For example: **Chocolaterie de l'Île d'Orléans** *(150 Chemin Royal, Ste-Pétronille, ☎828-2252)* makes, great little homemade sweets during the summer; **Ferme Mona**

(723 Chemin Royal, St-Pierre) concocts delicious liqueurs and crème de cassis (blackcurrent liqueur); and **La Boulange** *(2001 Chemin Royal, ☎829-3162)*, located in the Saint-Jean presbytery, prepares wonderful bread.

Paingruël
Tue-Sat
375-B Rue Saint-Jean
☎ *522-7246*
Paingruël, which has only been in operation for a few years, is already one of the favourite bakeries of Québec City residents, so much so that the store had to be expanded to keep up with the demand. The bakery is constantly filled with the aroma of freshly baked: bread, brioches and pastries which are created with skill and originality.

Halles du Petit-Quartier
1191 Rue Cartier
Halles du Petit-Quartier offers some of the finer things in life: a charcuterie, a bakery, a fruit store, a butcher shop, a fish shop, a pastry shop, and more. An ideal place to plan a great meal or a fun picnic!

SAQ Signature
1 Rue des Carrières
☎ *692-1182*
Housed in the Château Frontenac, this branch of the Société des Alcools du Québec specializes in liqueurs and spirits.

Shopping

Incredibly chic, it offers a great selection.

Sweets

When the weather is warm, Québécois are very fond of ice cream, frozen yogurt and sorbet. You have only to stroll along Avenue Cartier and spot the many ice cream shops to discover this is true. This short thoroughfare has at least half a dozen places that sell these tempting treats.

Arnold
1190-A Avenue Cartier
☎ 522-6053
On Avenue Cartier, Arnold announces its "*chocolats cochons*" (chocolate pigs) on a sign featuring a pig. Not only the chocolates, but also the ice cream (the fresh strawberry flavour is irresistible) will tempt you to eat more and more, just like a pig!

Érico
634 Rue Saint-Jean
☎ 524-2122
Rue Saint-Jean harbours a treasure trove for chocolate enthusiasts. Érico is a small establishment that makes these delights from the best products available, including cocoa, vanilla, caramel, hazelnuts, and much more. In the summer, Érico also sells rich homemade ice cream and sorbet. Even if you don't

have a sweet tooth, take the time to stop by, because its window design is always creative and amusing: it is made entirely of chocolate!

Au Palais d'Or
60 Rue Garneau
☎ 692-2488
The pastry shop Au Palais d'Or sells rich pastries made with real butter and cream. Absolutely delicious.

Le Panetier
764 Rue Saint-Jean
☎ 522-3022
Le Panetier makes great bread, delicious cakes and real croissants baked to perfection.

Tutto Gelato
716 Rue St-Jean
closed in winter
On Rue Saint-Jean, Tutto Gelato serves ice cream prepared from traditional Italian recipes. The result is absolutely divine! This is a definite must for ice cream lovers.

Newspapers and Tobacco

For all kinds of cigars, cigarettes and cigarillos, visit the store at the corner of Rue Crémazie and Avenue Cartier, **Tabac Tremblay** (*955 Avenue Cartier* ☎ *529-3910*), or opposite the Cathedral, **J.E. Giguère** (*59 Rue de Buade, ☎ 692-*

2296). Local newspapers are also sold there.

For magazines and newspapers from around the world, drop by either **Maison de la Presse Internationale** *(1050 Rue Saint-Jean)* or **Au Coin du Monde** *(1150 Avenue Cartier)*.

Outdoor Clothing and Equipment

L'Aventurier
710 Rue Bouvier
☎ *624-9088*
L'Aventurier is a little far from the Haute-Ville, but here you will find outdoor specialists to help you select the right equipment especially if you are interested in water sports. Kayaks, tents, clothing, hiking boots and other equipment are sold here.

Azimut
1194 Avenue Cartier
☎ *648-9500*
Azimut sells quality tents, sleeping bags, backpacks, hiking boots… everything for Québec's great outdoors.

Course à Pied
25A Rue Marie-de-L'Incarnation
☎ *688-7788*
Course à Pied is the shoe store to visit if you want comfortable footwear, no matter what your activity or sport. Clothing and accessories are also sold.

DLX/Deluxe
2480 Chemin Ste-Foy
Ste-Foy
☎ *653-0783*
This is where to buy or rent equipment such as a snowboard, a skate board, or a BMX. There are also well-known brands of clothing and shoes. This is the place in Québec City for fans of extreme sports!

Latulippe
637 Rue Saint-Vallier Ouest
☎ *529-0024*
Latulippe is a store popular with workers who need to be well-equipped as well as outdoor enthusiasts. All sorts of articles are sold at reasonable prices.

Les Fous du Plein Air
15 Rue De St-Vallier Est
☎ *522-1333*
This charming shop offers outdoor equipment for sale or rental.

Tourisme Jeunesse
94 Boulevard René-Lévesque Ouest
☎ *522-2552*
Tourisme Jeunesse lives up to its name. It sells everything from airline tickets to backpacks to guide books for young and not-so-young adventurers who want to explore the world.

Shopping

Stationery

Papeterie du Faubourg
545 Rue Saint-Jean
☎525-5377
The Papeterie du Faubourg
sells paper and greeting
cards, and provides a
photocopy and fax service.

Les Petits Papiers
1170 Avenue Cartier
☎524-3860
Les Petits Papiers has
greeting cards, writing
paper, notebooks and
wrapping paper, among
other items.

Miscellaneous

Animalerie Boutique Tropicale
1028 Avenue Cartier
☎522-6744
If you're travelling with
Buddy the dog or Fluffy the
cat, you will certainly
appreciate the following
address: Animalerie
Boutique Tropicale.

Excalibur
1055 Rue Saint-Jean
☎692-5959
Obviously, it is rare
nowadays that you would

need to shop for a sword or
a chain mail. However, if
you are a Medieval history
buff or just curious, you will
enjoy visiting Excalibur.

L'Attitude
71 Rue Crémazie Ouest
☎522-0106
If being on vacation is not
enough to relieve your
stress, drop by the boutique
in the L'Attitude Relaxation
and Massotherapy Centre.
Here you will find many
things to help you unwind,
including essential oils,
candles, discs, tapes and
books. You can also take
this opportunity to enjoy a
relaxing therapeutic
massage.

Musée de l'Abeille
8862 Boulevard Sainte-Anne,
Château-Richer
☎824-4411
Adjoining the Musée de
l'Abeille (bee museum) (see
p 161) is a small shop
selling a host of objects
related to bees, such as
beauty products made from
honey, mead and, of
course, honey. There's also
a pastry shop offering
delicacies that are made
with honey instead of
sugar.

Glossary

GREETINGS

Hi (casual)	*Salut*
How are you?	*Comment ça va?*
I'm fine	*Ça va bien*
Hello (during the day)	*Bonjour*
Good evening/night	*Bonsoir*
Goodbye, See you later	*Bonjour, Au revoir, à la prochaine*
Yes	*Oui*
No	*Non*
Maybe	*Peut-être*
Please	*S'il vous plaît*
Thank you	*Merci*
You're welcome	*De rien, Bienvenue*
Excuse me	*Excusez-moi*
I am a tourist.	*Je suis touriste*
I am American (m/f)	*Je suis Américain(e)*
I am Canadian (m/f)	*Je suis Canadien(ne)*
I am British	*Je suis Britannique*
I am German (m/f)	*Je suis Allemand(e)*
I am Italian	*Je suis Italien(ne)*
·I am Belgian	*Je suis Belge*
I am Swiss	*Je suis Suisse*
I am sorry, I don't speak French	*Je suis désolé(e), je ne parle pas français*
Do you speak English?	*Parlez-vous anglais ?*
Slower, please.	*Plus lentement, s'il vous plaît.*
What is your name?	*Quel est votre nom?*
My name is...	*Je m'appelle...*
spouse (m/f)	*époux(se)*
brother, sister	*frère, soeur*
friend (m/f)	*ami(e)*
son, boy	*garçon*
daughter, girl	*fille*
father	*père*
mother	*mère*
single (m/f)	*celibataire*
married (m/f)	*marié(e)*
divorced (m/f)	*divorcé(e)*
widower/widow	*veuf(ve)*

DIRECTIONS

Is there a tourism office near here?	*Est-ce qu'il y a un bureau de tourisme près d'ici?*

There is no...	*Il n'y a pas de...,*
Where is...?	*Où est le/la ... ?*
straight ahead	*tout droit*
to the right	*à droite*
to the left	*à gauche*
beside	*à côté de*
near	*près de*
here	*ici*
there, over there	*là, là-bas*
into, inside	*à l'intérieur*
outside	*à l'extérieur*
far from	*loin de*
between	*entre*
in front of	*devant*
behind	*derrière*

GETTING AROUND

airport	*aéroport*
on time	*à l'heure*
late	*en retard*
cancelled	*annulé*
plane	*l'avion*
car	*la voiture*
train	*le train*
boat	*le bateau*
bicycle	*la bicyclette, le vélo*
bus	*l'autobus*
train station	*la gare*
bus stop	*un arrêt d'autobus*
The bus stop, please	*l'arrêt, s'il vous plaît*
street	*rue*
avenue	*avenue*
road	*route, chemin*
highway	*autoroute*
rural route	*rang*
path, trail	*sentier*
corner	*coin*
neighbourhood	*quartier*
square	*place*
tourist office	*bureau de tourisme*
bridge	*pont*
building	*immeuble*
safe	*sécuritaire*
fast	*rapide*
baggage	*bagages*
schedule	*horaire*
one way ticket	*aller simple*

return ticket	*aller retour*
arrival	*arrivée*
return	*retour*
departure	*départ*
north	*nord*
south	*sud*
east	*est*
west	*ouest*

CARS

for rent	*à louer*
a stop	*un arrêt*
highway	*autoroute*
danger, be careful	*attention*
no passing	*défense de doubler*
no parking	*stationnement interdit*
no exit	*impasse*
stop! (an order)	*arrêtez!*
parking	*stationnement*
pedestrians	*piétons*
gas	*essence*
slow down	*ralentir*
traffic light	*feu de circulation*
service station	*station-service*
speed limit	*limite de vitesse*

MONEY

bank	*banque*
credit union	*caisse populaire*
exchange	*change*
money	*argent*
I don't have any money	*je n'ai pas d'argent*
credit card	*carte de crédit*
traveller's cheques	*chèques de voyage*
The bill please	*l'addition, s'il vous plaît*
receipt	*reçu*

ACCOMMODATION

inn	*auberge*
youth hostel	*auberge de jeunesse*
bed and breakfast	*gîte*
hot water	*eau chaude*
air conditioning	*climatisation*
accommodation	*logement, hébergement*
elevator	*ascenseur*
bathroom	*toilettes, salle de bain*
bed	*lit*

breakfast	*petit déjeuner*
manager, owner	*gérant, propriétaire*
bedroom	*chambre*
pool	*piscine*
floor (first, second...)	*étage*
main floor	*rez-de-chaussée*
high season	*haute saison*
off season	*basse saison*
fan	*ventilateur*

SHOPPING

open	*ouvert(e)*
closed	*fermé(e)*
How much is this?	*C'est combien?*
I would like...	*Je voudrais...*
I need...	*J'ai besoin de...*
a store	*un magasin*
a department store	*un magasin à rayons*
the market	*le marché*
salesperson (m/f)	*vendeur(se)*
the customer (m/f)	*le / la client(e)*
to buy	*acheter*
to sell	*vendre*
t-shirt	*un t-shirt*
skirt	*une jupe*
shirt	*une chemise*
jeans	*un jeans*
pants	*des pantalons*
jacket	*un blouson*
blouse	*une blouse*
shoes	*des souliers*
sandals	*des sandales*
hat	*un chapeau*
eyeglasses	*des lunettes*
handbag	*un sac*
gifts	*cadeaux*
local crafts	*artisanat local*
sun protection products	*crèmes solaires*
cosmetics and perfumes	*cosmétiques et parfums*
camera	*appareil photo*
photographic film	*pellicule*
records, cassettes	*disques, cassettes*
newspapers	*journaux*
magazines	*revues, magazines*
batteries	*piles*
watches	*montres*
jewellery	*bijouterie*

gold	or
silver	argent
precious stones	pierres précieuses
fabric	tissu
wool	laine
cotton	coton
leather	cuir

MISCELLANEOUS

new	nouveau
old	vieux
expensive	cher, dispendieux
inexpensive	pas cher
pretty	joli
beautiful	beau
ugly	laid(e)
big, tall (person)	grand(e)
small, short (person)	petit(e)
short (length)	court(e)
low	bas(se)
wide	large
narrow	étroit(e)
dark	foncé
light (colour)	clair
fat (person)	gros(se)
slim, skinny (person)	mince
a little	peu
a lot	beaucoup
something	quelque chose
nothing	rien
good	bon
bad	mauvais
more	plus
less	moins
do not touch	ne pas toucher
quickly	vite
slowly	lentement
big	grand
small	petit
hot	chaud
cold	froid
I am ill	je suis malade
pharmacy, drugstore	pharmacie
I am hungry	j'ai faim
I am thirsty	j'ai soif
What is this?	Qu'est-ce que c'est?
Where?	Où?

fixed price menu   *table d'hôte*
order courses separately *à la carte*

WEATHER
rain   *pluie*
clouds   *nuages*
sun   *soleil*
It is hot out *Il fait chaud*
It is cold out *Il fait froid*

TIME
When?   *Quand?*
What time is it?   *Quelle heure est-il?*
minute   *minute*
hour   *heure*
day   *jour*
week   *semaine*
month   *mois*
year   *année*
yesterday   *hier*
today   *aujourd'hui*
tommorrow   *demain*
morning   *le matin*
afternoon   *l'après-midi*
evening   *le soir*
night   *la nuit*
now   *maintenant*
never   *jamais*
Sunday   *dimanche*
Monday   *lundi*
Tuesday   *mardi*
Wednesday   *mercredi*
Thursday   *jeudi*
Friday   *vendredi*
Saturday   *samedi*
January   *janvier*
February   *février*
March   *mars*
April   *avril*
May   *mai*
June   *juin*
July   *juillet*
August   *août*
September   *septembre*
October   *octobre*
November   *novembre*
December   *décembre*

COMMUNICATION

post office	*bureau de poste*
air mail	*par avion*
stamps	*timbres*
envelope	*enveloppe*
telephone book	*bottin téléphonique*
long distance call	*appel outre-mer*
collect call	*appel collecte*
fax	*télécopieur, fax*
telegram	*télégramme*
rate	*tarif*
dial the regional code	*composer le code régional*
wait for the tone	*attendre la tonalité*

ACTIVITIES

recreational swimming	*la baignade*
beach	*plage*
scuba diving	*la plongée sous-marine*
snorkelling	*la plongée-tuba*
fishing	*la pêche*
recreational sailing	*navigation de plaisance*
windsurfing	*la planche à voile*
bicycling	*faire du vélo*
mountain bike	*vélo tout-terrain (VTT)*
horseback riding	*équitation*
hiking	*la randonnée pédestre*
to walk around	*se promener*
museum or gallery	*musée*
cultural centre	*centre culturel*
cinema	*cinéma*

TOURING

river	*fleuve, rivière*
waterfalls	*chutes*
viewpoint	*belvédère*
hill	*colline*
garden	*jardin*
wildlife reserve	*réserve faunique*
peninsula	*péninsule, presqu'île*
south/north shore	*côte sud/nord*
town or city hall	*hôtel de ville*
court house	*palais de justice*
church	*église*
house	*maison*
manor	*manoir*
bridge	*pont*
basin	*bassin*

workshop	*atelier*
historic site	*lieu historique*
train station	*gare*
stables	*écuries*
convent	*couvent*
door, archway, gate	*porte*
customs house	*douane*
market	*marché*
seaway	*voie maritime*
museum	*musée*
cemetery	*cimitière*
mill	*moulin*
windmill	*moulin à vent*
hospital	*Hôtel Dieu*
high school	*école secondaire*
lighthouse	*phare*
barn	*grange*
waterfall(s)	*chute(s)*
sandbank	*batture*
neighbourhood, region	*quartier*

NUMBERS

1	*un*	22	*vingt-deux*
2	*deux*	23	*vingt-trois*
3	*trois*	24	*vingt-quatre*
4	*quatre*	25	*vingt-cinq*
5	*cinq*	26	*vingt-six*
6	*six*	27	*vingt-sept*
7	*sept*	28	*vingt-huit*
8	*huit*	29	*vingt-neuf*
9	*neuf*	30	*trente*
10	*dix*	40	*quarante*
11	*onze*	50	*cinquante*
12	*douze*	60	*soixante*
13	*treize*	70	*soixante-dix*
14	*quatorze*	80	*quatre-vingt*
15	*quinze*	90	*quatre-vingt-dix*
16	*seize*	100	*cent*
17	*dix-sept*	200	*deux cents*
18	*dix-huit*	500	*cinq cents*
19	*dix-neuf*	1,000	*mille*
20	*vingt*	10,000	*dix mille*
21	*vingt-et-un*	1,000,000	*un million*

Index

Index

Index

Index

Travel Notes

El placer de viajar mejor

Le plaisir de mieux voyager

Travel Notes

_____

_____

_____

_____

_____

_____

_____

_____

_____

_____

_____

_____

_____

_____

_____

_____

_____

_____

_____

_____

_____

_____

_____

Travel Notes

Order Form

Ulysses Travel Guides

☐ Acapulco . . . . . $14.95 CAN $9.95 US	☐ Guadalajara . . . $17.95 CAN $12.95 US
☐ Alberta's Best Hotels and Restaurants . . . $14.95 CAN $12.95 US	☐ Guadeloupe . . . $24.95 CAN $17.95 US
☐ Arizona– . . . . . $24.95 CAN Grand Canyon $17.95 US	☐ Guatemala . . . . $24.95 CAN $17.95 US
☐ Atlantic Canada $24.95 CAN $17.95 US	☐ Haiti . . . . $24.95 CAN $17.95 US
☐ Beaches of Maine $12.95 CAN $9.95 US $10.95 US	☐ Havana . . . . . . $16.95 CAN $12.95 US
☐ Belize . . . . . . $16.95 CAN $12.95 US	☐ Hawaii . . . . $29.95 CAN $21.95 US
☐ Boston . . . . $17.95 CAN $12.95 US	☐ Honduras . . . . . $24.95 CAN $17.95 US
☐ British Columbia's Best Hotels and . . . $14.95 CAN Restaurants $12.95 US	☐ Huatulco– . . . . $17.95 CAN Puerto Escondido $12.95 US
☐ Calgary . . . . . $17.95 CAN $12.95 US	☐ Inns and Bed & Breakfasts in Québec . . . . $14.95 CAN $10.95 US
☐ California . . . . . $29.95 CAN $21.95 US	☐ Islands of the . . $24.95 CAN Bahamas $17.95 US
☐ Canada . . . . $29.95 CAN $21.95 US	☐ Jamaica . . . . . . $24.95 CAN $17.95 US
☐ Cancún & . . . . . $19.95 CAN Riviera Maya $14.95 US	☐ Las Vegas . . . . . $17.95 CAN $12.95 US
☐ Cape Cod, ... $24.95 CAN Nantucket and Martha's Vineyard $17.95 US	☐ Lisbon . . . . $18.95 CAN $13.95 US
☐ Cartagena . . . . . $12.95 CAN (Colombia) $9.95 US	☐ Los Angeles . . . $19.95 CAN $14.95 US
☐ Chicago . . . . . . $19.95 CAN $14.95 US	☐ Los Cabos . . . . $14.95 CAN and La Paz $10.95 US
☐ Chile . . . . $27.95 CAN $17.95 US	☐ Louisiana . . . . . $29.95 CAN $21.95 US
☐ Colombia . . . . . $29.95 CAN $21.95 US	☐ Martinique . . . . $24.95 CAN $17.95 US
☐ Costa Rica . . . . $27.95 CAN $19.95 US	☐ Miami . . . . $9.95 CAN $12.95 US
☐ Cuba . . . . $24.95 CAN $17.95 US	☐ Montréal . . . . . $19.95 CAN $14.95 US
☐ Dominican . . . . $24.95 CAN Republic $17.95 US	☐ New England . . $29.95 CAN $21.95 US
☐ Ecuador and . . $24.95 CAN Galápagos Islands $17.95 US	☐ New Orleans . . $17.95 CAN $12.95 US
☐ El Salvador . . . . $22.95 CAN $14.95 US	☐ New York City . $19.95 CAN $14.95 US
	☐ Nicaragua . . . . . $24.95 CAN $16.95 US
	☐ Ontario . . . . . . $27.95 CAN $19.95US

- ☐ Ontario's Best Hotels and Restaurants ... $27.95 CAN $19.95US
- ☐ Ottawa–Hull ... $17.95 CAN $12.95 US
- ☐ Panamá ...... $27.95 CAN $17.95 US
- ☐ Peru .... $27.95 CAN $19.95 US
- ☐ Phoenix ...... $16.95 CAN $12.95 US
- ☐ Portugal ...... $24.95 CAN $16.95 US
- ☐ Provence & the Côte d'Azur $29.95 CAN $21.95US
- ☐ Puerto Plata– Sosua $14.95 CAN $9.95 US
- ☐ Puerto Rico ... $24.95 CAN $17.95 US
- ☐ Puerto Vallarta . $14.95 CAN $10.95 US
- ☐ Québec ...... $29.95 CAN $21.95 US
- ☐ Québec City ... $17.95 CAN $12.95 US
- ☐ San Diego .... $17.95 CAN $12.95 US
- ☐ San Francisco .. $17.95 CAN $12.95 US
- ☐ Seattle .... $17.95 CAN $12.95 US
- ☐ St. Lucia ...... $17.95 CAN $12.95 US
- ☐ St. Martin– St. Barts $17.95 CAN $12.95 US
- ☐ Toronto ...... $19.95 CAN $14.95 US
- ☐ Tunisia .... $27.95 CAN $19.95 US
- ☐ Vancouver .... $17.95 CAN $12.95 US
- ☐ Washington D.C. $18.95 CAN $13.95 US
- ☐ Western Canada $29.95 CAN $21.95 US

budget.zone

- ☐ Central America $14.95 CAN $10.95 US
- ☐ Western Canada $14.95 CAN $10.95 US

Ulysses Travel Journals

- ☐ Ulysses Travel Journal (Blue, Red, Green, Yellow, Sextant) .... $9.95 CAN $7.95 US
- ☐ Ulysses Travel Journal (80 Days) ..... $14.95 CAN $9.95 US

Ulysses Green Escapes

- ☐ Cross-Country Skiing and Snowshoeing .. $22.95 CAN in Ontario $16.95 US
- ☐ Cycling in France $22.95 CAN $16.95 US
- ☐ Cycling in ..... $22.95 CAN Ontario $16.95 US
- ☐ Hiking in the ... $19.95 CAN Northeastern U.S. $13.95 US
- ☐ Hiking in ..... $22.95 CAN Québec $16.95 US
- ☐ Hiking in ..... $22.95 CAN Ontario $16.95 US
- ☐ Ontario's Bike Paths and Rail Trails . $19.95 CAN $14.95 US

Ulysses Conversation Guides

☐ French for . . . . $9.95 CAN
   Better Travel $6.50 US

☐ Spanish for Better Travel in
   in Latin America $9.95 CAN
   $6.50 US

Title	Qty	Price	Total
Name:		Subtotal	
		Shipping	$4.75CAN $5.75US
Address:		Subtotal	
	GST in Canada 7%		
		Total	

Tel: Fax:

E-mail:

Payment: ☐ Cheque ☐ Visa ☐ MasterCard

Card number_____

Expiry date_____

Signature_____

ULYSSES TRAVEL GUIDES

4176 St. Denis Street,
Montréal, Québec,
H2W 2M5
☎(514) 843-9447
Fax: (514) 843-9448

305 Madison Avenue,
Suite 1166,
New York, NY 10165

Toll-free: 1-877-542-7247
Info@ulysses.ca
www.ulyssesguides.com